JUL 1 2 2018

W9-DEK-950

"We are delighted with Deborah Lubera Kawsky's efforts to draw focus and attention to a lesser–known aspect of our grandfather's career. It was from his architectural training and foundation that Girard approached every project. This book adds an important chapter to the larger biography of his diverse life and career."

  —Aleishall Girard Maxon, Girard Studio LLC

"Alexander Girard was extraordinarily good at every facet of design, and his elegant views on modernity feel just as fresh and relevant today. *Alexander Girard, Architect* is a smart study of his purposefully revolutionary designs for living filled with never–before–seen drawings and photographs."

  —Todd Oldham, designer

"*Alexander Girard, Architect* is an enlightening glimpse into Girard's lesser-known, early career—before he partnered with the modernist powerhouse Herman Miller. Kawsky's thorough research and generous use of archival imagery uncover a fresh understanding of Girard's architectural practice and a fascinating account of his evolution as a designer."

  —Shelley Selim, associate curator of design and decorative arts, Indianapolis Museum of Art and the Miller House

"Before Alexander Girard joined the 'dream team' at Herman Miller as the head of the fabric division and moved to Santa Fe in the early 1950s, he spent more than a decade living and working in Detroit. This previously undocumented and virtually unknown chapter of the designer's career is the subject of Deborah Lubera Kawsky's groundbreaking research in *Alexander Girard, Architect*. Kawsky's lavishly illustrated book, with both archival and contemporary photographs, convincingly claims that it was in Michigan that Girard conceived and developed the ideas that would define his later career as a designer. The book is a must-read for all scholars and enthusiasts of midcentury modern design."

  —Gregory Wittkopp, director of the Cranbrook Center for Collections and Research

Advance Praise for *Alexander Girard, Architect*

"While Alexander Girard's remarkable body of work finds new and receptive audiences today, many still associate the multifaceted designer only with his beloved desert of the American Southwest or his exotic travels abroad. However, as Kawsky painstakingly demonstrates, Girard's formative years in Detroit were essential to the development of his unique approach to design. A key player in the crucible of mid-century modernism that was birthed in Michigan, Girard's time there was, like the rest of his life, an extended series of rich and layered experiments in exploring design in all of its many dimensions."
  —Andrew Blauvelt, director of Cranbrook Art Museum

"Kawsky delves into Girard's prolific design career in Michigan: his midcentury residential work, his exhibition curation, and his impact on fabric, furniture, and graphic design. Richly illustrated with rarely seen historic photographs, this book places Girard at the center of the extraordinary synergy that revolved around modern design in Michigan and led the artist to collaborate with icons Ray and Charles Eames, Eero Saarinen, Minoru Yamaski and George Nelson."
  —Brian D. Conway, Michigan's state historic preservation officer

"Alexander Girard's years in Michigan proved to be a turning point. In and around Detroit he became exposed to modernism and started his career as one of the most important textile designers of the twentieth century. In Grosse Pointe, Girard built a house for himself and his family and designed several modern residences for progressive–minded clients in the neighborhood. Deborah Lubera Kawsky's book sheds light on this little–known but important and fascinating part of the trained architect's work."
  —Dr. Jochen Eisenbrand, chief curator at Vitra Design Museum

"With the publication of this book, a critical piece of the Alexander Girard puzzle has been uncovered. By bringing Girard's contributions and connections to the fore, Michigan's rich history of mid-century design just gets richer."
  —Sam Grawe, global brand director at Herman Miller

DISCARD
CADL

Alexander Girard, Architect

DISCARD
CADL

1. Alexander Girard in his Lothrop home, 1953. Photographer: Andrew Plotchay. © 2017 Girard Studio LLC. All rights reserved.

Alexander Girard, Architect

Creating Midcentury Modern Masterpieces

Deborah Lubera Kawsky
Foreword by Ruth Adler Schnee

A Painted Turtle Book
Detroit, Michigan

© 2018 by Wayne State University Press, Detroit, Michigan 48201. All rights reserved. No part of this book may be reproduced without formal permission. Manufactured in the United States of America.

ISBN: 978-0-8143-4365-4 (jacketed cloth); 978-0-8143-4366-1 (ebook)

Library of Congress Cataloging Number: 2017960025

Wayne State University Press
Leonard N. Simons Building
4809 Woodward Avenue
Detroit, Michigan 48201-1309

Visit us online at wsupress.wayne.edu

To my parents Elizabeth and Richard Lubera—without your support and enthusiasm, none of this would have been possible.

2. Alexander Girard for Herman Miller Textile Division, "Love Heart," environmental enrichment panel, 1971. Courtesy Herman Miller Archives.

ontents

Preface

The current resurgence of Detroit has gone hand in hand with a rediscovery of its history. Perhaps the most potent instruments of this process are historic buildings, which enable the modern viewer to revisit a city's aesthetic and cultural past, while providing new opportunities for its future. However, as we have experienced in Detroit, urban regeneration is often a double-edged sword, bringing both restoration and destruction to architectural landmarks. This paradox is particularly evident in the study of midcentury modern architecture, which has soared in popularity yet too often has succumbed to demolition. A case in point is Alexander Girard's architecture, which came to my attention in 2009, when I was asked to research a house designed by Girard in the Detroit suburb of Grosse Pointe. I had grown up in Grosse Pointe but never noticed the single-story, wood and glass, minimalist-style house on Vendome Road, the only modern structure on an exclusively traditional street—and one of only a handful in the entire area. I discovered that while Girard had lived in Grosse Pointe and designed a number of houses there, this house alone (the McLucas house) had survived intact.

Thus began my eight-year quest to uncover several interrelated histories, relating not only to Girard's architecture and the McLucas house but also to his connection with key clients, designers, and institutions in Detroit during a pivotal time in its history. My years of research have led me down some unexpected paths, from archives to upscale exhibition openings, encompassing architectural drawings, building permits, social registries, and interviews with those who knew Girard and grew up in the spaces he designed. Little by little, the fascinating backstory of the McLucas house, of Girard the architect, his structures and patrons, and of Detroit at midcentury, revealed itself. This process paralleled the painstaking restoration of the McLucas house to its midcentury glory. Although I never met Alexander Girard in person, I feel as if I have come to know him in the course of writing this book. I am inspired by the work of this soft-spoken, endlessly creative genius, and I am proud to bring to light the untold story of his architecture.

3. Alexander Girard for Herman Miller Textile Division, "Ribbons," 1957. Courtesy Herman Miller Archives.

Foreword

I first had the pleasure to meet Alexander Girard in 1948. He had rented a small storefront space on Fisher Road in Grosse Pointe, Michigan, where he practiced architecture and interior design.

It was spring.

I had returned to Detroit to establish my own interior-planning studio and to complete an order for large, silkscreen-printed, abstract-patterned drapery fabrics in very bold colors; the idea had never been explored, and I was very anxious to develop it. Girard was a vast repository of information and advice. He, with great patience, outlined the responsibilities and possible pitfalls of such a venture. In looking back, I now wonder what gave me the courage to move forward.

Girard was enthusiastic to share his new idea of designing a "conversation pit" within the confines of a large living-room space, a space that would create a stage for intimate discussion. He invited my husband, Eddie, and me to his house, where we learned that Girard shared my love of color and of Mexican folklore and the beautiful artifacts that culture achieved in so many materials.

Charlie Eames and Eero Saarinen joined us, and we all agreed that "design" should educate and delight; it should provide a framework to structure our thinking, a guide for how we look at things, and should help us to identify limitations and rules. Living within the rules embodied in good design is not submitting to them but conforming to them out of respect for their existence. Girard and his friends had the ability to recognize and give form to these restrictions, creating beautiful spaces and beautiful works in many media.

In the fall of 2011, I had the opportunity to revisit my experiences with Girard when I was first interviewed by Deborah Lubera Kawsky on the subject of Girard's architecture and his time in Detroit. In the intervening years, she and I have had many discussions about her research on midcentury modern design and its Michigan roots. Since 2014, I have served as design consultant on the restoration of the Mr. and Mrs. John N. McLucas House, the sole surviving residence designed entirely by Girard during his career in Detroit and the centerpiece of this book. After all these many years, we still find pleasure and aesthetic rewards in Girard's work and in the work of the many good designers who have followed the path blazed by him and his contemporaries.

Ruth Adler Schnee

May 2016

4. View of the Great Hall and exhibition rooms, *For Modern Living* exhibition, Detroit Institute of Arts, Detroit, MI, 1949. Courtesy, Alexander Girard estate, Vitra Design Museum. MAR-04762-32.

ntroduction

If these designers have been able to show us here, in a great center of modern technology, an answer good for American life, they have something to offer important not only for Detroit but for the nation. Not only for the nation but for the world.

—E. P. Richardson, director of the Detroit Institute of Arts

Visitors entering the Detroit Institute of Arts (DIA) on Sunday, September 11, 1949, were in for a shock. A "strange, many colored forest" of slender poles filled the galleries.[1] Old Master paintings were swapped for everyday objects, from plastic containers and printed textiles to stackable aluminum chairs and slinky toys. The classically styled Great Hall (fig. 4) had been transformed into a "fantastic jungle" in which viewers journeyed on a winding pathway over hills and through trees to view a series of nine, fully furnished rooms.[2] As one observer noted, "solid citizens of Detroit were acting like guinea pigs in an art experiment . . . and liking it."[3] The displays, orchestrated by the Detroit-based designer Alexander Girard, were part of a groundbreaking exhibition, *For Modern Living*, which ran from September 11 through November 20, 1949, at the DIA (fig. 5). While other museums had showcased modern design, the focus of *For Modern Living* was new: the adaptation of modern design—through new materials, products, and technologies—to modern American life and the identification of modern design as a new, uniquely American, form of beauty. The popularity of the exhibition, which attracted 149,553 viewers (45,000 more than any previous exhibition), likely reflected not only the dramatic nature of Girard's installation but also its timing and setting: at midcentury and in Detroit.[4]

By 1949, Detroit was the fifth-largest city in America, with a population of nearly two million people (fig. 6).[5] Celebrated for its wartime role as the "arsenal of democracy," it was also the epicenter of the auto industry, which employed (directly or indirectly) one in every six Americans.[6] However, during the postwar period, Detroit was redefining itself, leading the way in the adaptation of its innovative design heritage—in automobiles and wartime machinery but also in architecture and interior design—to the new modern era. The connection between *For Modern Living* and Detroit's revamped image was reiterated by DIA director E. P. Richardson, who called modern design for the home a "subject of the greatest importance" for the new generation and Detroit

5. View of the Detroit Institute of Arts, Detroit, MI, during the *For Modern Living* exhibition, September–November 1949. Courtesy Detroit Institute of Arts.

6. Skyline, downtown Detroit from Windsor, 1941. Courtesy Walter P. Reuther Library, Archives of Labor and Urban Affairs, Wayne State University.

7. Alexander Girard for Herman Miller Textile Division, "Eden," 1966. Courtesy Herman Miller Archives.

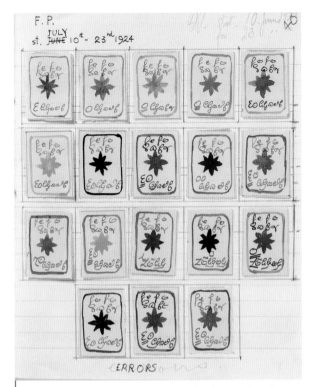

8. Alexander Girard, Republic of Fife notebook, 1918–24. Courtesy Alexander Girard Estate, Vitra Design Museum. MAR-00218-0007.

9. Alexander Girard for Herman Miller Textile Division, "Arabesque," 1954. Courtesy Herman Miller Archives.

10. Alexander Girard, matchbook covers for La Fonda del Sol restaurant, New York, 1960. Courtesy Herman Miller Archives.

"one of the great reservoirs of the technological skills of the twentieth century."[7] Echoing the utopian tone of many postwar projects, he referenced the "large implications" of the exhibition, "not only for Detroit but for the nation. Not only for the nation but for the world."[8] However, Richardson saved his highest praise for the exhibition's director, Alexander Girard, telling him that Museum of Modern Art curators were "green with envy" over its success.[9] Another reviewer praised Girard's "epic production, world's fair style—with all the complexities of financing, promotion, dramatics, glamour effects, [and] public relations"—as a model for museum practice and for the integration of art into a changing postwar society.[10]

The same visionary quality is evident in Girard's later work as director of the Fabric Division of the Herman Miller furniture company, where he worked from 1951 to 1972. At Herman Miller, Girard created hundreds of innovative textile and furniture designs, characterized by bold colors and patterns (fig. 7). By providing designers and consumers a vibrant alternative to the prevailing minimalist, monochromatic modernist aesthetic, he helped to define the modern age of interior design. Yet despite his pervasive influence and popularity, Girard's name—and his work in Detroit, in which he applied many of the aforementioned principles in architectural projects—is still not widely known. Indeed, Jochen Eisenbrand called Girard "the great unknown pioneer" of American midcentury design.[11]

Museum of Modern Art curator Edgar Kaufmann Jr. traced Girard's "artistic mastery" to his cosmopolitan background and training.[12] Alexander Hayden Girard was born in New York City on May 24, 1907, to an American mother, Lezlie Cutler, and a French and Italian father, Carlo Matteo Girard, an international antiques dealer.[13] The family moved to Florence, Italy, in 1909. There young Alexander, known as "Sandro," was immersed in the family's collections of antique prints, textiles, and furnishings and in Florentine intellectual and artistic culture; indeed, Kaufmann characterized Girard as a

11. Alexander Girard, studio and apartment, Florence, Italy, 1928. Photographer: F. Barsotti. © 2017 Girard Studio LLC. All rights reserved.

12. Poster from the Stockholm Exhibition (1930). Stockholmsutstallningen Plakat, 1930 © Anita Christiansen 08-4633130 for Sigurt Lewerentz / Svensk Form / Wikimedia Commons / CC-BY-SA-3.0 / GFDL.

13. Ludwig Mies van der Rohe, German Pavilion, Barcelona, Spain, 1929 (reconstructed 1986). Photographer: Pepo Segura. Courtesy Pepo Segura and Fundació Mies van der Rohe.

"Renaissance man."[14] At the age of ten, while away at a London boarding school, young Sandro conceived his "first comprehensive design project": a "fantastic universe" called the Republic of Fife (fig. 8), consisting of imaginary countries, represented by coats of arms, banners, postage stamps, and currency, all communicated with family and friends through a coded visual language.[15] This fusion of design and play—through symbol, color, and pattern—was a recurrent theme throughout Girard's career, manifested not only in his later textile and graphic designs (figs. 9 and 10) but also in his designs for exhibitions and interior and architectural projects.[16] Girard's imagination was fueled by his studies at the Architectural Association School in London (1924–29), where he received both technical training and exposure to landmark developments in European architecture.[17] These included iconic movements such as the Bauhaus and De Stijl, monuments such as Le Corbusier's Pavilion de l'Esprit Nouveau at the Paris world's fair (1925), and publications such as the *Wendingen* issues on the American architect Frank Lloyd Wright (1921–25).[18]

These influences coalesced in Girard's 1928 design (fig. 11) for an apartment on the third floor of his parents' home, La Lucciola, in Florence, which blended elements of De Stijl (the multicolor walls), Neo-Rococo (the ornamental metal grill), and modernism (the use of geometric forms and metal tubes).[19] After graduating in 1929, Girard witnessed two groundbreaking exhibitions: the 1929 International Exposition in Barcelona and the 1930 Stockholm exhibition (fig. 12). The undisputed highlight of the Barcelona Exposition was the German Pavilion by Ludwig Mies van der Rohe (fig. 13). Composed of glass, steel, and stone in a minimalist design, the work is considered a masterpiece of International Style modernism.[20] While in Stockholm, Girard was exposed to a modernist movement called functionalism; he later described his own work as "aesthetic functionalism."[21] Between 1930 and 1931, Girard worked as a designer for the Stockholm department store Nordiska and on architectural projects in Rome and Paris.[22]

Girard's career as an independent designer began in 1932, after his move to New York City. There he designed furniture and interiors—aided by connections from his father, Matteo—for wealthy New York clients and institutions.[23] These included a model interior designed for the Permanent Exhibition of Decorative Arts and Crafts at Rockefeller Center, which was praised by *Vogue* magazine for the "dozens of ideas it incorporates."[24] In 1935, he completed a degree program at New York University, which established him as a "registered architect" in the United States.[25] On March 15, 1936, Girard married Susan Needham, the daughter of Winifred and Thomas Needham, a vice president of the

14. Alexander Girard for Herman Miller Textile Division, "Sansusie," 1969. Courtesy Herman Miller Archives.

influential US Rubber Company.[26] Girard set up a design studio in the couple's Upper East Side New York City apartment, located at 159 East Seventieth Street; this fusion of work and home was a practice that he continued for the rest of his career.[27] While the role of Susan Girard in her husband's career has never been fully explored, it is clear that her support—both personal and professional—was instrumental in his success.[28] Indeed, their son, Marshall Girard, once stated, "There would have been no Sandro Girard without Susan Girard."[29] Fittingly, Girard demonstrated Susan's status as his lifelong partner through design: a logo (dubbed "sansusi" for Sandro and Susan) composed of two intertwining heart-shaped *S* letters (fig. 14).[30]

Girard's career took a decisive turn in 1937, when he and Susan moved from New York City to Detroit. Facilitated by his father's personal connections, Girard had secured work—hard to come by during the Depression years—at the Thomas Esling Company, an interior design firm.[31] In 1943, Girard went to work for International Detrola, a Detroit radio communications firm. However, by 1945, he and Susan had opened an independent design studio on Fisher Road in Grosse Pointe; they opened a studio on Kercheval Place in 1950.[32] One could say that Girard's Detroit design work—launched from his Grosse Pointe home and studios—served as the springboard for his later career. It was during this Detroit period (1937–53) that Girard first met his Michigan modernist colleagues Charles and Ray Eames, Eero Saarinen, Minoru Yamasaki, and George Nelson; established connections with iconic design institutions such as the Cranbrook Academy of Art, Herman Miller, and the Detroit Institute of Arts; and met key patrons, including the McLucas, Rieveschl, and Miller families. He was also involved in several iconic postwar design projects, including the St. Louis Arch (1948), the General Motors Technical Center (1948–56), and the *For Modern Living* exhibition (1949) at the DIA. These projects were diverse, encompassing interior, industrial and graphic design, folk art collection, exhibition curation, and residential architecture, the latter of which reached its fullest expression during Girard's last years in Detroit (1947–51). Girard stayed in Detroit until 1953, when he moved with his family to Santa Fe, New Mexico, likely inspired by his new position as textile director at Herman Miller.

Perhaps surprisingly, during Girard's time in Detroit, he lived with his wife, Susan, and their two children in the exclusive, traditional suburb of Grosse Pointe. At the time, the standard for Grosse Pointe architecture was epitomized by the homes designed by architects in the circle of Albert Kahn. Kahn designed his industrial projects in Detroit in a utilitarian, modernist style, featuring steel frames and glass skins.[33] However, he built the residences of his wealthy industrialist clients, including the estate of Edsel and Eleanor Clay Ford on Lakeshore Drive (fig. 15), in historically inspired styles, primarily of stone and brick.[34] In contrast, Girard's architectural projects of the years 1947–51— characterized by wood and glass, single-story structures, with open floor plans and bold color accents—represented a dramatic departure from traditional Grosse Pointe architecture and patronage of the time.

Sadly, little remains of Girard's Grosse Pointe architecture, which included two design studios and four private residences. However, there is one notable exception: the residence of Mr. and Mrs. John N. McLucas (1950), the only surviving home designed entirely by Girard (fig. 16). Located on a prominent corner lot at the intersection of Vendome Road and Grosse Pointe Boulevard, its site and style made a bold statement, embodying Girard's ideas about how modern design could enhance modern living in the postwar era. More importantly, however, 55 Vendome is a monument, a sort of midcentury time capsule, documenting the mind of a modernist master at work. While much has been written about Girard and his later work for Herman Miller, the story of his Detroit period—and of his architectural projects in Grosse Pointe—has not been told; it lives on in the McLucas house.

15. Façade of the Edsel and Eleanor Clay Ford house, Grosse Pointe, MI, 1926. Architect: Albert Kahn. Photographer: Katie Doelle.

16. View of the McLucas house from Vendome Road, Grosse Pointe Farms, MI. Architect: Alexander Girard. Photographer: Robert R. Lubera.

17. Alexander Girard at his desk at Detrola Corporation, Detroit, MI, circa 1940s. © 2017 Girard Studio LLC. All rights reserved.

Connections
Modern Design in Postwar Michigan

Eventually everything connects—people, ideas, objects. . . .
The quality of the connections is the key to quality per se.

—Charles Eames

While Alexander Girard's quiet demeanor earned him the nickname "mouse," his work was adamantly outspoken. This was the case in 1944, when the designer Charles Eames, then working for Evans Products, "met" Alexander Girard during a visit to the International Detrola Corporation, a Detroit radio manufacturer (fig. 17). At the time, Detrola was shifting its focus from wartime communications to the postwar, consumer radio market and had hired Girard as head designer.[1] Like Eames, Girard was experimenting with modern styles and materials, including plastic and plywood (then manufactured by the Evans Molded Plywood Division). Indeed, one critic praised the "fresh, progressive spirit" of Girard's designs for Detrola, evident not only in radios but in factory offices, which incorporated curving plywood walls and oval-shaped desks.[2] While Girard was not in his office at the time, Eames saw the myriad of radio designs on his desk. Recognizing a similar aesthetic sensibility, he left a note, stating, "I see you already have all of this so you don't need me."[3] The "meeting" between Eames and Girard launched a lifelong friendship and a collaborative working relationship, one of the many that Girard formed during his time in Detroit (1937–53). The anecdote also illustrates the status of Detroit—and Michigan as a whole—as a design mecca during the midcentury period, not only in architectural and automotive design but in the design of furniture and of everyday objects, previously considered "artless."[4]

The key role of Michigan as a "midcentury powerhouse of Modern design" has only recently been recognized and celebrated.[5] Detroit's primacy in the styling, production, and marketing of automobiles has been universally accepted. However, Alan Hess has noted that its role in the development and dissemination of modernism in America—not only in automobiles but in "buildings, planning, decorative arts, factories, furniture, and household goods"—has been consistently "underplayed."[6] Brian Conway and Amy Arnold credit a "synergy of industry, prosperity and educational leadership" with attracting visionary architects, designers, and theorists to Michigan between 1900 and 1970.[7] They trace Michigan's key role in three "intersecting tracks" of design, including industry (war production as well as

18. Close-up of Tritons in the Triton Pool, with Cranbrook Academy of Art in the background. Photographer: Balthasar Korab. © Balthasar Korab / Cranbrook Archives.

the automotive and furniture industries), architecture (industrial and residential projects), and education (design education programs at Cranbrook Academy of Art and the University of Michigan).[8] At midcentury, Alexander Girard was one of the pioneers of modernist design in Michigan, among a group that included Charles and Ray Eames, Eero Saarinen, Minoru Yamasaki, and George Nelson.[9] The personal and professional relationships between these designers—each of whom was directly connected with Alexander Girard—took shape in institutions such as Cranbrook Academy of Art and Herman Miller and in projects such as the General Motors Technical Center. This creative vortex produced an atmosphere of collaborative cross-pollination that had repercussions both within and beyond Michigan.

Cranbrook Academy of Art

In many ways, it was the founding of the Cranbrook educational community in Bloomfield Hills, Michigan, that set the stage for the development of modernism in America. The creation of an artistic community, a "school, atelier and art colony," was the brainchild of George Gough Booth and Ellen Scripps Booth.[10] In 1906, the Booths had commissioned the Detroit architect Albert Kahn to build a country estate, Cranbrook

19. Cranbrook's Maija Grotell with pot, 1947. Photographer: Harvey Croze. Courtesy Cranbrook Archives (P369).

House, on their 175-acre site in the Detroit suburb of Bloomfield Hills, Michigan.[11] The Booths had used their newspaper fortune to support arts organizations in Detroit, including the Detroit Society of Arts and Crafts (1906), its affiliated Detroit School of Design (1911), and the Detroit Institute of Arts.[12] However, after a trip to Rome in 1922, George Booth conceived a plan to create an art academy at Cranbrook.[13] In 1924, he asked the Finnish architect Eliel Saarinen—then a visiting professor at the University of Michigan—to draw up master plans for the complex, including a school for boys and an art academy, and to develop an educational plan for the art academy (fig. 18).[14]

20. Eliel Saarinen (with hat) with Cranbrook Academy of Art students on the steps of Cranbrook Art Museum, including Eero Saarinen (center left) and Charles Eames (behind the camera), May 1941. Courtesy Cranbrook Archives (5699-3).

By the mid-1920s, Eliel Saarinen was designing buildings for the campus and running the Architectural Office (1926), although the Academy of Art—the heart of Booth's plan—did not open officially until 1932.[15] As Leslie Edwards writes, by 1937–38, the academy's major departments included Architecture, Sculpture, and Painting, although an Intermediate School offered instruction in modeling, design, and weaving.[16] Despite the devastating impact of the Depression, Cranbrook continued to grow during the '30s, gaining important European faculty members such as the sculptor Carl Milles (1931), the textile designer and weaver Marianne Strengell (1937), and the ceramicist Maija Grotell (1938), making it a "rich melting pot for the exchange of ideas and design principles" (fig. 19).[17]

During the mid-1930s and '40s, Cranbrook became a think tank for modern design, with the influx of talented faculty and design students, including Eero Saarinen, Florence Schust Knoll, Charles and Ray Eames, Ralph Rapson, Harry Bertoia, and Ruth Adler Schnee (fig. 20).[18] Eliel Saarinen, with the help of visiting architects such as Alvar Aalto and Walter Gropius, inspired students and faculty alike in new collaborative—and competitive—ventures (fig. 21).[19] In 1940, Charles Eames, instructor of design, and Eero Saarinen, then teaching city planning, submitted joint furniture designs in the "Organic Design in Home Furnishings" competition sponsored by New York's Museum of Modern Art (MOMA). The mission of the exhibition was to create furniture that would "reflect today's social, economic, technological and aesthetic tendencies," merging good design with mass production.[20] The entries by Eames and Saarinen to the MOMA competition, which included chairs made with innovative plywood shells in organic shapes (fig. 22), won their respective categories.[21]

After Eames left Cranbrook, he and Eero Saarinen continued to collaborate on architectural projects, including the "Entenza" house, part of the influential postwar architectural experiment the Case Study House program.[22] However, from 1941 onward, Charles's full-time design partner was another former Cranbrook student, Ray Kaiser (Eames); their work for Herman Miller was to revolutionize modern design in America. Beginning in 1943, Eero Saarinen worked with another longtime Cranbrook friend, Florence Schust Knoll, to design mass-produced furniture for Knoll Associates. His earliest (and perhaps most iconic) Knoll piece is the "Womb" chair of 1948 (fig. 23), which—with its chrome steel frame and upholstered fiberglass shell—epitomized the merging of innovative technologies, materials, and shapes for a postwar consumer market.[23]

While Alexander Girard was never officially affiliated with Cranbrook, he was connected with faculty and former students Eliel and Eero Saarinen, Charles and Ray Eames, Florence Knoll, Marianne Strengell, and Maija Grotell and with the Museum of Cranbrook Academy of Art. In a letter dated April 6, 1946, the museum director Albert Christ-Janer asked Girard to participate in a Cranbrook exhibition, titled *Varieties in Abstraction*.[24] In a letter dated August 9, 1946, Christ-Janer inquired about the possibility of a Girard-only show at Cranbrook.[25] The exhibition, titled *Paintings and Sculpture of Alexander Girard*, ran during the month of January 1947. The show included abstract paintings and sculptures, in wood and molded corrugated cardboard (fig. 24), which were selected by the director after a visit to Girard's home/studio on Lakeland Avenue in November 1946.[26] At the close of the exhibition, Christ-Janer purchased one of Girard's paintings,

21. Eero Saarinen and Charles Eames with a lightweight tensile structure designed for the 1939 faculty exhibition held at the Cranbrook Academy of Art Pavilion, 1939. Photographer: Richard G. Askew. Courtesy Cranbrook Archives (5624-2).

22. Eero Saarinen and Charles Eames, competition drawing for a side chair, Organic Design in Home Furnishings exhibition, Museum of Modern Art, New York, 1940. Pencil on white poster board covered with cellophane, 76 × 50 cm. Gift of the designers. Digital image © The Museum of Modern Art. Licensed by Scala / Art Resource.

23. Eero Saarinen, model 70 "Womb" chair for Knoll, 1946. Courtesy Knoll Inc.

24. Alexander Girard, corrugated cardboard sculptures from Paintings and Sculptures of Alexander Girard exhibition, Museum of Cranbrook Academy of Art, January 1947. Courtesy Alexander Girard Estate, Vitra Design Museum. MAR-04729-03.

Fish, and thanked Girard for a seminar that he had given for Cranbrook students.[27] In 1948, Girard included Marianne Strengell, head of the Department of Weaving at Cranbrook Academy of Art, as part of the Committee of Advisors for the *For Modern Living* exhibition that he was curating at the DIA. The list of exhibitors included notable Cranbrook instructors and alumni Charles Eames, Florence Knoll, Harry Bertoia, Maija Grotell, and Ruth Adler Schnee.[28] In 1953, Girard exhibited three textiles at the *Fourth Biennial Exhibition of Textiles and Ceramics*, held at the Museum of Cranbrook Academy of Art from February 14 to March 15, 1953. According to an exhibition pamphlet, a Girard textile, *Squares* (1952), was purchased by the museum.[29]

Herman Miller

During the postwar period, the Herman Miller furniture company, based in the western Michigan city of Zeeland, was on the forefront in the design of modern home furnishings. However, its innovative roots dated back to the 1930s, when the visionary designer Gilbert Rohde convinced Herman Miller's president, D. J. De Pree, that manufacturing furniture in period styles was not only old-fashioned but downright dishonest. As De Pree later stated, "I came to see that the starting point of our design had been immoral."[30] Modern life required more "honest" designs, devoid of heavy moldings and carvings that often hid sloppy workmanship (referred to by De Pree as "sins"). More importantly, modern designs were free of historical reference, more compact and easier to care for, and composed of new industrial materials such as steel, Plexiglas, Formica, and plywood. As Rohde told De Pree, "I know how people live and I know how they are going to live. Modern living . . . calls for a different kind of furniture."[31] The wider implications are evident in another Rhode comment to De Pree: "You're not making furniture anymore. You're providing a way of life."[32]

These ideals were implemented by Rohde but carried on after his death (1944) by his successor, George Nelson, who assembled a "dream team" of design at Herman Miller (fig. 25).[33] Nelson had been trained as an architect but had published an influential handbook, *Tomorrow's House*, which promoted the adaptation of modern technology and design ideas in postwar American homes.[34] Indeed, *Tomorrow's House* set out many of the key elements of midcentury modern design, including large glass windows, open plans, and built-in storage, orchestrated to increase the efficiency of life in the modern era.[35] It was likely Nelson's Storagewall (fig. 26), an innovative modular, built-in storage unit— published in *Life* magazine in 1945—which inspired D. J. De Pree's choice of Nelson as

25. The designers of Herman Miller, circa 1975 (from left to right: Robert Propst, Alexander Girard, George Nelson, D. J. De Pree, Ray and Charles Eames). Photographer: Melissa Brown. Courtesy Herman Miller Archives.

26. George Nelson exhibition room from the *For Modern Living* exhibition, Detroit Institute of Arts, Detroit, MI, 1949, showing Storagewall concept. Courtesy Detroit Institute of Arts.

27. Herman Miller advertisement showing Eames plywood chairs. Courtesy Herman Miller Archives.

28. View of Herman Miller furniture and textiles, circa 1960, showing George Nelson "Coconut" chair and Alexander Girard "Triangles" textile. Photographer: Dale Rooks. Courtesy Herman Miller Archives.

29. Alexander Girard for Herman Miller Textile Division, "International Love Heart," environmental enrichment panel, 1972. Courtesy Herman Miller Archives.

the new design director for Herman Miller.[36] Beginning in 1947, Nelson promoted an image and design aesthetic for Herman Miller that matched postwar attitudes about modern design and technology. The primary characteristics of postwar society—utopian idealism and commercialism—would be reflected in furniture and interior design that demonstrated key modernist principles: honesty, simplicity, technology, economy, and flexibility.[37]

Significantly, it was Nelson who brought Charles Eames to Herman Miller, after seeing the designs by Eames for MOMA's *Organic Design* exhibition (1941) and for Evans Products. In 1946, George Nelson hired Charles Eames as a consultant designer, cementing both his (and Ray's) relationship with Herman Miller.[38] Beginning in 1947, Herman Miller retained the marketing and distribution rights for Eames-designed furniture and after 1949 gained production rights as well.[39] The molded plywood chairs designed by Charles and Ray Eames (fig. 27), marketed in the 1948 Herman Miller furniture catalogue, were heralded as modernist icons, translating the "ideas and forms of abstract

art . . . into three-dimensional plastic form."[40] The adaptation of cutting-edge materials, including plywood and plastic reinforced with fiberglass, ensured the status of Herman Miller as America's preeminent modernist furniture company.

Charles Eames, in turn, brought Alexander Girard to the attention of George Nelson. In October 1951, Nelson hired Girard as director of Herman Miller's new Textile Division, created to supply the boldly colored and patterned textiles to cover and complement the new modern furniture and interiors created by Herman Miller designers.[41] D. J. De Pree recalled that there "was a dearth of good design" and that Girard was the one to "supplement and lend excitement to the work of Nelson and Eames."[42] Perhaps surprisingly, Girard's designs for this "mid-century modernizing culture" were inspired by "contemporary non-industrialized and non-technological cultures, such as Mexico," characterized by bold patterns and colors.[43]

However, Girard's textiles served a deeper role beyond the decorative. Inspired by his architectural training, Girard stated, "Textiles are a building material, as much a part of a

30. Aerial view of General Motors Technical Center, circa 1956. Photographer: Balthasar Korab. Courtesy Library of Congress.

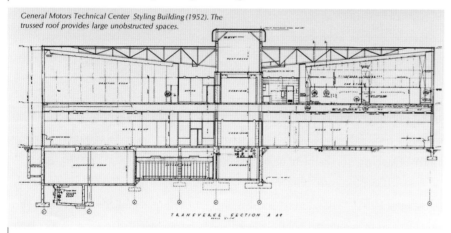

General Motors Technical Center Styling Building (1952). The trussed roof provides large unobstructed spaces.

31. Eero Saarinen and Associates, transverse section of Styling Building, General Motors Technical Center, 1952. Courtesy Smith Group JJR.

32. Exterior showing glazed-brick wall, General Motors Technical Center, Warren, MI, 1945–56. Photographer: Balthasar Korab. Courtesy Library of Congress.

ones as well (fig. 28).[46] Indeed, while Girard's creation of a systematic process for textile design at Herman Miller reflects his analytical side, he is most often characterized as a "humanist."[47] Perhaps inspired by his lifelong love of folk art, Girard never forgot that his works were designed for people, who craved personal expression in their surroundings.[48] Environmental enrichment panels such as "International Love Heart" (fig. 29) demonstrate his desire to connect clients with the "intangible activities of the mind and soul," which he believed were "in far greater need of consideration than are our purely practical functions in life."[49]

Eero Saarinen

The postwar boom was particularly advantageous for Eero Saarinen, who started working with his father, Eliel Saarinen, after graduating from Yale University. The firm began as Saarinen and Swanson, before transforming to Saarinen, Saarinen, and Associates, and finally (after Eliel's death) to Eero Saarinen and Associates.[50] In July 1945, the firm of Saarinen and Swanson, headed by Eliel Saarinen, won an iconic postwar commission: the

room as are the conventional materials of brick, glass, wood and plaster."[44] Susan Brown has aptly dubbed Girard a "textile architect" for his recognition of the "functional and aesthetic role of textiles as part of a cohesive interior environment."[45] During his tenure at Herman Miller from 1951 to 1972, Girard designed more than three hundred textiles, each calculated to address not only aesthetic and functional concerns—color, pattern, texture, durability, privacy, light control, and sound dampening—but emotional

33. Alexander Girard (second from left), Dan Kiley, Lillian Saarinen, and Eero Saarinen (second from right) receiving first prize for the Jefferson National Expansion Memorial in St. Louis, MO, 1948. Courtesy Alexander Girard Estate, Vitra Design Museum.

34. Second-floor studio hallway showing Alexander Girard color scheme, Design Center Building, General Motors Technical Center, Warren, MI, 1961. Courtesy GM Design Archive & Special Collections.

design of the new General Motors Technical Center (GMTC) in Warren, Michigan.[51] The project represented a new concept: the consolidation of all new product development into one corporate campus, located outside the city rather than in downtown Detroit.[52] At the behest of Harley Earl, General Motors vice president, the design of the complex—architecture and interior furnishings—would match the modern spirit and technology of the products designed within.[53] While the project was suspended in October 1945, work resumed in 1948, although with Eero Saarinen as lead architect.[54] Indeed, the new design concept—featuring rectilinear steel and glass buildings housing GM's design, engineering, research, manufacturing, and service activities, clustered around a twenty-two-acre lake—matches Eero's description of the design as "based on steel—the metal of the automobile."[55]

The impact—both architectural and technological—of the General Motors Technical Center cannot be overestimated. While the complex (fig. 30) represented a new corporate concept, it also represented a new collaborative design model, in which designers and engineers shared ideas and new technologies.[56] The results are evident in the use of innovative building technologies such as thin glass-and-metal curtain walls and neoprene window gaskets.[57] Steel roof trusses, designed in triangular sections (fig. 31), allowed for large, unobstructed spaces and for the integration of structural, mechanical, and electrical systems.[58] The use of boldly colored, double-glazed ceramic brick on the end walls of the buildings (fig. 32)—the first application of ceramics in architecture—was an integral part of the revised design. The bricks have been interpreted as a humanistic (and uniquely American) counterpoint to the severe geometry and impersonality of International Style modernism.[59] Indeed, it was the Cranbrook ceramicist Maija Grotell (known for her innovative glaze experiments) who first developed the low-fire glazes in bright colors that could be applied to bricks.[60]

However, while the textured surface of the bricks—specified by Eliel Saarinen—gave the bricks a "hand-crafted aesthetic," their production followed the industrial standards adopted elsewhere at the GMTC.[61] Indeed, additional research and testing on issues such

35. Interior view of the Power Plant, General Motors Technical Center, Warren, MI, circa 1956. Note the multicolored pipes. Published in the historical brochure "Where Today Meets Tomorrow," GM Design Archive. Photograph: Ezra Stoller. © Ezra Stoller/Esto.

as whether the glazes would adhere under extreme cold temperatures was conducted by the GM designer Joseph Lacy, in conjunction with ceramic experts at GM's AC Spark Plug division.[62] The bricks themselves—glazed in deep crimson, scarlet, tangerine orange, lemon yellow, chartreuse, royal blue, sky blue, tobacco gray, brown, black, and white—were produced in a special kiln designed for General Motors by Claycraft Corporation of Columbus, Ohio.[63] The Engineering buildings, the first of the five building clusters, opened to the press during the summer of 1951; the complex as a whole, hailed as an "industrial Versailles," was dedicated in May 1956.[64]

The bold color palette of the GMTC, not only evident in the glazed brick walls but employed strategically throughout the campus, provides a direct connection between Eero Saarinen and Alexander Girard. Saarinen and Girard likely met through their mutual friend Charles Eames. Their first direct collaboration was in 1946, when Girard, Saarinen, and Eames entered a textile competition at the Museum of Modern Art in New York; their joint entry was given honorable mention.[65] The following year, Girard was part of Eero Saarinen's winning team (fig. 33) for the Jefferson National Expansion Memorial in

36. View of the New Union Trust (Guardian) Building, Detroit, MI, circa 1930–45. Courtesy Tichnor Brothers Collection, Boston Public Library.

37. View of the Detroit Federal Reserve Bank with Yamasaki addition (*rear right*), Detroit, MI. Photographer: Andrew Jameson.

38. Minoru Yamasaki (center), Joseph Leinweber, and George Hellmuth with model for the Pruitt-Igoe housing development, St. Louis, MO, circa 1950. Courtesy Archives of Michigan.

St. Louis.[66] Girard's contribution to the project was a mural with views of St. Louis, which was never executed.[67]

During the early 1950s, Girard served as color consultant for Saarinen's GMTC project.[68] According to GM designer George Moon, Saarinen consulted Girard on the color scheme of Harley Earl's office, the Styling Building (fig. 34), and the Power Plant (fig. 35).[69] One writer commented that the bold color scheme of the Power Plant—which included pipes painted blue, motors and valves red, and stairs and balustrades yellow—reminded him of paintings by Fernand Léger.[70] However, Moon added that "while some color was used for décor," the interior was "color coded to standards."[71] The fact that the exterior glazed brick walls of the GMTC demonstrate a similar juxtaposition of bright primary colors suggests that Girard may have been consulted on that color scheme as well (see fig. 213 in chapter 5). Indeed, Girard was in close contact with Eero Saarinen in 1948 when the concept originated, and he certainly had direct access to GMTC bricks in 1950.[72]

Minoru Yamasaki

Minoru Yamasaki was at the center of postwar developments in Detroit architecture, after coming to Detroit in 1945 to work for the seminal firm Smith, Hinchman & Grylls

(SH&G).[73] As Detroit grew in size and influence during the 1920s, firms such as Albert Kahn Associates and SH&G were instrumental in shaping the architectural image of the city and its suburbs.[74] Major commissions of SH&G ranged from iconic corporate skyscrapers such as the Buhl (1925), Penobscot (1928), and Guardian (1929) buildings (fig. 36) to grand, private commissions such as the John Dodge residence (1920), the Country Club of Detroit (1926), and Meadowbrook Hall (1929). The boom of the 1920s was followed, however, by the Great Depression and by World War II, both of which brought an end to the construction of large-scale office buildings, factories, churches, and homes. However, with the end of the war in 1945, many clients who had postponed projects proceeded with their plans for new facilities.

SH&G responded to this postwar expansion by hiring a new head of design: Minoru Yamasaki.[75] Yamasaki's first assignment, an addition to Detroit's Federal Reserve Bank, made a bold statement about the new direction of the firm—and of Detroit. Yamasaki's design incorporated traditional elements—the marble material and the horizontal division of the façade—with new styles and technologies, including the thin, curtain wall construction and wide expanses of glass. The end result (fig. 37) marked both a continuity and a "clean break between the old and the new."[76] In 1948, SH&G was named the

39. Minoru Yamasaki, Alexander Girard, Charles Eames, and Eero Saarinen, Eero Saarinen and Associates party, Eero Saarinen residence on Vaughn Road, Bloomfield Hills, MI, circa 1950. Courtesy, Margueritte Kimball Papers, Cranbrook Archives.

41. Alexander Girard, drawing for the Edelman residence, Lake Angelus, MI, showing the "Cave" seating area, 1949. Courtesy Alexander Girard Estate, Vitra Design Museum. MAR-00157-11.

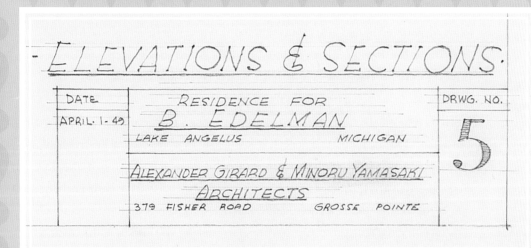

40. Alexander Girard & Minoru Yamasaki Architects, elevation and sections for Bernard Edelman residence, Lake Angelus, MI, April 1, 1949. Detail shows the name and address of the partnership: Alexander Girard & Minoru Yamasaki Architects, 379 Fisher Road, Grosse Pointe, MI. Courtesy Alexander Girard Estate, Vitra Design Museum, with the permission of the estate of Minoru Yamasaki. MAR-00157-07.

coarchitects (with Saarinen, Saarinen & Associates) of the General Motors Technical Center, the project that epitomized innovative style and technology in postwar Detroit.[77] Yamasaki played a huge role in securing the landmark project for the firm, which eventually utilized 125 engineers, architects, and draftsmen and cost more than $70 million.[78] Given the unique concept and scale of the project, SH&G architects and designers collaborated both with architects from Saarinen's office and with their clients, GM executives and engineers. Indeed, while it is Eero Saarinen's name that is most commonly associated with the GMTC, the division of labor in the final project was 20 percent to Saarinen's firm and 80 percent to Yamasaki's firm, SH&G.[79] However, in 1949—just as the GMTC project was getting under way—Yamasaki left the firm to set up two partnerships, with George Hellmuth and Joseph Leinweber (fig. 38), both formerly of SH&G.[80] According to Dale Gyure, the architect served as chief designer for both the Detroit office (Leinweber, Yamasaki, and Hellmuth) and the St. Louis office (Hellmuth, Yamasaki, and Leinweber).[81] The projects of the new firms included both municipal and residential projects, from the Lambert–St. Louis Municipal Air Terminal to a Japanese-inspired residence in Greenwich, Connecticut.[82]

While the date of the men's first meeting is not known, by the summer of 1948, Yamasaki, Girard, and Eero Saarinen (fig. 39) were working together on the Design Committee in charge of planning the *For Modern Living* exhibition at the DIA.[83] Around the same time, Yamasaki and Girard formed an official partnership, documented in an unsigned contract, dated May 1, 1949.[84] According to the contract, the purpose of the partnership was to provide "architectural services, and interior and industrial designing . . . and to engage in the business of interior decorating." Girard would contribute the lease, equipment, and merchandise from his Grosse Pointe design studio on 379 Fisher Road and the "good will" of his preexisting business, while Yamasaki would contribute a cash equivalent.[85] The products of the Girard-Yamasaki partnership include two 1949 designs, each part of a planned complex of modern homes: one for the real estate developer Bernard Edelman in Lake Angelus, Michigan (never built), and another for Daniel and Margaret Goodenough in Grosse Pointe. In each case, project blueprints, drawings, and models are dated 1949 and include the name and address of the partnership: Alexander Girard & Minoru Yamasaki Architects, 379 Fisher Road (fig. 40).[86] While the contract does not specify the design responsibilities of each partner, Yamasaki was likely the principal architect and Girard the designer of interior spaces and furnishings. Indeed, the Edelman house featured an interior design concept (fig. 41) that is clearly a

Girard invention: a sunken, semicircular hearth area (cut into the rock foundations and referred to on the design drawings as the "cave") with a built-in, curving couch and table unit.[87] Yamasaki's comment, "I designed some houses on my own" after leaving SH&G in 1949, strengthens the theory that he was the primary architect.[88]

It is interesting to speculate whether the Girard-Yamasaki partnership was influenced not only by the affiliated business and design concerns of the partners but also by anti-Japanese sentiment in the postwar period. Yamasaki recalled in his autobiography, *A Life in Architecture*, that his attempts to buy or rent a house in Grosse Pointe (as well as in Birmingham and Bloomfield Hills) were thwarted by discriminatory practices.[89] The architect eventually settled with his family on a seven-acre lot in Troy, Michigan, then a rural suburb. A partnership with Girard, based out of Girard's Grosse Pointe design studio, would have facilitated commissions from prominent clients in the Detroit suburbs. However, the arrangement seems to have been short-lived, given that the architectural projects completed by Girard in Grosse Pointe after 1950 (including the Jackson, McLucas, and Rieveschl residences) bear Girard's name alone. Indeed, in 1949, Yamasaki had entered into the aforementioned partnerships, with Joseph Leinweber and George Hellmuth, after all three left SH&G. No doubt, as the new firms received more high-profile projects, Yamasaki spent more time outside Detroit.[90] However, the connections established by Girard with Yamasaki, as well as with Eero Saarinen, Charles and Ray Eames, and George Nelson, would come together in his Grosse Pointe design work of the years 1947–51.

42. Exterior of Alexander Girard's studio, 379 Fisher Road, 1947. Photographer: Elmer Astelford. © Girard Studio LLC. All rights reserved.

Promotion

Girard's Studios and Exhibitions

> If attention and interest can be stimulated in good design—
> resulting in the same attitude and enthusiasm that is lavished
> on baseball and fashion—it will no longer be relegated to the
> intellectual privacy of the aesthete.
>
> —Alexander Girard

January 13, 1947, was opening night for an exhibition (figs. 43–45) featuring furniture by Charles Eames and Florence Knoll, fabrics by Marianne Strengell, and sculpture by Lily Swann Saarinen—all in an old hamburger stand. The site was Alexander Girard's new design studio on 379 Fisher Road in Grosse Pointe, converted by Sandro and Susan for a mere $2,000.[1] Equipped with a showroom, drafting room, workshop, and two offices (one for Sandro, the other for Susan), the studio demonstrated the breadth of his design work, which ranged from interior design to typography, from exhibit curation to architecture. It also demonstrated his desire to promote modern design to a wider audience, through exhibitions held both at his own Grosse Pointe studios and at other institutions, culminating in the groundbreaking *For Modern Living* exhibition at the Detroit Institute of Arts.

Girard's Grosse Pointe Studios

While Susan and Sandro lived in Detroit when they first moved from New York City, Girard's earliest commission was in Grosse Pointe: the redesign of the Junior League Little Shop on Kercheval Avenue. The store, run by a prominent women's charitable group, the Junior League of Detroit, connected Girard with key society clients, including future patrons Mrs. Richard Jackson and Mrs. Daniel Goodenough. Indeed,

● OPENING EXHIBITION

ALEXANDER GIRARD
379 FISHER ROAD, GROSSE POINTE 30, MICHIGAN

Furniture by Charles Eames — Evans Products

Sculpture by Lilly Swann Saarinen

Fabrics by Marianne Strengell

Paintings by Wallace Mitchell

Collection of Prints — Buchholz Gallery, New York

Books — Special Editions — Buchholz Gallery

Furniture by Knoll Associates, Inc.

JANUARY 13 TO 30, 1947

43. Invitation to opening exhibition (January 13–30, 1947) at Alexander Girard's studio, 379 Fisher Road, Grosse Pointe, MI. Courtesy Alexander Girard Estate, Vitra Design Museum. MAR-00921-01.

44. Exterior of Alexander Girard's studio, 379 Fisher Road, 1947. Photographer: Elmer Astelford. Courtesy Alexander Girard Estate, Vitra Design Museum. MAR-04744-03.

45. Interior view of Alexander Girard's studio, 379 Fisher Road, Grosse Pointe, MI, during opening exhibition. This photo shows the Roualt prints and Eames plywood furniture, featured in the opening exhibition. Photographer: Elmer Astelford. © Girard Studio LLC. All rights reserved.

46. Exterior of Junior League Little Shop, Kercheval Avenue, Grosse Pointe, MI, 1938. Photographer: Elmer Astelford. Courtesy Alexander Girard Estate, Vitra Design Museum. MAR-04693-03.

47. View of Kercheval Avenue, Grosse Pointe, MI, during the 1940s, showing Girard's design for the Junior League Little Shop. Courtesy Grosse Pointe Historical Society.

the grand reopening was covered on the society page of the *Detroit Free Press* on Sunday, November 20, 1938.[2] The design (figs. 46 and 47) praised as "modernistic" and "pictorial but practical" for its curved front window and counters, innovative storage solutions, painted ceiling, and indirect lighting, gave Girard national visibility when it was featured in the 1945 publication *Contemporary Shops in the United States*.[3]

By 1941, Susan and Sandro had moved to Grosse Pointe, settling at 380 Lakeland Avenue.[4] The residence—like those in Florence and New York City—served as home, studio, and showroom for Girard's latest design ideas. In May 1944, Girard advertised a public sale of furnishings at 380 Lakeland, likely spurred by a renovation of the home that year.[5] Funded by his work at Detrola, the redesign included curving partition walls, which subdivided the large living-dining room into separate dining, living, and working spaces (fig. 48). George Nelson had promoted a similar multifunctional room (which he called the "room without a name") in his book *Tomorrow's House*.[6] Partition walls became a characteristic feature of Girard's architectural projects. Girard also custom designed plywood tables and chairs, which in their organic shapes echoed the designs of Eames and Saarinen for the MOMA competition of 1941.

Around the same time, Girard partnered with H. Beard Adams to open an interior design firm, Girard and Adams, at 16906 Kercheval Avenue, just down the street from the Junior League Little Shop. In 1946, Girard opened an independent studio in the same space.[7] While the modern aesthetic may have run counter to Grosse Pointe tradition, the opening was attended by Mrs. Eugene du Pont and Mrs. Henry Ford and featured in *Town and Country* magazine.[8] Indeed, during these years, Girard designed interiors for many prominent Grosse Pointe families, including Thayer and William Laurie Jr., Susan and Sandro's closest Grosse Pointe friends.[9] While the Lauries lived in a traditional-style Grosse Pointe home on Merriweather Road, they were avid supporters of Girard's modernist aesthetic. This was evident in Girard's 1946 redesign of the Lauries' living room (fig. 49), which included a built-in unit that ran the length of the living room, incorporating bookshelves and a radio, record player, and speaker system. Even more unusual was the mesh material applied to the surface of the wall, which—along with the adjacent ledge—created a changeable display surface for a variety of objects, both traditional and exotic, including a vase of flowers, art prints, books, and a kachina doll.[10] Girard also designed the seating group and the plywood tables, similar to the ones in his own home on Lakeland. The same modern approach is evident in a book plate (fig. 50), designed by Girard for William Laurie, incorporating a typewriter, a modern artwork, a poodle, and a bust of his wife, Thayer.[11]

48. Alexander Girard, living room with custom-designed plywood furniture, 380 Lakeland, Grosse Pointe, MI. Photographer: Elmer Astelford. Courtesy Alexander Girard Estate, Vitra Design Museum. MAR 04633-LB17.

49. Alexander Girard, living room of William and Thayer Laurie residence, Grosse Pointe, MI, 1946. Photographer: Elmer Astelford. Courtesy Alexander Girard Estate, Vitra Design Museum. MAR-04736-02.

50. Alexander Girard, book plate for William Laurie. Courtesy Duncan Laurie.

On January 13, 1947, Girard opened his new Fisher Road design studio, offering "complete design services for the home, office and industrial field" and promoting the "intelligent use of contemporary methods, materials and ideas."[12] The studio contrasted with its surroundings not only in its merchandise but in its exterior and interior form.[13] This would have been evident at first glance in the unique, rigidized steel entrance door and the picture window, allowing both light and views into the interior spaces (fig. 42). Once inside, the interior featured modern, industrial materials such as corrugated cement, asbestos board painted gray-blue and striated plywood on the walls, black-painted fiber board on the ceilings, and metal lath.[14] The chairs—all in molded plywood—were designed by Charles Eames, although Girard's own plywood tables (the same ones visible in his

51. Interior view of Alexander Girard's studio from Girard's office, 379 Fisher Road, Grosse Pointe, MI. Photographer: Elmer Astelford. © 2017 Girard Studio LLC. All rights reserved.

Lakeland living room) were also on display. The interior spaces (fig. 51) included a lobby, showroom, and office—separated by a glass partition wall (which could be screened by a curtain)—along with a second office (for Susan Girard), a drafting room, and workshop.

Rotating exhibitions (nine in less than twelve months) in the studio featured work by Girard as well as other designers and artists from across the world. The list included jewelry by Alexander Calder and Harry Bertoia (fig. 52), prints by Pablo Picasso, textiles by Henry Moore, along with gifts, rugs, ceramics, textiles, and glassware from China, Finland, India, Italy, Mexico, Portugal, and Sweden.[15] The fact that the shop windows were backed with cellulose fabric to block the "continual peering of sightseers" suggests that Girard's avant-garde, exotic aesthetic did not mesh fully with Grosse Pointers at the time.[16] However, when the *Everyday Art Quarterly* published its 1948 guide to "discriminating" retail shops (those offering "modern products exclusively"), there were only two Midwest studios featured: one of them was Alexander Girard's on 379 Fisher Road in Grosse Pointe.[17]

52. Invitation to exhibition of contemporary jewelry at Alexander Girard's studio, 379 Fisher Road, Grosse Pointe, MI. The exhibition featured jewelry by Bertoia and Calder. Courtesy Alexander Girard Estate, Vitra Design Museum. MAR-00921-02.

For Modern Living at the Detroit Institute of Arts

Fittingly, it was an offhand remark made by Alexander Girard in July 1948 that inspired the groundbreaking 1949 *For Modern Living* exhibition at the Detroit Institute of Arts. According to one account, James B. Webber Jr., vice president of J. L. Hudson Company, Detroit's leading department store, was a guest in the Grosse Pointe home of Susan and Sandro Girard. When Webber asked for ideas to promote the DIA, Girard responded, "Give them something interesting to look at and they'll come in."[18] Soon afterward, Webber proposed to DIA director E. P. Richardson that the store sponsor an exhibition to "raise the level of taste" among Detroit consumers and to "stimulate their interest in [modern] design."[19] Richardson suggested a focus on "living," with the idea of commissioning designers to create rooms, as an approach that would be "easier for the public to grasp."[20] The approach differed from that of previous exhibitions at MOMA and the Walker Art Center, which had focused on objects and designers and had included price lists.[21] The resulting exhibition—which mobilized key figures in Detroit artistic, commercial, and industrial circles—was to have a huge impact both within and beyond Detroit (fig. 53).

By July 28, 1948, Alexander Girard was identified as the "one person" tasked with directing the project.[22] Girard was paid the sizeable sum of $11,500 total for his efforts by the J. L. Hudson Corporation.[23] Hudson's also paid $41,500 to fund the exhibition as a whole, which included an estimated $13,500 for construction, $8,000 for publicity, $1,000 for landscaping, and $2,500 for artwork and murals.[24] The implementation of the exhibition was entrusted to an executive committee consisting of Girard and Richardson, along with the architects Minoru Yamasaki and Eero Saarinen, General Motors styling director LeRoy Kiefer, and the Maxon advertising agency vice president William Laurie Jr.[25] Each headed subcommittees, including Publicity (Laurie), Special Exhibits (Saarinen), Construction Materials Procurement (Yamasaki), and Special Techniques and Procurement (Kiefer), with Girard in charge of Planning, Exhibition Objects, Space Design, and Production. Additional subcommittees included Catalogue, Finances, and Budgeting, led by DIA secretary William Bostick, and Legal Advice, led by Daniel Goodenough.[26]

The innovative nature of the exhibition encompassed not only the products exhibited and their unique presentation—all overseen by Girard himself—but also the overall conception of the exhibition as an educational rather than a commercial enterprise.

53. Publicity photo, *For Modern Living* exhibition, Detroit Institute of Arts, Detroit, MI, 1949. Shown from left to right: K. T. Keller, president of Chrysler Corp.; James B. Webber Jr., general manager of J. L. Hudson's; Mrs. Edsel Ford, Art Institute commissioner; Alexander Girard; and Edgar P. Richardson, DIA director. Photographer: Elmer Astelford. Courtesy Alexander Girard Estate, Vitra Design Museum. MAR-04762-52.

As stated by Richardson, the goal was to demonstrate the principles of "good" modern design to the American public.[27] The educational intent was reiterated by public-relations director Laurie, who insisted that there be "no tie-ins whatsoever; no instructions on who makes what; where to get this or that" but that the exhibition "stimulate among the general public . . . a broader understanding . . . of contemporary creative effort."[28] The particular relevance of the show to Detroit was noted by Richardson, who stated, "This city is dedicated to streamlining and beautifying automobiles but its people are often afraid to apply these principles to daily living."[29] He also noted the larger implications of the exhibition beyond Detroit, given its midcentury timing, its industrial context, and its inclusion of "objects actually in production—not dreams but things actually available today."[30] Echoing the ongoing dialogue on the role of art in postwar society, Richardson asked, "What shall we see in the second half of this troubled but remarkable century? . . . It is for the designers to answer it with their work."[31]

space

-- a small space grows large
- space is valueable - keep it
- space is freedom
- space is our greatest luxury
- bulk and weight kill space
- lightness and economy make space

romance - magic

- modern has romance --
    - of today's inventions
    - of today's progress
    - of liberty (freedom)
    - of making the most of ourselves
    - of the pioneer

- modern has magic --
    - of modern science
    - of new discoveries
    - of a new world
    - of a better way of life

nature - beauty

- let the sun in.
- natural materials are beautiful
- God made nature don't spoil it.
- make the most of nature
- respect nature.
- natures' inspiration is honesty
- beauty can be simple too
- the richness of color is beautiful
- the richness of texture is beautiful
- space is beautiful.

morals   honesty

- lets believe in ourselves
- let a thing be honestly itself
- be honest with your home
- dont disguise your home
- lets wake up to our day!
- dont live in the past!
- look for the honest thing - not the "cute"
- beware of things that look like others.
- let yourself live!
- make the most of today!
- modern is a way of living not a "style"
- modern is not new - it is ageless honesty.
- modern of today is 50 years old.
- modern is here now. not tomorrow.
- thought + reason = modern.
- good modern makes sense - it isnt a tricky fad.
- be suspicious of things used for purposes other than for what they were originally intended.
- "all that's modern is not chrome" there's a right material for every use.
- a good thing has its place wherever it is useful.
- modern is your way of life - not that of an early settler. not that of a spanish Grandee or an english manor, or a french chateau.
- what is new will last longer than some thing already old.
- borrowing and copying are the sure signs of weakness

tradition

- respect the past - they believed in themselves.
- in the greatest tradition - be yourself!
- lets find our way - our forefathers found theirs!
- all that was Good - was modern in its day.

periods vs. modern

- are we to live with scenery or sense?
- scenery or sense?
- period fake or modern honesty?
- you dont wear a hooped skirt - why sit in a victorian chair?
- live your way - not your Grandmas!

fashion & 'Styles'

- fashion dictates - modern leaves you free -
- dont live for a style - live for yourself -
- dont look for a "style" in modern look for a way of living honestly.
- "styles" are habits - modern you enjoy
- streamlining doesn't make modern
- Colors are yours to use - not for fashion to dictate

54. Exhibition notes on "modern" style, written by Alexander Girard for the *For Modern Living* exhibition, Detroit, MI, 1949. Courtesy Alexander Girard Estate, Vitra Design Museum.

Surviving correspondence documents the evolution of the exhibition theme during the months July–November 1948. While a July 28, 1948, letter from Richardson to J. L. Hudson president Reuben Ryding referenced several potential names, by October "Modern Living" was the favorite.[32] However, during a November 7, 1948, meeting, Girard, Yamasaki, and Saarinen rejected that concept in favor of a new one: "A New Concept of Beauty," nicknamed "the Victorian Room."[33] This new concept–presented at an executive meeting on November 10, 1948, attended by Richardson and Ryding–was premised on the idea that contemporary architects and designers must reject the "prevailing decadence [that is, the revival style] of the arts of their time" in order to "reintegrate art with life" through modern design.[34] The theme would be evident in the exhibition design: the visitor would enter through a Victorian room, emblematic of this "decadent period," before viewing the modern exhibits, intended to illustrate the "new way of life" made possible by modern design."[35] After criticism by Richardson–who rejected the negative, "straw man" approach–Girard and his committee reverted to the original concept and by late November approved the title "For Modern Living."[36]

While the "Victorian room" concept was rejected, the document presented at the November 10 executive committee meeting–prepared by Girard, Laurie, Yamasaki, and Saarinen–is significant in that it identified the essential qualities of "modern" design."[37] These included (1) freedom, (2) honesty, (3) simplicity, (4) lightness, and (5) naturalness. Bullet points defined the terms. "Freedom" signified a "new understanding of the quality and use of space, the opening up to sun, air and sky, letting the outside in, the breaking down of the 'box' house and room, and the use of space as form." "Honesty" referred to the "use and expression" of materials and manufacturing methods, with particular attention to the clear "expression of function with regards to form and use." "Simplicity" and "lightness" dictated the economical use of materials as opposed to "the ostentation of over-elaboration and over-ornamentation." "Naturalness" was defined literally as "the enjoyment of the form and variety of natural objects–in themselves and in their contrasting relation to the geometry of man's creations"–but also symbolically as "the urge to achieve a natural way of life, as against the outmoded formalities of the past."[38] Other exhibition documentation references additional design qualities, including the "free use of color" and "new forms due to new material," reflecting the importance of new technology in modern design.[39]

According to the document, adherence to the aforementioned qualities resulted in an additional, "intangible quality": "A New Concept of Beauty."[40] However–echoing the utopian tone of many postwar projects–Girard emphasized that "truly modern" objects must address functional and spiritual as well as aesthetic concerns. In a *New York Times* article, Girard posed the question, "Have imagination, ingenuity and invention been used to answer new problems . . . with the aim of creating better products for more people? To the extent . . . that those answers can be answered positively, will indicate to what extent an object is truly modern."[41] Similar criteria appear in a series of exhibition notes, handwritten by Girard (fig. 54), which delineate the key elements of "modern" style, including economy, freedom, invention, nature, reason, and honesty, as well as beauty.[42]

Girard used these criteria to select the more than two thousand objects in the exhibition, noting that each shared essential qualities that "uniquely express our predominantly mechanized age."[43] Girard had surveyed lists of previous modern design shows, in order to select "only the best examples of contemporary design for the home," showing both a "culmination of 50 years of effort in the modern design field and . . . a preview of much important work-in-progress."[44] He had also contacted prominent designers and theorists–both within and beyond Detroit and from diverse design fields–to form an advisory committee. Key advisers, invited to help assemble the objects to be exhibited, included the Cranbrook weaver Marianne Strengell (woven fabrics), the architectural historian W. Hawkins Ferry (historical data and objects), DIA curator John S. Newberry (modern painting and sculpture), and MOMA industrial design director Edgar Kaufmann Jr.[45] Others included Herman Miller president D. J. De Pree; designers Florence Knoll, George Nelson, and Charles Eames; General Motors vice president Harley Earl; and *Arts and Architecture* editor John Entenza.[46]

The educational and aesthetic impact of the objects was maximized by the organizational flow of the exhibition (fig. 55). Despite the rejection of the "Victorian room" concept, both the exhibition banner (fig. 5) and the catalogue cover (fig. 56) denigrated historical revival styles. Both featured a humorous image: a Saul Steinberg drawing of a man sitting on a modern, streamlined chair, putting his feet up on an ornate, Baroque-style chair.[47] The concept evolved through a dialogue (via letter and telegram) between Girard and Steinberg in July 1949.[48] This theme was reiterated in the exhibition entrance (fig. 57), which offered the visitor a choice between two doorways / ways of life: one (featuring Chippendale chairs) labeled "the dead end of repetition" and another promising "a new road."

This promotion of modern American design as an antidote to the "affliction" represented by historical revival styles and by the "monotonous uniformity" of European

floor plan of exhibition

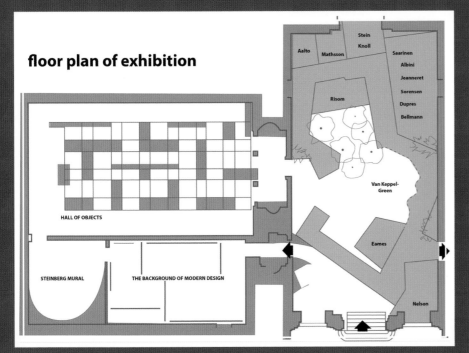

Labels on floor plan: Aalto, Mathsson, Stein, Knoll, Saarinen, Albini, Jeanneret, Sorensen, Dupres, Bellmann, Risom, Van Keppel-Green, Eames, Nelson, HALL OF OBJECTS, STEINBERG MURAL, THE BACKGROUND OF MODERN DESIGN

55. Floor plan of the exhibition, *For Modern Living*, Detroit Institute of Arts, Detroit, MI, 1949. Artwork: adapted from the exhibition catalogue by Rachel Goad. Courtesy Detroit Institute of Arts.

A DEADEND OF REPETITION - OR - A NEW ROAD?

57. Entrance to the *For Modern Living* exhibition: "A Dead End of Repetition or a New Road?" Detroit Institute of Arts, Detroit, MI, 1949. Photographer: Elmer Astelford. Courtesy Alexander Girard Estate, Vitra Design Museum. MAR-04762-11.

an exhibition

STEINBERG

for
modern
living

THE DETROIT INSTITUTE OF ARTS • DETROIT, MICHIGAN, U.S.A.

56. Exhibition catalogue, *For Modern Living* exhibition, Detroit Institute of Arts, Detroit, MI, 1949. Cover art by Saul Steinberg. Courtesy Saul Steinberg Foundation and Detroit Institute of Arts.

58. Evolution of the cantilevered chair from the Historical Section, room 1, *For Modern Living* exhibition, Detroit Institute of Arts, Detroit, MI, 1949. Photographer: Elmer Astelford. Courtesy Alexander Girard Estate, Vitra Design Museum. MAR-04762-18.

59. Detail of Saul Steinberg mural from the *For Modern Living* exhibition catalogue, Detroit Institute of Arts, Detroit, MI, 1949. Courtesy Saul Steinberg Foundation.

60. Detail of Saul Steinberg mural from the *For Modern Living* exhibition catalogue, Detroit Institute of Arts, Detroit, MI, 1949. Courtesy Saul Steinberg Foundation.

modernism was a recurrent theme.[49] The first exhibition room, which presented a historical overview of modern design, set out to dispel the notion that modern design was not "cooked up by long-haired nuts and radicals across the Atlantic" but instead was rooted in American life.[50] One display (fig. 58) presented the Mies cantilevered chair (1927) as derived from design principles dating back to two American inventions: an R. L. Howard mower spring seat of 1857 and the jump seat of a 1917 Owen Magnetic touring car.[51] In the next room, a sixty-foot-long mural by Saul Steinberg (figs. 59 and 60) caricatured the discrepancy between modern American life and the revivalist preferences of American homeowners. The drawings, dubbed by Steinberg as "modern and not so modern living," featured humorous, aesthetically and technologically incongruous vignettes such as a family moving modern art, furnishings, and appliances (including an ornate yet electrified fireplace) into a Tudor-style home.[52] These themes were reiterated in a catalogue essay by John Kouwenhoven, who encouraged Americans to embrace their own modern heritage ("the vernacular tradition of our machine-age democracy") by choosing furnishings—as they would cars and appliances—on the basis of form, technology, and function.[53] Edgar Kaufmann Jr. asserted in his catalogue essay a distinction between "intrinsic design" (design based on function and "native ingenuity") and "superficial styling" (based on copying from the past, with no link to modern time or place), characterizing the latter as an attitude that "still afflict[s] us."[54]

The next phase of the exhibition, the Hall of Objects, included more than two thousand objects—selected from some six thousand gathered by Girard—intended to represent the "spirit" of the modern world.[55] Examples (figs. 61 and 62) were culled from every aspect of modern life, from home furnishings (chairs and lamps), home décor (silverware, textiles, and ceramics), and personal items (jewelry, footwear and toys) to household appliances (fans, radios, typewriters, and tools).[56] In keeping with the American focus of the show, the majority of the objects—if not the designers—were American (and machine) made.[57] One exception was a magnificent ceramic pot (fig. 63), handcrafted by the Cranbrook ceramist Maija Grotell and singled out by Charles and Ray Eames as "the best we have seen done in these times."[58] Indeed, true to Girard's love

61. Three-speed fan, O. A. Sutton Corporation, from the Hall of Objects, *For Modern Living* exhibition, Detroit Institute of Arts, Detroit, MI, 1949. Photographer: Elmer Astelford. Courtesy Detroit Institute of Arts.

62. Toys from the Hall of Objects, exhibition catalogue, *For Modern Living* exhibition, Detroit Institute of Arts, Detroit, MI, 1949. Courtesy Detroit Institute of Arts.

63. Maija Grotell, vase, 1940, 14 × 14 in. While this is not the exact Maija Grotell pot exhibited in the Hall of Objects of the *For Modern Living* exhibition in 1949, it is very similar to the one illustrated in the catalogue. Museum Purchase, from the artist, CAM 1952.3. Courtesy Cranbrook Art Museum.

64. View of the Hall of Objects exhibition area, *For Modern Living* exhibition, Detroit Institute of Arts, Detroit, MI, 1949. This photo showcases the innovative "jungle gym" system of display and the variety of objects exhibited. Photographer: Elmer Astelford. © 2017 Girard Studio LLC. All rights reserved.

of folk art, handcrafted items were displayed side by side with machine-made items, with design alone as the prime determinant of modernity.[59] As noted by Monica Obniski, the installation of the objects without retail information "removed them from the commercial realm and sanctioned them as art objects."[60]

The modern character of the objects was matched by their display: the more than two thousand objects were arranged in a custom-designed Girard installation (fig. 64). The system of display, aptly nicknamed the "jungle gym," consisted of a grid-like structure of white, plastic-covered pipes and shelves at varying heights.[61] Decorative screens of "contemporary materials in vivid colors and rich textures" were hung between the pipes to enliven the displays.[62] As in Girard's architectural projects, he conceived the design with the aid of drawings and small-scale, 3-D models. Indeed, a model for the Hall of Objects is visible in the foreground of the aforementioned publicity photo (fig. 53). The bold visual effect of the display system is best captured in a Girard colored-pencil drawing (figs. 65 and 66). Here we see a floor plan of the Hall of Objects and an elevation, which shows a multilevel display of textiles, glassware, and plantings, complete with rapt viewers.

The dramatic climax of the exhibition was a series of nine rooms, set in a "fantasy landscape" in the DIA's Great Hall (fig. 4).[63] An early concept sketch for the Great Hall documents Girard's experimentation with bold color—reminiscent of the GMTC brick scheme—on the walls of the Great Hall (see fig. 212 in chapter 5). However, in the final design (fig. 67), Girard transformed the Beaux-Arts–style space by recovering floors and ceilings, adding live trees and bushes, and constructing a three-hundred-foot-long, multilevel ramp. The ramp led visitors past a series of complete rooms, designed by Alvar Aalto, Jens Risom, Bruno Mathsson, Florence Knoll, Charles Eames, and George Nelson. While the focus was on the designers, Obniski notes that each had connections with major manufacturers, including Knoll, Evans Products, and Herman Miller, which could cover the installation costs.[64] Each room demonstrated the extent to which modern design—with its integration of seemingly incompatible concepts such as function and beauty, mass production and personal expression—could meet the needs of modern American life.

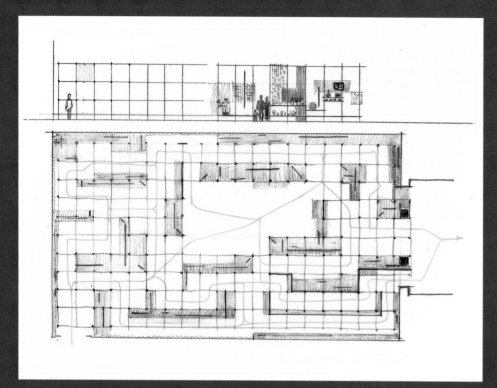

65. Alexander Girard, floor plan and elevation of the Hall of Objects, *For Modern Living* exhibition, Detroit Institute of Arts, Detroit, MI, 1949. Colored pencil on paper. Courtesy Alexander Girard Estate, Vitra Design Museum. MAR-17168-02.

67. View of the Great Hall and exhibition rooms under construction, *For Modern Living* exhibition, Detroit Institute of Arts, Detroit, MI, 1949. Courtesy Alexander Girard Estate, Vitra Design Museum. MAR-04762-42.

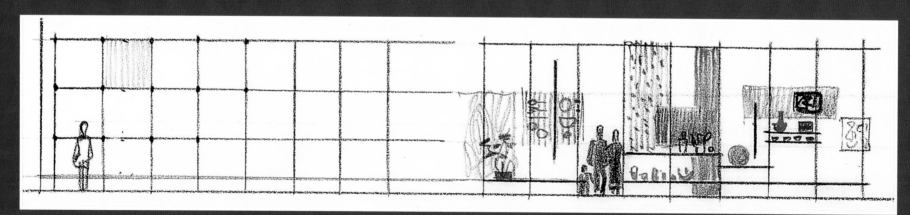

66. Alexander Girard, detail of fig. 65 showing display shelves for Hall of Objects. Colored pencil on paper. This detail showcases not only the bold, visual effect of Girard's display but also its powerful effect on viewers, including young families. Courtesy Alexander Girard Estate, Vitra Design Museum.

68. Florence Knoll exhibition room, *For Modern Living* exhibition, Detroit Institute of Arts, Detroit, MI, 1949. This photograph shows the living room with furnishing by Knoll, Inc., including the model 198 Hardoy "Butterfly" chair and the model 92 "Scissors" chair. Photographer: Elmer Astelford. Courtesy Detroit Institute of Arts.

Florence Knoll designed a series of rooms, including a combined living-dining room (fig. 68) and a bedroom, featuring furnishings by Pierre Jeanneret ("Scissors" chair; fig. 69), Jorge Ferrari-Hardoy ("Butterfly" chair), Eero Saarinen, Isamo Noguchi, and others. Knoll's spaces demonstrated her conception that "good modern" furniture must be "practical, durable, and inexpensive" but also customizable to personal tastes, through choices of fabrics and colors.[65] Materials were easy-care, in order to "withstand the daily impact of heavy use," including washable plastic, jute, and sailcloth upholstery and Formica "Realwood" tabletops, "resistant to scratching, burning and heat."[66] The George Nelson room (fig. 70) showcased the designer's belief that furniture should be "incorporated within the design and construction of the room itself."[67] All seating, apart from two chairs, was built in, including a raised, upholstered platform in the foreground of the room, which demonstrated the fact that "built-in facilities need not duplicate even the forms of existing furniture."[68] Storage was concentrated in one, multifunctional unit: the Storagewall concept developed in 1945 for *Life* magazine (but by 1946 manufactured

by Herman Miller), incorporating a built-in desk, record player, and speaker and a myriad of storage spaces. Despite the increased functionality of the space—intended to simplify housekeeping—Nelson insisted that its "clean lines" and "trim surfaces" combined "beauty and function into a pleasing whole."[69]

The room designed by Charles Eames (fig. 71) included more customizable elements, such as modular, multicolored storage units and chairs, including the Eames DCM molded plywood chair and La Chaise, a lounge chair composed of two bonded fiberglass shells (fig. 72).[70] As explained in the catalogue essay, the room represented a more "expansive" attitude

69. Pierre Jeanneret, model 92 "Scissors" chair, 1947, for Knoll Furniture Company. Courtesy Knoll, Inc.

70. George Nelson exhibition room, showing built-in Storagewall unit, *For Modern Living* exhibition, Detroit Institute of Arts, Detroit, MI, 1949. Photographer: Elmer Astelford. Courtesy Alexander Girard Estate, Vitra Design Museum. MAR-04762-04.

71. Charles Eames exhibition room, showing the studded wall, display unit, and Eames plywood chairs, *For Modern Living* exhibition, Detroit Institute of Arts, Detroit, MI, 1949. Photographer: Elmer Astelford. Courtesy Detroit Institute of Arts.

toward modern living, one that maximized the individual's "opportunity and facilities for free expression" through the variety of colors and objects chosen.[71] Key to this concept was the studded display wall, which showcased a vase of flowers, a mask, an enlarged photograph, and a colorful box kite. The value placed by Eames on aesthetic enjoyment is evident in the ceiling light, conceived not "as an efficient machine for illumination but for its special sparkly optic sensation."[72] Sadly, while correspondence from DIA secretary William Bostick indicates that color slides of the exhibition were shot, the most comprehensive photographs of the exhibition known to date were shot by Elmer Astelford in black and white.[73] However, a collage by Ray Eames (fig. 73) and a 1949 advertisement for Pittsburgh Paints (fig. 74) capture the "free use of color" in the exhibition rooms by Eames, Knoll, and Nelson.[74] Indeed, one visitor commented, "I never thought the pinks, reds and greens Charles Eames used in his room would work together. . . . It gives me courage to try something like that."[75]

The exhibition received high praise from D. S. Defenbacher of the Walker Art Gallery for its marriage of museum and industry and for its dramatic style, both within the galleries and behind the scenes in financing, promotion, and public relations.[76] MOMA

72. Alexander Girard seated in La Chaise in the Charles Eames exhibition room, *For Modern Living* exhibition, Detroit Institute of Arts, Detroit, MI, 1949. Photographer: Elmer Astelford. Courtesy Alexander Girard Estate, Vitra Design Museum. MAR-04629-01.

73. Ray Eames, color collage of the Charles Eames exhibition room from the *For Modern Living* exhibition, Detroit Institute of Arts, Detroit, MI, 1949. © 2017 Eames Office, LLC.

curator Edgar Kaufmann Jr. wrote that it was "the most comprehensive statement yet made in favor of modern design rooted in the necessities and character of the American community today."[77] The show also drew record crowds: total attendance was 149,553 (the highest in the museum's history), and 6,783 copies of the catalogue were sold.[78] Richardson told Girard that MOMA curators were "fluttered and upset that Detroit should have put on such an important show, instead of their museum."[79] In a letter to Webber, he credited Girard specifically, calling the exhibition "a superb piece of installation" and a "triumph for Sandro Girard."[80]

Girard hoped to build on the success of the show by setting up a permanent gallery, "the new 20th Century Department," at the DIA to promote "good contemporary art and design."[81] Inspired by this concept, the DIA secretary Bostick requested that J. L. Hudson's donate exhibition materials—80 percent of the pipes and all of the shelving and supports from the "jungle gym," 80 percent of the lighting fixtures, and the entire Steinberg mural—for the creation of a "permanent modern living exhibition gallery in the museum."[82] A *Detroit News* article dated January 15, 1950, reiterated the plan, soliciting

Widely hailed for its influence on present-day living patterns, Detroit's *For Modern Living* Exhibition featured the most significant trends in home engineering and decorations. The beautiful room above is by Florence Knoll. Pittsburgh Paints were used for their outstanding quality and beauty.

The modern way to decorate your home for lasting satisfaction...

Paint Right with *Color Dynamics!* *

Paint Best with *Pittsburgh Paints!*

Clean lines and trim surfaces are blended into a harmonious whole through the free use of color in this handsome room designed by George Nelson. The room was a feature of the Detroit Institute of Arts' *For Modern Living* exhibit, A. H. Girard, director.

FREE and daring use of color is today's first commandment in home decoration. The exciting, new rooms reproduced here are from the famous Detroit Institute of Arts' exhibition "For Modern Living". They suggest the charming, distinctive effects you can have in your own home when you *let yourself go* with Pittsburgh's COLOR DYNAMICS!

By following the principles of this scientific system, you can plan striking color arrangements with absolute assurance that your results will be beautiful and artistically correct!

COLOR DYNAMICS uses the *energy in color* to enhance the beauty of your home inside and out. It helps you wake up dull, drab rooms—make them lively and interesting. You can paint cool effects into rooms of southern exposure or bring the sunshine of warm, cheerful colors into those that face the north.

You can in effect re-model your home with COLOR DYNAMICS—make small, stuffy rooms seem large and airy—narrow halls and cramped areas appear spacious —ceilings seem higher or lower!

And the lovely effects you obtain in decorating your home are made more enduring by the Live Paint Protection of Pittsburgh Paints. Enriched with "*Vitolized Oils*," these quality paints afford a smoother, richer finish that far outlasts ordinary paints.

Visit your Pittsburgh dealer and let him explain how much more lasting satisfaction you enjoy when you paint *right* with COLOR DYNAMICS—paint *best* with fine-quality Pittsburgh Live Paints!

*Trade Mark Registered

• Ask your Pittsburgh dealer for a FREE copy of our interesting booklet, "Color Dynamics for Your Home," Or send this coupon.

Pittsburgh Plate Glass Co., Paint Division, Department AH-50, Pittsburgh 22, Pa.

Please send me a FREE copy of your new Booklet, "Color Dynamics for Your Home."

Name

Street

City   County   State

PITTSBURGH PAINTS
PAINTS • GLASS • CHEMICALS • BRUSHES • PLASTICS

PITTSBURGH PLATE GLASS COMPANY

74. Advertisement for Pittsburgh Paints Color Dynamics showing the Florence Knoll and George Nelson exhibition rooms, *For Modern Living* exhibition, Detroit, MI, 1949. Courtesy PPG.

75. Ruth Adler Schnee with her design "Slits and Slats," 1947. Courtesy Edward and Ruth Adler Schnee Papers, Cranbrook Archives.

76. Ruth Adler Schnee, "Germination," 1948. Photographer: R. H. Hensleigh and Tim Thayer. Courtesy Cranbrook Art Museum.

"friends of modern art who will roll up their sleeves to help build a dream."[83] In the article, DIA curator William Woolfenden indicated that the planned modern gallery would include "changing displays of good furniture and home objects" as well as work by contemporary Michigan artists.[84] Sadly, the plan was never executed.

A letter written by Richardson to Webber, dated November 22, 1949, documents the director's hope that the exhibition would have a lasting influence on the buying—and, perhaps, viewing—habits of everyday Americans.[85] A *Business Week* article indicated that J. L. Hudson carried the modern merchandise on display in the exhibition, although a contemporary photograph of its "Modern Galleries" suggests otherwise.[86] Girard commented that the modern items carried by Hudson's—including Eames chairs, released to the public for the first time—were not well received. He stated that "people used to come and look at this as if it were some sort of freak show or museum, and they didn't buy much."[87] However, the exhibition did boost sales for one Detroit designer, Ruth Adler Schnee (fig. 75), whose textile design Ship Shape was included in the Hall of Objects.[88]

77. Adler Schnee Associates' first showroom at 9842 Twelfth Street, Detroit, MI, September 1949. Photographer: Detroit News. Courtesy Edward and Ruth Adler Schnee Papers, Cranbrook Archives.

Adler Schnee had opened her first design studio in Detroit in 1947, after completing an MFA degree at Cranbrook Academy of Art and winning the "Better Rooms for Better Living" competition, sponsored by the *Chicago Tribune*.[89] Her textile designs include "Germination" (fig. 76), which was inspired by the landscapes of Arizona and Colorado. Adler Schnee recalls that when *For Modern Living* enthusiasts flocked to Hudson's, they were devastated to discover that the store did not carry the modern merchandise exhibited in the show.[90] Salespeople recommended the Adler-Schnee "showroom" (fig. 77) on Livernois Avenue in Detroit—in actuality, a refurbished garage—which she had opened with her husband, Edward Schnee.[91] Adler-Schnee Associates was a true partnership: while Ruth worked behind the scenes designing textiles, husband Eddie named the designs, silk-screened, and actively promoted modern design to customers inspired by the exhibition. Ruth recalls that her customers "were so desperate to buy modern merchandise" that they even ordered from drawings (evident in the photo) sketched on the wall of their garage showroom (fig. 78).[92]

The success of the *For Modern Living* exhibition clearly enhanced Girard's reputation as a designer, allowing him to further promote modern design, both within and beyond

78. Detail of showroom wall, Adler Schnee Associates' first showroom at 9842 Twelfth Street, Detroit, MI. Due to financial constraints, drawings on the showroom wall were used in lieu of catalogues. Photographer: Detroit News. Courtesy Edward and Ruth Adler Schnee Papers, Cranbrook Archives.

79. "Good Design for Modern Living" advertisement for Girard Studio, 16841 Kercheval Place, Grosse Pointe, MI, 1950. © 2017 Girard Studio LLC. All rights reserved.

80. Interior of Alexander Girard's studio, 16841 Kercheval Place, Grosse Pointe, MI, circa 1950. © Girard Studio LLC. All rights reserved.

81. Exterior of Alexander Girard's studio, 16841 Kercheval Place, Grosse Pointe, MI. The photograph shows the same rigidized steel door from Girard's previous studio at 379 Fisher Road. Photographer: Elmer Astelford. © 2017 Girard Studio LLC. All rights reserved.

82. Advertisement for exhibition of Eskimo crafts, October 1–11, 1951, at Girard's studio, 16841 Kercheval Place, Grosse Pointe, MI. © 2017 Girard Studio LLC. All rights reserved.

83. Advertisement for exhibition of Steinberg drawings, October 15–20, 1951, at Girard's studio, 16841 Kercheval Place, Grosse Pointe, MI. © 2017 Girard Studio LLC. All rights reserved.

84. Advertisement for exhibition of Picasso lithographs, November 1–12, 1951, at Girard's studio, 16841 Kercheval Place, Grosse Pointe, MI. © 2017 Girard Studio LLC. All rights reserved.

Detroit. In January 1950, Girard served as a juror for MOMA's "Good Design" competition, conceived by Edgar Kaufmann Jr. as a partnership between the MOMA and the Merchandise Mart in Chicago.[93] In the fall of 1950, Girard moved into a new studio space on 16841 Kercheval Place in Grosse Pointe, advertising "good design for modern living" (fig. 79). Once again, he transformed a stark, industrial space with concrete floors, cement walls, and exposed I beams and heating ducts into a workable studio. An article in *Interiors* notes that Girard "hid none of the structural elements, but used color to organize them," explaining that steel beams were painted black, steel columns blue-white, ducts white, and nuts and bolts orange vermillion.[94] He subdivided the interior space (fig. 80) through the use of split bamboo screens, plywood, and cabinets. An exterior view (fig. 81) demonstrates that Girard reused the same rigidized steel door but added black Bakelite trim with white wood letters, spelling out "Girard."

Building on the momentum of the *For Modern Living* exhibition, Girard held a series of exhibitions (figs. 82–84) at his Kercheval Place studio between October and November 1951. The exhibitions, which featured Eskimo crafts, Steinberg drawings, Picasso lithographs, and The Toy by Charles and Ray Eames, showcased Girard's expansive conception of modern design.[95] However, one could say that Girard's most concrete expression of "design for modern living" and its guiding principles—freedom, honesty, simplicity, lightness, naturalness, free use of color, and new materials—came in his Grosse Pointe architecture of the period 1947–51.

85. Alexander and Susan Girard in the master bedroom of their Lothrop home, 222 Lothrop Road, Grosse Pointe Farms, MI. Photographer: Elmer Astelford. © 2017 Girard Studio LLC. All rights reserved.

Tradition and Innovation

Girard and Grosse Pointe Architecture

Modern is your way of life—not that of an early settler, not that of a Spanish grandee, nor an English manor or a French chateau. . . . Let us find our way. . . . All that was good was modern in its own day.

—Alexander Girard

During a search for a home site in 1947, Sandro and Susan Girard discovered a pair of run-down houses overlooking a pine forest on the dead end of Lothrop Road in Grosse Pointe Farms. The first two blocks of Lothrop nearest the lake shore were prime real estate, home to Colonial- and Regency-style estates. However, this area—home to a Prohibition-era speakeasy—was described as the "hinterland side of Grosse Pointe's fashionable Lake Shore Drive."[1] While the wooded location and the somewhat unsavory associations of the site had scared off previous buyers, it resonated with the Girards, who likely sought some separation from traditional Grosse Pointe society—and architecture. Indeed, their new, hybrid home—created by renovating the two preexisting structures and joining them with a new two-story unit—clashed with the historical revival styles prevalent in Grosse Pointe at the time. Girard's new, modernist vision is clearly expressed in a photograph (fig. 85) of Sandro and Susan Girard in the master bedroom of their new home, which features an innovative, cantilevered staircase, built-in furniture, and folk art. Indeed, despite the home's traditional

86. Map of Grosse Pointe township from C. Sauer (1893). Detailed official atlas of Wayne County, Michigan. Courtesy Geography and Map Division, Library of Congress.

87. Photo of Horace and John Dodge. Courtesy Meadowbrook Hall Archives.

88. Bloodgood Tuttle, John Dodge estate, Grosse Pointe, MI (demolished circa 1940). Courtesy Meadowbrook Hall Archives.

89. Edsel and Eleanor Ford with their children, Henry, Benson, Josephine, and William, at Gaukler Point, circa 1938. Courtesy Benson Ford Research Center, The Henry Ford.

address, 222 Lothrop marked a dramatic departure from Grosse Pointe architectural design and patronage at the time—and a springboard for future projects, including the Goodenough and Jackson houses.

Tradition: Style and Status in Grosse Pointe

In order to understand the innovative nature of Girard's work in Grosse Pointe, one must first understand the traditional nature of Grosse Pointe society and architecture. Grosse Pointe had been settled in the nineteenth century as a site of summer cottages for wealthy Detroit businessmen but evolved during the early decades of the twentieth century into an exclusive residential district (fig. 86).[2] This geographic (and architectural) shift was influenced by both social and economic factors, centering on the "new aristocracy of the automobile" that had emerged as a result of Detroit's booming automotive industry.[3] Newly rich businessmen attempted to solidify their social status among the old-money Detroit elite by commissioning houses in historically inspired styles as "proof of arrival."[4] Prime examples include the estates designed for the automotive elite in the first decades of the twentieth century by the Detroit architectural firms SH&G and Albert Kahn. While Albert Kahn designed innovative factories for both the Ford and Dodge motor companies, utilizing new technologies such as reinforced concrete, steel frames, and wide expanses of glass, in the families' private residences, he catered to their "extravagant and anachronistic tastes."[5]

The first examples of this phenomenon include the residences built for the Dodge brothers. Horace and John Dodge (fig. 87) had moved to Detroit in 1900 to supply engines for Ransom E. Olds and Henry Ford, before forming their own car company, Dodge Brothers, in 1914.[6] In 1912, Kahn built an English Renaissance–style estate, dubbed "Rose Terrace," for Horace and Anna Dodge on Lakeshore Drive.[7] Not to be outdone, in 1918, Horace's brother and partner, John Dodge, hired SH&G to design a massive, Tudor-style estate farther down the lakeshore, complete with a small artificial peninsula and private dock.[8] The estate (fig. 88) was designed by SH&G's Bloodgood Tuttle, an English, Beaux-Arts–trained architect, and was crafted by stonecutters from Scotland. The mansion would have contained over 110 rooms, each filled with ornately carved woodwork, rich tapestries, and English furniture.[9] As W. Hawkins Ferry stated, the "massive walls, cavernous interiors and heraldic devices . . . conveyed a message of awesome masculine dignity and prestige."[10] Sadly, John Dodge's estate, Harbor Hill, remained unfinished after his death in 1920; it was demolished in 1941 and its property subdivided.[11]

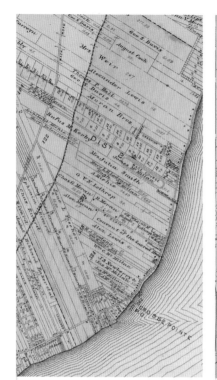

90. Detail, 1893 map of Grosse Pointe township. At center is the land owned by George V. N. Lothrop, which stretches from the lake shore all the way to current-day Mack Avenue. Farther north is the land owned by James McMillan, site of a racecourse (visible as an oval shape near the lake shore). Courtesy Geography and Map Division, Library of Congress.

91. Detail of Baist's Real Estate Atlas, Detroit Suburbs, vol. 1, Subdivisions to 1938. This detail shows the new subdivisions, including Lothrop's Subdivision and Hamilton Park, developing west of Grosse Pointe Boulevard on Lothrop and Vendome Roads. The land closest to the lake shore is still owned by the Lothrop and Joy families, although a considerable part of Lothrop's land is owned by John Dodge's widow (Mrs. Alfred Wilson). Courtesy Grosse Pointe Historical Society.

In 1926, Albert Kahn began construction on an English Tudor–style estate (fig. 15) for Edsel Ford (fig. 89), son of Henry Ford and president of Ford Motor Company.[12] Adhering to the English Cotswold-cottage style, Kahn imported stones, fireplaces, staircases, paneling, and other materials from England, creating a "domestic environment . . . in marked contrast to the industrial world of which he [Edsel Ford] was a leader."[13] Historically inspired styles predominated in Grosse Pointe residential architecture throughout

the 1920s, '30s, and '40s in the work of the architects Robert O. Derrick, John Russell Pope, Charles Platt, C. Howard Crane, Hugh T. Keyes, and H. H. Micou.[14] These architectural styles reflected the predominant social and aesthetic concerns of the families that built them, many of whom strived for innovation in business but maintained a staid, traditional image at home.[15] Examples include the residences built in the 1920s and '30s on Lothrop and Vendome, streets that later admitted—albeit, reluctantly—the modern-style homes designed by Girard.

Lothrop Road was developed on land purchased in 1830 by George V. N. Lothrop, a Detroit lawyer and politician, who is cited as one of the founders of the summer colony in Grosse Pointe.[16] A detail of the 1893 Grosse Pointe map (fig. 90) shows the extent of Lothrop's land, which originally encompassed 130 acres, stretching from the lake shore to Mack Road (now Avenue).[17] There he built a cottage named Summerside and planted a pine forest, marking one of the first reforestation efforts in the United States.[18] Lothrop's land was kept intact after his death in 1897; it was managed first by his heirs and after 1899 by the newly formed Lothrop Estate Company.[19] On June 5, 1905, a residential subdivision (Lothrop's Subdivision) was platted on the first block of Lothrop, west of Grosse Pointe Boulevard.[20] The Lothrop Estate land nearest the lake was subdivided in 1918, when a large section was purchased by John Dodge to build his Harbor Hill estate. As evident in a map of Grosse Pointe Farms dated 1938 (fig. 91), the Lothrop Estate Company continued to own a narrow strip of the land east of Grosse Pointe Boulevard (closest to the lake shore and adjacent to the land purchased by John Dodge) and west of the platted subdivision (home to the remains of George Lothrop's pine forest).[21] A building boom in Grosse Pointe in the 1920s resulted in new estates on the first block of Lothrop. These included the Allen F. Edwards house on 99 Lothrop (fig. 92), designed in 1928 by Charles Platt in a Colonial style, and the J. Stewart Hudson house on 114 Lothrop (fig. 93), built in 1937 by Hugh T. Keyes in a Regency style.[22]

During the 1930s and '40s, the size of the Lothrop Estate Company—and of Lothrop's pine woods—diminished as new subdivisions were developed. Indeed, by 1945, the "Pine Woods" (as the wooded area is known to local residents) were reduced to a small patch at the dead end of Lothrop Road between Ridge and Charlevoix Roads. During the Prohibition era, the area was reportedly the site of a popular speakeasy, the Pines, which operated out of a clapboard farmhouse.[23] Indeed, according to one source, as much as 80 percent of the nation's bootleg smuggling took place on the waterways of the Detroit River

92. Charles Platt, Allen F. Edwards house, 99 Lothrop, Grosse Pointe Farms, MI, 1928. Photographer: Katie Doelle.

93. Hugh T. Keyes, J. Stewart Hudson house, 114 Lothrop, Grosse Pointe Farms, MI, 1937. Photographer: Katie Doelle.

94. Robert O. Derrick, 70 Vendome, Grosse Pointe Farms, MI. Photographer: Katie Doelle.

95. Robert O. Derrick, F. Caldwell Walker house , 211 Vendome, Grosse Pointe Farms, MI. Photographer: Katie Doelle.

96. Map of Lothrop's Subdivision lots at the dead end of Lothrop Road past Ridge Road, Grosse Pointe Farms, MI, circa 1945. The highlighted area shows the land (lot 53 and part of lot 51) and the preexisting houses purchased by Alexander and Susan Girard in 1947. Artwork by Rachel Goad. Based on "1945 Sanborn Fire Safety" map (vol. 20, sheet 98), Sanborn Map Collection.

97. Color photograph of the Pine Woods at the dead end of Lothrop Road past Ridge Road, Grosse Pointe Farms, MI, circa 1947. Courtesy Alexander Girard Estate, Vitra Design Museum. MAR-04509-14.

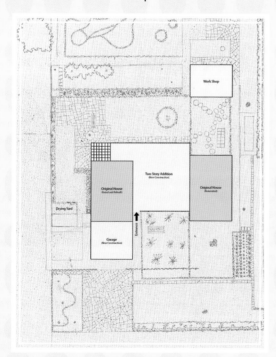

98. Site map of 222 Lothrop showing old and new structures. Artwork by Rachel Goad. Adapted from "1949 Lothrop Road Plan," Alexander Girard Estate, Vitra Design Museum. MAR-04799-01.

99. 222 Lothrop during the construction of the Alexander and Susan Girard house, 1947. Photograph shows preexisting structures on site adapted by Girard with new two-story structure. Courtesy Alexander Girard Estate, Vitra Design Museum. MAR-04509-11.

and Lake St. Clair.[24] After the repeal of Prohibition, however, the area became a popular recreational site for Grosse Pointe residents.[25]

Vendome Road, another bastion of traditional style later infiltrated by Girard's modernism, was first developed from land owned by the entrepreneur James McMillan. McMillan had earned millions in the mid- to late 1800s in the railroad-car and steam-transit business.[26] McMillan's land, nicknamed "Hamilton Park" after his birthplace in Ontario, was the site of a racetrack, visible in the 1893 Grosse Pointe map detail (fig. 90) as a large oval.[27] However, in 1910, the land was purchased by Henry B. Joy, president of Packard Motor Company, who hired Albert Kahn to build a country estate, Fair Acres, on the site.[28] On May 26, 1926, the Joy Realty Company platted a residential subdivision, Hamilton Park, on the part of Joy's land west of Grosse Pointe Boulevard, as shown in the map of 1938 (fig. 91).[29] Historical revival styles prevailed on Vendome in the works of H. H. Micou, Gustav Steffens, and Robert O. Derrick. Derrick studied architecture at Columbia University, before moving in 1921 to Grosse Pointe, where he designed more than twenty private residences and several public buildings, primarily in Colonial, Georgian, and Tudor styles.[30] With a hipped roof, horizontal transoms, dormer windows, and stone detailing, 70 Vendome (fig. 94) was clearly influenced by the English estates that Derrick visited during a 1927 trip to England.[31] The following year, Derrick built a massive, Georgian-style mansion on two and a half acres at 211 Vendome (fig. 95) for the whiskey heir F. Caldwell Walker, although Walker never moved in.[32] During the 1940s and '50s, Vendome was home to many leading Grosse Pointe businessmen, including Henry T. Bodman, chairman of NBD Bank (78 Vendome), and Wilbur Brucker, former Michigan governor (56 Vendome).[33] However, between 1947 and 1951, sections of Lothrop and Vendome Roads were transformed by an outsider, Alexander Girard, whose modern style appealed to a new breed of socially prominent yet architecturally adventurous patrons.

Innovation: The Alexander and Susan Girard House

Fittingly, Girard's first departure from Grosse Pointe architectural tradition came in his own home at 222 Lothrop Road. On June 27, 1947, Sandro and Susan Girard purchased lot 53 and part of lot 51 on the dead end of Lothrop Road (fig. 96), complete with two dilapidated houses (one of them, reportedly, the old speakeasy).[34] The remote nature of the site is evident in a color photograph (fig. 97)—taken before the construction of the Girard house—which shows an unpaved road leading to the remaining pine woods. Girard applied for a building permit on August 11, 1947, and began the estimated $20,000

project.[35] The construction process reflected Girard's conception of modern design as a "cocktail" of "economy, common sense and functionalism."[36] While the comment comes from an interview relating to the *For Modern Living* exhibition, it certainly applies to Girard's architecture. By serving as architect, contractor, and interior designer, Girard cut construction costs to as low as nine dollars per square foot.[37]

However, the greatest cost savings came with Girard's decision to reuse the preexisting structures on site. "Visualizing a single modern structure in place of the two existing dwellings," Girard renovated one house, razed and rebuilt the other, and connected the two preexisting structures with a new, two-story unit (fig. 98).[38] The resulting "hybrid" home included a large master suite (in the renovated house), a dining room and kitchen (in the razed and rebuilt house), and an added garage.[39] The new, two-story structure (fig. 99) included a large, multifunctional living/work room (thirty-four by nearly thirty-eight feet) on the ground floor and a suite of children's bedrooms and a playroom on the upper floor. One author commented that Girard had "knit two and purled one" in order to create "a surprisingly successful home in which the owner (Girard himself) can live, work, receive clients, and entertain."[40]

The house was completed by September 24, 1948, when it was featured on the front page of the *Detroit News* Home section.[41] As one author wrote, the façade of 222 Lothrop (fig. 100) offered "nothing but indifference to the taste for high style and big effects" prevalent in the other houses on Lothrop.[42] Indeed, the vertical board-and-batten pinewood treatment of the exterior was described in one article as "somewhat barnlike."[43] Girard's playful nature was evident in the bold color of the house exterior: the garage wing was painted white and the bedroom wing orange. On October 15, 1948, the new Girard residence was one of five stops on a Grosse Pointe home tour organized by the Radcliffe College Club of Michigan.[44] The tour consisted primarily of traditional-style homes, including the residences of Mr. and Mrs. Frederick Ford (Georgian), Mr. and Mrs. Richard O. Burr (Nantucket), and Mr. and Mrs. Alvan Macaulay (Tudor).[45] A *Grosse Pointe News* article described the Girard house as "functional modern."[46] Girard, who viewed his home as an "experimental laboratory" and a "showcase for his ideas of a modern lifestyle," would have likely agreed with that definition.[47] Indeed, at 222 Lothrop (fig. 101), Girard utilized many cutting-edge architectural concepts, including an open plan, partition walls, cove/spot/sky lighting, varying ceiling/floor levels, integrated indoor and outdoor spaces, built-in furniture/storage/display areas, natural and modern materials, and bold color.[48]

100. Exterior view of the Girard house, 222 Lothrop, Grosse Pointe Farms, MI, 1947. Architect: Alexander Girard. Photographer: Maynard Parker. Courtesy Huntington Library.

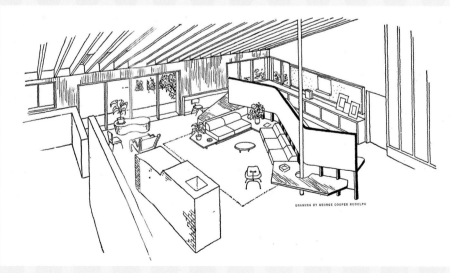

102. Diagram of the Girard house living room. Artwork George Cooper Rudolph Architects. Courtesy Rudolph Architects.

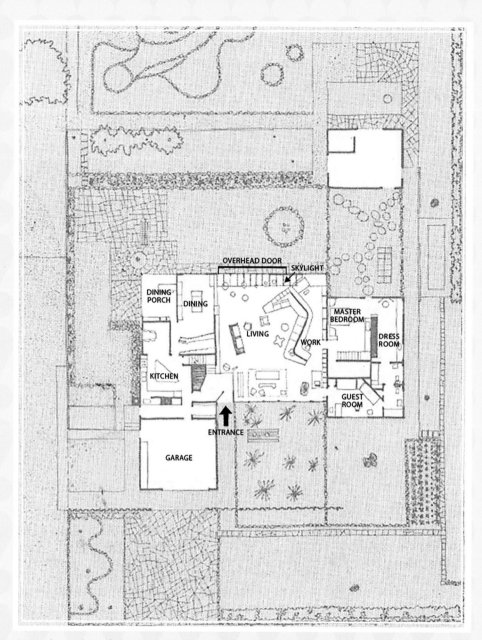

101. Floor plan of the Girard house, 222 Lothrop, Grosse Pointe, MI. Adapted by Rachel Goad from 1949 "Lothrop Road Plan," Alexander Girard Estate, Vitra Design Museum (published in "Serendipity in the Woods"). MAR-04799-01.

103. View of the entrance hall toward the front door, Girard house, 222 Lothrop, Grosse Pointe, MI. This photo shows the front entrance with the tree-stump step. At left, a partition wall and the fireplace screen the entrance hall from the living room. At right, a partition wall separates the entrance hall from the dining room. © 2017 Girard Studio LLC. All rights reserved.

104. View of the entrance hall from the front door, Girard house, 222 Lothrop, Grosse Pointe, MI. This photo shows the view from the entrance down the hall. At left, the partition wall separates the hall from the dining room; at right is the back of the fireplace. In the distance at left, a step connects the living room with the dining room, separated by a low partition wall. In the distance at center is the seating area near the garage door / window wall (here screened with wood panels for winter). © 2017 Girard Studio LLC. All rights reserved.

105. View of the living room from the fireplace toward the built-in couch / table / partition wall, Girard house, 222 Lothrop, Grosse Pointe, MI. Photographer: Elmer Astelford. Courtesy Alexander Girard Estate, Vitra Design Museum. MAR-04758-14.

106. Color photo of the built-in couch / table / partition wall, Girard house, 222 Lothrop, Grosse Pointe, MI, shot for House Beautiful, 1953. Photographer: Maynard Parker. Courtesy Huntington Library.

107. Color photo of the built-in couch / table / partition wall with lit candles, Girard house, 222 Lothrop, Grosse Pointe, MI. © 2017 Girard Studio LLC. All rights reserved.

Girard's characteristic blend of "function, fantasy and advanced technology" was showcased in the large, multifunctional space at the center of the house, captured best in a 3-D diagram (fig. 102).[49] Like Nelson's "room without a name," Girard's room combined all the activities of modern living, encompassing both work and play, public and private.[50] The novelty of Girard's design was immediately apparent upon entering the house (figs. 103 and 104). The visitor walked down steps (one of them a tree trunk) and through a corridor, framed by partition walls and by the freestanding brick fireplace. A chestnut-wood wall screened the sitting area at the front of the house from the entrance, and a black plywood wall, fronted by a chestnut-wood cabinet with a red-lacquered top, separated the living room from the dining room. In the distance, the viewer looked out the window wall (screened off in the winter) to the backyard.

Moving down the narrow corridor and around the fireplace (fig. 105), the viewer was treated with a spatial surprise: the sloping ceiling of the living room with its exposed pine beams, rising upward to the height of the freestanding brick fireplace (thirteen feet).

The central living area—facing the fireplace—was defined by a unique Girard design: a custom-designed, couch/table complex, built into an angled partition wall. Like the partition walls he had designed previously for Detrola Corporation and for his Lakeland home, this unit divided the large living room into separate, multifunctional spaces. The living-room side featured a conversation area, complete with couches, chairs, and a triangular table with built-in radio, record player, and record storage, essential for modern living. However, building on the concept that he had experimented with in the Laurie living room in 1946, the surface of the wall was a display area, a sort of "moveable collage."[51] Photos taken throughout the period 1947–53 (figs. 105–107) document the chameleon-like nature of the wall, which featured a changing array of objects and images, from folk art to lit candles.

The opposite side of the partition wall (fig. 108) housed Girard's studio. Girard maximized efficiency of space and privacy here by designing storage cabinets, a drafting table, and skylights to maximize natural light. Tack-up boards provided an additional

108. View of the living room / home studio (rear of partition wall), Girard house, 222 Lothrop, Grosse Pointe, MI. Photographer: Maynard Parker. Courtesy Huntington Library.

109. View of the living-room sitting area, Girard house, 222 Lothrop, Grosse Pointe, MI. This view of the seating area at the south (front) side of the house shows the Girard custom-designed magazine rack and bookshelves. Photographer: Maynard Parker. Courtesy Huntington Library.

exhibition space. The meandering wall ended on the south (front) side of the house in another seating area (fig. 109), set apart by a low, suspended plaster ceiling and by the chestnut-wood partition wall, which separated it from the entrance. Large windows, facing south to receive the winter sun, and chairs by Eames and Saarinen made this a cozy spot for reading. Reading material was stored in two Girard custom designs: a magazine rack and floor-to-ceiling oak bookcases with adjustable glass shelves. True to his industrial design background, this area was lit by cold cathode light tubes, adapted for residential use.[52]

On the north side of the house—facing onto the backyard—Girard found an inventive solution to Michigan's hot summers and cold winters: a wall with a built-in, custom-designed, swinging aluminum garage door (figs. 110 and 111). The door could be

110. View of the living room, Girard house, 222 Lothrop, Grosse Pointe, MI. This photo shows the swinging garage door open, exposing the house to the backyard, and shows the mugo-pine-tree stump/table that Girard later gave to his friend Daniel Goodenough. Photographer: Maynard Parker. Courtesy Huntington Library.

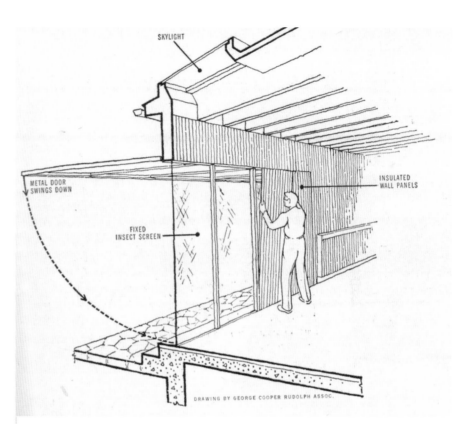

111. Diagram of the living room swinging garage door/wall, Girard house, 222 Lothrop, Grosse Pointe, MI. Artwork by George Cooper Rudolph Associates. Courtesy Rudolph Architects.

opened in summer to serve as an awning, providing a direct connection to the outdoor terrace—and to the landscape. During the winter months, the door could be closed and covered with a plywood panel, which served as an insulated wall.[53] Girard displayed his love of nature by displaying an enormous mugo-pine-tree stump near the door/wall, repurposed as a table.[54]

Girard maximized function and cost-efficiency by designing much of the furniture himself. This was particularly true in the dining room (figs. 112 and 113), which was separated from the living room by the black partition wall, steps, and a low balustrade. Here Girard custom designed a multipiece dining-room table, a sideboard, and a wall of built-in cupboards (cleverly shielded from the entryway by the black partition wall).

The individual "butcher block" cherry tables (sized eighteen by thirty-six, thirty-six by thirty-six, and fifty-four by eighteen inches) were designed to be used—individually or grouped together in various configurations—for seating up to sixteen people.[55] Notes written on the back of the black-and-white photos of the dining room at the Vitra Design Museum provide some indication of Girard's original bold, coloristic effects, indicating that the buffet-bar counter legs were "all different very bright colors."[56] Girard added another touch of color by hanging a Chinese paper kite from the ceiling.

The storage wall (visible in the background of figure 113) had shelves and drawers of various sizes and depths to accommodate the Girards' eclectic collection of glassware, textiles, and a myriad of other items. A twenty-two-page feature on the Girard house in

112. View of the living room, Girard house, 222 Lothrop, Grosse Pointe MI. This view is taken from the north side of the living room looking west toward the dining room. Photographer: Elmer Astelford. © 2017 Girard Studio LLC. All rights reserved.

the February 1953 issue of *House Beautiful* captured the Girards' playful rejection of conventional formulas not only in architectural matters but in everyday elements such as their table settings.[57] The bare butcher-block table top was viewed as a blank canvas to showcase such diverse items as a Guatemalan monk holding a stick of Chinese incense and a Mexican bone-handled knife (fig. 114) and Bohemian crystal and French flatware, paired with a porcelain chemist's beaker used as serving dish (fig. 115).

The same use of custom-designed, built-in components was evident in the kitchen and master suite. In the kitchen (fig. 116), a triangular island (described in one article as "larger than a concert grand piano") featured black linoleum counter tops with an inset maple cutting surface.[58] Built-in cupboards with sliding, black Masonite doors ensured maximum work space and storage. Another wall featured a built-in radio, likely a novel idea at the time. Notes on black-and-white photographs in the Vitra Design Museum indicate that the kitchen was accented in "brilliant orange and ultramarine blue."[59] The same

113. View of the dining room, Girard house, 222 Lothrop, Grosse Pointe, MI. This view shows the dining room from the far northwest side of the living room. Visible in the foreground are the custom-designed dining tables, here clustered together. In the background is the custom-designed buffet and storage wall. Photographer: Maynard Parker. Courtesy Alexander Girard Estate, Vitra Design Museum. MAR-04786-14.

115. Place setting from the House Beautiful photo shoot, Girard house, 222 Lothrop, Grosse Pointe, MI. Photographer: Maynard Parker. Courtesy Huntington Library.

114. Place setting from the House Beautiful photo shoot, Girard house, 222 Lothrop, Grosse Pointe, MI. Photographer: Maynard Parker. Courtesy Huntington Library.

116. View of the kitchen with built-in island, Girard house, 222 Lothrop, Grosse Pointe, MI. Photographer: Maynard Parker. Courtesy Huntington Library.

117. View of the master bedroom and open stairway, Girard house, 222 Lothrop, Grosse Pointe, MI. Photographer: Elmer Astelford. Courtesy Alexander Girard Estate, Vitra Design Museum.

118. View of the master dressing room, Girard house, 222 Lothrop, Grosse Pointe, MI. The photograph shows the built-in cabinets; full-length, tripartite mirror; and display area for the Girards' collection of folk art. Photographer: Elmer Astelford. © 2017 Girard Studio LLC. All rights reserved.

119. Alexander, Susan, Marshall, and Sansi Girard with masks and kachina doll, Girard house, 222 Lothrop, Grosse Pointe, MI. Photographer: Ezra Stoller. © Ezra Stoller/Esto.

120. View of the backyard with swinging garage door/porch open, Girard house, 222 Lothrop, Grosse Pointe, MI. Photographer: Maynard Parker. Courtesy Huntington Library.

combination of bold color and clever practicality was evident in the attached breakfast room (visible in the distance in figure 116), which included a blue wall panel and connected the space directly to the dining terrace outside.

The master suite (fig. 117), located in the renovated/preexisting house, incorporated built-in storage and display areas for the Girards' developing art collection, focused increasingly on folk art. The master dressing room (fig. 118) featured oak cabinets with built in-storage, linoleum countertops with pull-out towel bars, and a black-lined display cabinet, showcasing Mexican figurines. Other folk art objects, among the more than one hundred thousand donated in 1978 by Sandro and Susan Girard to the Museum of International Folk Art in Santa Fe, were showcased in the master bedroom.[60] As noted by Obniski, Sandro and Susan Girard—like their good friends Charles and Ray Eames—collected folk art objects and toys for their aesthetic and humanistic rather than economic value.[61] Viewed as "playthings for both children and adults"—an attitude captured in an

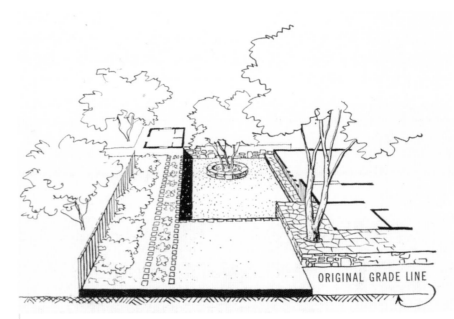

ORIGINAL GRADE LINE

121. Diagram of the multilevel backyard, Girard house, 222 Lothrop, Grosse Pointe, MI. Artwork by George Cooper Rudolph Associates. Courtesy Rudolph Architects.

Ezra Stoller family photograph (fig. 119), showing Sandro, Susan, Sansi, and Marshall Girard with folk art masks—these objects reflected Girard's more expansive approach to modern design.[62] Indeed, Girard was a pioneer in his integration of handcrafted folk art objects and displays into modern interiors.[63] One overtly modern element in the master bedroom was the open, cantilevered staircase, which connected the master bedroom to the upper floor with the children's bedrooms and playroom. There the theme of play was reiterated through plywood walls stained in bright yellow, magenta, blue, and purple.[64]

Girard's "outside the box" ideas were not limited to the house's interior: he also enhanced the beauty and functionality of the exterior spaces—and at a minimum of expense. As noted in the 1953 *House Beautiful* feature, there were two problems with the existing site: (1) the land surrounding the house was flat and lacked "character," and (2) the house stood eighteen inches above the ground.[65] By removing several inches of dirt from the backyard, Girard created a sunken garden terrace (figs. 120 and 121). He used the extra dirt to raise the ground level at the front and sides of the house. Broken pieces of concrete, salvaged from the construction process, and wood from old logs were used as paving stones. The resulting multilevel effect is similar to that adopted by Girard in the house's interior. Other outdoor terraces, located off the front yard, master suite, and dining room, connected the Girards directly with views of the surrounding pine woods; in one case, they even cut through a privacy fence to create a "picture window."[66]

Perhaps surprisingly, it was on the wall of the outdoor dining terrace (fig. 122) that Girard created an abstract composition, which *House Beautiful* called the "climax" not only of the Girard house but of Girard's idiosyncratic modernist aesthetic.[67] The work (fig. 123) consisted of hundreds of pieces of wood and found objects, selected for their "delicate or unusual tone and texture," nailed into the bare, wooden wall.[68] These included boards from an old barn, the seat of an old swing, driftwood from Jamestown, and "masks of primitive cultures."[69] The Girard editorial in the 1953 *Monthly Bulletin, Michigan Society of Architects* emphasized the deeper significance of the work, stating, "Here on Girard's porch modern architecture re-enters the scene." The essay compared Girard's "assemblage" technique with the pasted paper of cubist collages, the richly ornamented surfaces of San Miniato in Florence, and the early modern architectural ornament of Louis Sullivan, Frank Lloyd Wright, Victor Horta, Gropius, Le Corbusier, and others.[70] Given that the layout of the bulletin where the editorial appeared was supervised by Girard, these statements were likely provided by him.[71] Indeed, one could say that the wall was a metaphor for Girard's collage-like approach to architecture, which integrated seemingly contradictory characteristics: progressive and traditional, playful and intellectually rigorous.[72]

122. View of the outdoor dining porch, Girard house, 222 Lothrop, Grosse Pointe, MI. This photo shows the dining porch before the addition of the wood wall collage. Photographer: Maynard Parker. Courtesy Huntington Library.

123. Detail of the outdoor dining porch with Alexander Girard wood collage, Girard house, 222 Lothrop, Grosse Pointe, MI. This photo shows the dining porch after the addition of Girard's innovative, abstract wood collage. Courtesy Alexander Girard Estate, Vitra Design Museum.

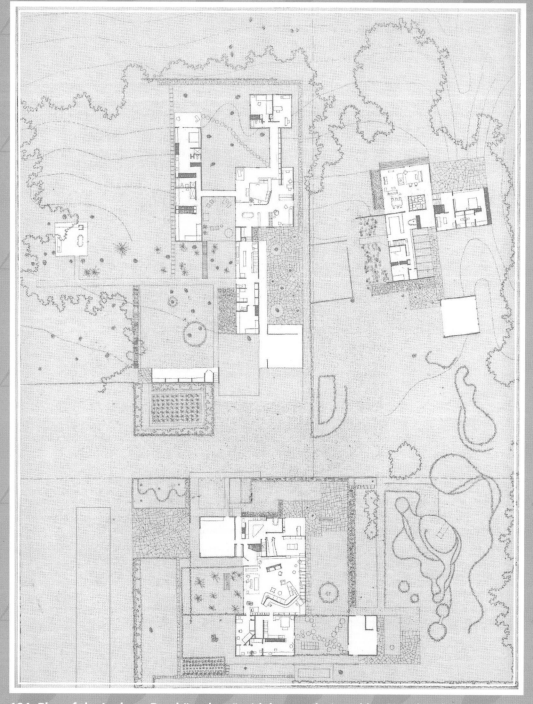

124. Plan of the Lothrop Road "enclave" with houses designed by Girard and Yamasaki in the Pine Woods. Adapted from "1949 Lothrop Road Plan," Alexander Girard Estate, Vitra Design Museum (published in "Serendipity in the Woods"). MAR-04799-01.

Collaboration and Experimentation
Girard, Yamasaki, and Lothrop Road (1949–50)

The American home has suffered from being the last stronghold of resistance to contemporary architecture. . . . Only the adventurous few are prepared to demand a domestic architecture that has been revitalized by the technical and aesthetic innovations of the twentieth century.

—W. Hawkins Ferry

In a 1956 article, "A Suburb in Good Taste," W. Hawkins Ferry wrote that the prospect for architecture in Grosse Pointe in the second half of the century was "not one of unmitigated gloom." Whereas he criticized Grosse Pointe architecture from the first half of the century as representative of an "escapist dream," he hoped that "changing concepts of taste" would bring about a new style, consistent with "the industrial civilization from which it has sprung."[1] In support of his optimism, he identified a "vanguard of skillfully designed modern dwellings and public buildings" as evidence of a turning tide.[2] No doubt these included Girard's designs for his own house and two others on Lothrop Road, dated 1949–50. The first, designed by Minoru Yamasaki in collaboration with Girard for Daniel and Margaret Goodenough, formed part of a planned modernist "enclave" (fig. 124) in the Pine Woods of Lothrop. The second house, designed by Girard alone for Richard and Margaret Jackson, was more

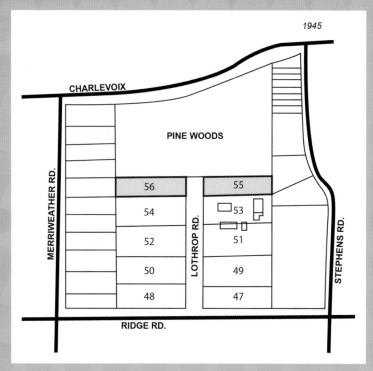

125. Map of Lothrop's Subdivision, lots 47–56 (dead end of Lothrop past Ridge), Grosse Pointe Farms, MI, in 1945. Artwork by Rachel Goad. Based on "1945 Sanborn Fire Safety" map (vol. 20, sheet 98), Sanborn Map Collection.

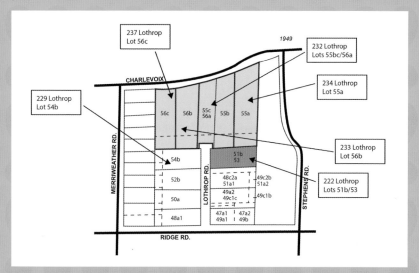

126. Map of the Lothrop Pines Subdivision, lots 47–56 (dead end of Lothrop Road past Ridge Road), Grosse Pointe Farms, MI in 1949. Artwork by Rachel Goad, based on the "1969 Grosse Pointe, Michigan Area Plat Book," Grosse Pointe Historical Society Archives.

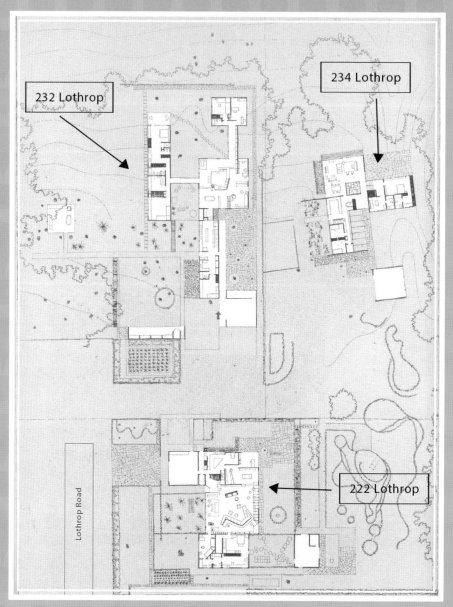

127. Plan of the houses designed by Girard and Yamasaki in the Pine Woods of Lothrop (1949–51), showing 222 Lothrop (Girard house), 234 Lothrop (Goodenough house), and 232 Lothrop (Rieveschl house). Adapted by Rachel Goad from "1949 Lothrop Road Plan," Alexander Girard Estate, Vitra Design Museum (published in "Serendipity in the Woods"). MAR-04799-01.

experimental in nature and planned for an exclusively traditional block of Lothrop. Girard likely viewed these residential projects on Lothrop as an expansion of his modernist principles on a larger scale and—in the case of the Jackson house—to a more prominent site. They also represented a small but significant cultural shift in Grosse Pointe, inspired by Girard and adopted by a new breed of Grosse Pointe patrons. Indeed, while Girard clients/friends William Laurie Jr., Richard Jackson, Daniel Goodenough, and George Rieveschl held prominent positions in the high-stress but socially acceptable advertising, legal, automotive, and pharmaceutical fields, modern design—particularly that of their own homes—represented a rare aesthetic escape.

Expansion: The Pine Woods "Enclave"

The impact of 222 Lothrop was significant, not only for Girard's career as an architect but also for attitudes about modern style in Grosse Pointe. While it was not the first modern home in the area, 222 Lothrop seems to have been the most influential, spurring real estate development in the area.[3] A 1949 article noted that local residents "still look warily at this newcomer (the first modern building in a radius of several miles)," yet the same article noted that surrounding lots, "never considered saleable, have been since cut up for market."[4] These included two lots (55 and 56) on the dead end of Lothrop near the Girard home. In 1945, lots 55 and 56 looked much like they did when they were platted in 1905 (fig. 125). However, by 1949, lots 55 and 56 had been split into five lots (55a, 55b, 55c/56a, 56b, and 56c), encompassing the last remains of the pine woods planted by George Lothrop (fig. 126).[5] Between the years 1949 and 1954, these lots were developed into four home sites (232, 233, 234, and 237 Lothrop); in 1950, another house was built on lot 54b (229 Lothrop), across the street from the Girards (222 Lothrop).

Surviving plans and documents suggest that Girard—possibly in conjunction with then-partner Minoru Yamasaki—conceived the area as an "enclave" of modern-style houses, integrated into the Pine Woods site (fig. 127).[6] This theory is supported by two 1953 articles, which identify a plan view of the houses on Lothrop (222, 234, and 232) as houses "built by Girard" and "planned as a group to preserve one of the few wooded sections remaining in Grosse Pointe."[7] Girard's role in developing the area was asserted by George Rieveschl (the original owner of 232 Lothrop) in an affidavit from a 2002 lawsuit. In his testimony, Rieveschl identified Girard as "the architect of Lothrop Estate Company," stating that he had designed 232 Lothrop in "contemporary styling similar to the other homes in the immediate area" and in conformity with the subdivision's deed

restrictions.[8] These deed restrictions, established by the Lothrop Estate Company on January 15, 1949, included specifications relating to the plan, size, materials, and location of the proposed homes in the Pine Woods site.[9] One key restriction was that the houses be constructed on the eastern part of the property and with access only from Lothrop Road, likely to preserve the woods on the western side. Another was that all proposed house plans be approved by "the architect designated for that purpose by the Lothrop Estate Company," who would determine whether

128. Margaret and Daniel Goodenough in front of 234 Lothrop, Grosse Pointe, MI. Courtesy Goodenough family.

the proposed structure was consistent with the aesthetics of the neighborhood.[10] No doubt the prescribed neighborhood aesthetic—as in the planned complex of homes conceived at the same time by Bernard Edelman in Pontiac, Michigan—was modern style.[11] Whether or not Girard was officially connected with the Lothrop Estate Company, the architectural development of the Pine Woods enclave represented an opportunity for him to showcase his modernist principles on a larger scale.

Collaboration: The Daniel and Margaret Goodenough House

The first of these new houses in the Pine Woods enclave was 234 Lothrop, built for Daniel and Margaret Goodenough (fig. 128), who were both directly connected with Sandro and Susan Girard. The Goodenough and the Girard families knew each other socially through their mutual friends Thayer and William Laurie. However, there were direct artistic as well as social ties. In 1948–49, Margaret Goodenough served as president of the Junior League, the organization that had commissioned Girard to design the Little Shop (1937). In October 1948, she served—along with Thayer Laurie and Margaret Jackson—as a hostess for the Radcliffe tour of the Girard house on Lothrop.[12] Beginning in September 1948, Daniel Goodenough, a Detroit attorney, served as the

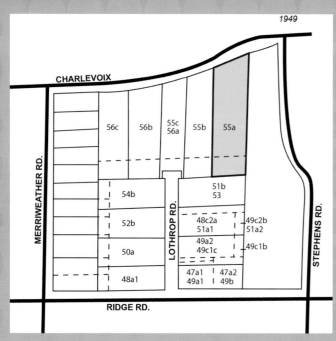

129. Map of Lothrop's Subdivision, showing lot 55a (234 Lothrop), purchased by Daniel and Margaret Goodenough. Artwork by Rachel Goad, based on the "1969 Grosse Pointe Michigan Area Plat Book," Grosse Pointe Historical Society Archives.

130. Model of the Goodenough house. Girard and Yamasaki, Associated Architects. Photographer: Elmer Astelford. Courtesy Goodenough Family.

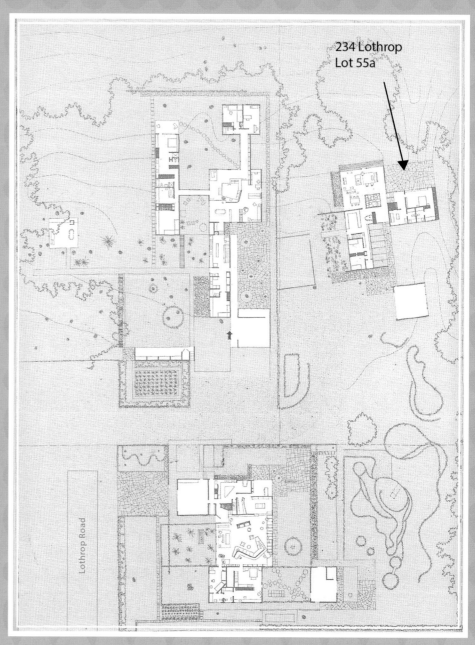

131. Plan of the houses designed by Girard and Yamasaki in the Pine Woods of Lothrop (1949–51). Highlighted area shows 234 Lothrop (Goodenough house). Adapted by Rachel Goad from "1949 Lothrop Road Plan," Alexander Girard Estate, Vitra Design Museum (published in "Serendipity in the Woods"). MAR-04799-01.

legal consultant for the *For Modern Living* exhibition; he knew Girard, Yamasaki, and Eero Saarinen personally and had an interest in modern design.[13] Indeed, Goodenough's work on the exhibition may have inspired him to purchase lot 55a (next to the Girard house) in the Lothrop's Subdivision on January 15, 1949 (figs. 129 and 131).[14]

However, Daniel Goodenough's interest in the Pine Woods site—the only wooded area then remaining in Grosse Pointe—may also relate to his father, Luman Goodenough. Inspired by his love of nature, Luman Goodenough commuted (via automobile) from his 440-acre country estate in Farmington, Michigan, to his law office in Detroit.[15] It is interesting to note that in 1915, Luman Goodenough encouraged other wealthy friends to buy property in the area.[16] These included Richard Webber, one of the owners of the J. L. Hudson department store and uncle of James B. Webber Jr., who sponsored the *For Modern Living* exhibition.[17] Therefore, Daniel Goodenough would have known the sponsors as well as the designers of the 1949 exhibition. Work on the house progressed quickly. In March 1949, Elmer Astelford shot several photographs of a model for the Goodenough house (fig. 130), credited to "Girard and Yamasaki, Associated Architects." The house is identified in the "Girard Editorial" as the "upper, smaller" house on the Lothrop Road plan and as a collaboration with Minoru Yamasaki.[18] On July 27, 1949, a building permit was filed for a house, estimated at $50,000.[19]

Both the Goodenough house and the house designed (but never built) in the same year for real estate developer Bernard Edelman (figs. 40 and 41) can be connected to the "contract of partnership" formed by Girard and Yamasaki on May 1, 1949.[20] Indeed, as in the Edelman house, the names Girard and Yamasaki are listed as architects on the Goodenough house blueprints (fig. 132). However, here there is clear evidence that Yamasaki (who was a good friend of Daniel and Margaret Goodenough) was the principal architect and Girard the designer of the interior furnishings. The first piece of evidence comes from the contract of partnership itself, which states, "It is understood that Girard will continue to devote a large part of his time during May, June, July and August, 1949, as Director in the management and execution of the exhibition titled 'For Modern Living.'"[21] Given that the Goodenough house was designed during the months leading up to the DIA exhibition, it is likely that Yamasaki served as the primary architect. Indeed, photographs of the Goodenough house are included among the project records of the Yamasaki Inc. architectural firm.[22] Further proof is provided by the Goodenough house blueprints, which bear an imprint of Yamasaki's seal (fig. 132), indicating both his status as a licensed architect and his role as the "person in responsible charge" of the project.[23]

132. First- and second-floor plans, residence for Mr. and Mrs. Daniel Goodenough, June 24, 1949. Detail showing name and address of partnership: Girard and Yamasaki, Associated Architects, 379 Fisher Road. Significantly, the blueprint lists the names of both Girard and Yamasaki as architects but includes only Yamasaki's embossed seal as a registered architect. Courtesy Shelley and John Schoenherr, with permission from the estate of Minoru Yamasaki.

133. Miller house architectural drawing label, 1955 (MHG_IIIa_FF043_003_crop). The blueprint includes the names of both Saarinen and Girard as architects but includes only Saarinen's embossed seal as a registered architect. Miller House and Garden Collection (M003). Courtesy IMA Archives, Indianapolis Museum of Art.

This division of responsibility was affirmed in an interview with Margaret Goodenough, one of the original owners, who credited Yamasaki as the architect and Girard as the interior designer.[24]

However, Girard's role in this and other collaborative projects is best described as interior architect rather than interior designer. Indeed, the inclusion of Girard's name as architect on the blueprints for all of his collaborative residential projects—including the Miller house (fig. 133), normally attributed to Eero Saarinen—reflects his uniquely

134. Exterior view of the Goodenough house, 234 Lothrop, Grosse Pointe, MI, 1950. Girard & Yamasaki Architects. Courtesy Goodenough family.

135. Exterior view of the Baker house, Greenwich, CT, 1950, Leinweber, Yamasaki, and Hellmuth. Courtesy Archives of Michigan.

136. Exterior view of the Goodenough house, 234 Lothrop, Grosse Pointe, MI. This photo shows (at left) the covered walk leading to the entrance. Courtesy Goodenough family.

137. View of shoin (main house), Katsura Imperial Villa, Kyoto, Japan. Photographer: Raphael Azevedo Franca.

138. Covered walk and entrance, Goodenough house, 234 Lothrop, Grosse Pointe, MI. This photo of the entrance showcases (in the front window) the mugo-pine-tree stump, given to Daniel Goodenough by Alexander Girard in 1953. Courtesy Goodenough family.

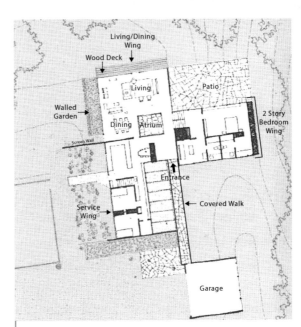

139. Floor plan of the Goodenough house, 234 Lothrop, Grosse Pointe, MI. Adapted by Rachel Goad from "1949 Lothrop Road Plan," Alexander Girard Estate, Vitra Design Museum (published in "Serendipity in the Woods"). MAR-04799-01.

expansive conception of architecture. As Girard once stated, "Since it is impossible to conceive of an architecture (a space-enclosing structure) as existing without an interior space, one cannot then think of 'interior design' . . . as a separate activity." He added, "consequently, my concept of architecture rarely exists as a total reality."[25] We will see that Girard's expansive concept of "architecture"—encompassing both structure and interior—did come to fruition in the McLucas and Rieveschl houses. Significantly, Girard's drawings for the McLucas house furnishings (figs. 193–96) do include his seal as a licensed architect in the state of Michigan.

The Goodenough house (fig. 134) includes many architectural elements found in other Yamasaki-designed residences, such as the Louis C. Baker house (fig. 135), also completed in 1950.[26] The flat roofline and vast expanses of glass in each house recall Miesian modernism. However, other elements—the rectilinear structure, the predominance of wood details, and the integration of the house into the surrounding wooded landscape—may have been inspired by traditional Japanese architecture.[27] The architectural historian W. Hawkins Ferry agreed, describing Yamasaki's use of white wall surfaces in the Goodenough house (fig. 136) as "closer to the Japanese ideal."[28] Indeed, Yamasaki later

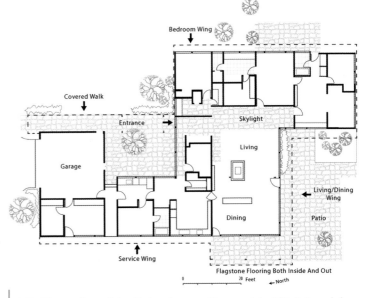

140. Floor plan of the Baker house, Greenwich, CT. Artwork by Emily Matt. Adapted by Rachel Goad.

141. View of the atrium with Christmas tree, Goodenough house, 234 Lothrop, Grosse Pointe, MI. The Goodenough house was centered on an open-air atrium. Courtesy Goodenough family.

142. View of the interior skylight, Baker house, Greenwich, CT. The Baker house was centered on a skylit gallery, allowing natural light into the entrance hall. Courtesy Archives of Michigan.

143. View of the living room, Goodenough house, 234 Lothrop, Grosse Pointe, MI. This photo shows the freestanding fireplace and the view out the living-room window walls into the surrounding landscape. Courtesy Archives of Michigan.

144. View of the living room, Baker house, Greenwich, CT. This photo shows the freestanding fireplace and the glass window walls, with views of the surrounding pine woods. Photographer: Ezra Stoller. © Ezra Stoller/Esto.

145. Rear view of the Goodenough house. Visible at right is the stone-wall-enclosed garden and at far right the wood screen wall. Courtesy Goodenough family.

146. View into the living room of the Goodenough house with Margaret, Liz, and Pixie Goodenough. The rear wall at left shows the adjustable, floor-to-ceiling bookshelves, custom designed by Girard. The open-air atrium is visible in the right rear of the photograph, and the pine woods are visible in the reflection on the glass window wall. Courtesy Goodenough family.

referenced the Katsura Imperial Villa in Kyoto (fig. 137) as exemplifying the ideal blend of aesthetics and function in Japanese architecture.[29]

The Goodenough and Baker houses are also very similar in their overall design. In each house, the integration of interior and exterior space is evident in the approach: the visitor walks down a long, covered breezeway and through a natural space to the front door. In each case, a glass window wall adjacent to the door allows a glimpse into the interior spaces. Significantly, the front window of the Goodenough house (fig. 138) featured a precious Pine Woods relic: the petrified mugo-pine-tree stump from the Girard living room, entrusted to Daniel Goodenough by his friend Alexander Girard upon his departure from Grosse Pointe for Santa Fe in 1953.[30] The integration of each house into its natural surroundings continued in the interior spaces (figs. 139 and 140), in which service, living, and sleeping areas occupied separate wings yet were clustered around a central space, open to the landscape. Indeed, such spaces provided what Yamasaki credited as an essential element of great architecture: the "architectural surprise."[31] In the Goodenough house, the visual surprise was an atrium (fig. 141), glassed in on three sides and open to the sky. In the Baker house, it was a skylit gallery (fig. 142) on axis with the entrance, which created the illusion of an open-air courtyard. One author wrote that the effect was the opposite of what was expected: "outdoors you were under the shade of an entrance canopy; indoors you are under the open sky."[32]

Consistent with architectural principles promoted at midcentury by Nelson, Eames, Girard, and others, each living room was subdivided into separate, multifunctional zones for entertaining, dining, and reading. Most importantly, each house was open to the outdoors, both looking inward toward the atrium/skylight (figs. 141 and 142) and outward through the glass window walls of the living room (figs. 143 and 144). In each house, these window walls provided uninterrupted views of the surrounding pine woods. The natural beauty of the wooded site of 234 Lothrop (fig. 145) was enhanced by Daniel Goodenough, who with the advice of his neighbor and friend Sandro Girard designed gardens and stone-lined, raised beds of shrubs and flowers on the half-acre lot. A wood deck, a two-story brick patio, and a stone-wall-enclosed garden further integrated the house into the landscape. In order to preserve the natural beauty of the site, a wood screen wall on the south side of the property blocked views of the service wing, including the driveway and a bridge built to facilitate access to the kitchen. The integration of indoor and outdoor space is clear in a photo of the Goodenough house (fig. 146): while the viewer looks into the *interior* spaces of the house, he or she sees two *outdoor* spaces—the open-air atrium (rear right) and the pine woods, glimpsed in the window wall's reflection.

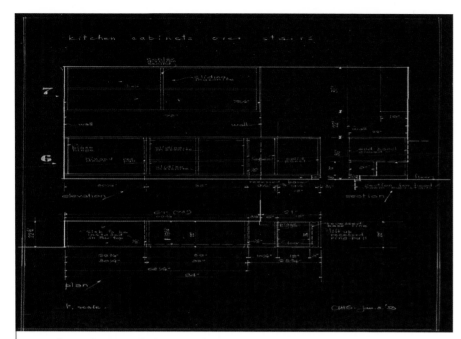

147. Alexander Girard, drawings for custom-designed cabinets, Goodenough house. Note Girard's initials (AHG) and the date January 3, 1950, at lower right. Courtesy Shelley and John Schoenherr.

148. Interior of the living room, Goodenough house, 234 Lothrop, Grosse Pointe, MI. This view shows the colorful, Girard-designed textiles, plywood table, and floor-to-ceiling, adjustable bookshelves (barely visible on the back wall). Courtesy Goodenough family.

Whereas Yamasaki can be considered the primary architect of the Goodenough house, Girard's involvement was predominant in the interior furnishings and textiles, which featured bold, strategically placed colors and custom-designed, built-in storage. Indeed, surviving drawings (fig. 147)—some with notes in Girard's handwriting and signed with his initials (AHG)—document his role in designing cabinets, dressers, and bookcases throughout the house. Consistent with the language in the Girard-Yamasaki contract, the initialed Girard drawings are dated January 3, 1950, after the close of the *For Modern Living* exhibition. A color photograph of the living room (fig. 148) shows a Girard plywood table (the same visible in the Girard home on Lakeland and in the Fisher Road studio) and a couch with colorful textiles, no doubt supplied by Girard. Barely visible on the back wall of the two living-room photographs (fig. 146 and 148) are the custom-designed, moveable shelves designed by Girard (as in his own home) to display the books and small objects—European, Asian, and Indian—that Margaret Goodenough had inherited from her Detroit forebears.[33] This eclectic, eye-catching display reflected Girard's attitude that modern interior decoration "doesn't call for the sweeping away of familiar

things or condemn to death everything associated with the past. Instead, it endeavors to reconcile the old with the new."[34]

Pixie Goodenough Dodge, who grew up in the Goodenough house, recalls hearing that it was the first in Grosse Pointe to demonstrate that it was possible to have a modern-style home that was furnished with antiques.[35] In contrast, the interior spaces of the Baker house (fig. 144) embody in their clean lines and restrained décor the simplicity inherent in Japanese tradition, later lauded by Yamasaki as an ideal alternative to the "clutter that we suffer in America."[36] Given these comments, one might consider the partnership between Yamasaki and Girard a union of opposites: restrained simplicity versus joyful exuberance. However, given their close, collaborative relationship, there was a decisive, reciprocal influence between the two partners. Indeed, many of the architectural elements present in the Goodenough house—the integration of indoor and outdoor, the use of screen walls, skylights, atrium spaces, and freestanding fireplaces—are evident in the independent residential projects executed by Girard during the years 1949–51: the Jackson, McLucas, and Rieveschl residences.

149. Richard, Margaret, and Linda Jackson in front of Jackson Lodge. Courtesy Jackson Family.

Experimentation: The Richard and Margaret Jackson House

While the Girard and Goodenough houses broke with Grosse Pointe tradition, both in their style and site, the Jackson house—had it been completed—would have pushed its limits even further. While the Jackson house was designed in 1949–50 for a site on Lothrop Road, it was located not in the Pine Woods enclave but rather on the first block, location of the aforementioned traditional-style homes.[37] The patrons, Richard and Margaret Jackson (fig. 149), knew Sandro and Susan Girard through their mutual friends William and Thayer Laurie. Both the Lauries and the Jacksons lived in traditional homes on Merriweather Road, and both men were then involved in promoting the upcoming *For Modern Living* exhibition at the DIA. Laurie was in charge of public relations for the exhibition, and Jackson, vice president of Hudson Motor Company, is listed in the exhibition catalogue as part of the committee of sponsors.[38]

However, Richard Jackson had deeper personal and professional connections to the exhibition sponsor, the J. L. Hudson department store. The Hudson Motor Company had received its initial funding—and name—from J. L. Hudson, store founder, in 1909.[39]

When J. L. Hudson died in 1912, he left the family department store to his nephews, Richard H., Oscar, James B., and Joseph L. Webber; their sister was Richard Jackson's mother.[40] It was Richard Jackson's cousin / best friend and J. L. Hudson's vice president, James B. Webber Jr., who had first suggested that the store sponsor the exhibition and that Girard be hired as director. The fact that Richard Jackson was connected to both Girard and Webber adds credence to the idea that it was Girard who provided the initial inspiration for the DIA exhibition. In a letter, written on February 11, 1949, to DIA director Richardson, William Laurie listed Richard Jackson as one of a group of men representing Detroit industry (along with Henry Ford II of the Ford Motor Company and George Fink of Great Lakes Steel) to be added to the list of sponsors for the exhibition. In support of Jackson, Laurie added that he "has just completed a large, modern house, is very interested personally, and can be helpful in other ways."[41]

The "large, modern house" that Laurie was referring to is likely the vacation house/lodge that Girard had designed in 1945 for Jackson in Hillman, Michigan, described in the "Girard Editorial" as his first "entirely new building."[42] According to Richard Jackson Jr., Jackson Lodge (figs. 150 and 151) was located near the Turtle Lake Club, a private hunting and fishing club, composed primarily of male members of the Jackson-Webber family.[43] Most members were involved in the J. L. Hudson and Hudson Motor companies, although other members included a Grosse Pointe banker, John N. McLucas.[44] The 1953 "Girard Editorial" described Girard's use in the lodge of "vernacular forms" such as board-and-batten skin over frame and a corrugated-cement shed roof, although the author also noted a parallel with Japanese architecture.[45] Indeed, the correspondence between the simplicity of its wood and glass structure and its rustic location/function may explain Laurie's description of the lodge as "modern." After all, Girard and the other organizers of the *For Modern Living* exhibition had listed economy in materials ("lightness" and "simplicity") among the criteria for good modern design.[46] The same could be said for the exposed wooden beams and the built-in storage and furnishings visible in photographs of the couch/table in the lodge's living room. Girard used a similar built-in couch/table concept in his own house a few years later, and built-in storage walls were promoted by George Nelson and others in the postwar period. However, Laurie could also have been referencing the proposed Jackson residence on Lothrop Road in Grosse Pointe.

Significantly, drawings for the Jackson house, dated between October 1949 and March 1950, are labeled "Alexander Girard Architect," with no reference to the

150. Exterior view of Jackson Lodge, Hillman, MI, 1945. Architect: Alexander Girard. Note the plywood treatment of the exterior, similar to that used later by Girard in his own home on 222 Lothrop. © 2017 Girard Studio LLC. All rights reserved.

151. Interior view of Jackson Lodge, Hillman, MI, with built-in furnishings and cabinets, 1945. Architect: Alexander Girard. Photographer: Elmer Astelford. © 2017 Girard Studio LLC. All rights reserved.

Girard-Yamasaki partnership.[47] Furthermore, the house was located not in the Pine Woods enclave on the dead end of Lothrop (with the Girard and Goodenough houses) but instead on the first, more architecturally conservative, block of Lothrop.[48] Drawings at the Vitra Design Museum document Girard's evolving design concept for the Jackson house, which would have contrasted dramatically with its traditional-style neighbors: the Allen Edwards house and the J. Stewart Hudson house (figs. 92 and 93). As in Jackson Lodge and in Girard's own house, wooden boards predominate on the façade (fig. 152), although disposed in vertical and horizontal bands, creating with the doorways and windows an overall geometric effect. While the flat roof and geometric emphasis recall the Goodenough house, the bold color accents are pure Girard—and reminiscent of another contemporary Girard project: the Fletcher Motel in Alpena, Michigan (fig. 153), commissioned by another Grosse Pointe resident, Ralph Fletcher.[49] The motel units, designed in 1949, presented Girard with an unprecedented opportunity to blend form, function, and fun. Walls, ceilings, and exterior wall panels were painted in bold, contrasting colors, and custom-designed Knoll furniture converted from day to night use. Given that Alpena is located in northern Michigan—not far from Hillman—it is interesting to speculate whether Ralph Fletcher was introduced to Girard's architecture by seeing Richard Jackson's lodge.

Girard's sketches for the Jackson residence clearly show his mind at work, experimenting with an inventive—if somewhat impractical—series of interlocking masses and courtyards (fig. 154). Here the simplicity employed by Yamasaki in the Goodenough and Baker house plans—living, sleeping, and service wings, clustered around a central open area—has been supplanted by Girardian exuberance. According to a note written by Girard on one of the drawings, the house would have totaled more than fifty-five hundred square feet: more than four thousand for the house itself and more than one thousand for the courtyards. Notes written on another concept sketch detail Margaret and Richard Jackson's "wish list," which included a telephone in the master bedroom, a basement laundry, and bedrooms for two maids. Other features indicate that Girard was willing to go above and beyond standard practice in order to customize the house to his clients/friends' personal and professional needs. These included up to three interior courtyards, a multitude of plantings, and an overhead skylight, all to satisfy Margaret Jackson's passion for gardening. According to Richard Jackson Jr., an early concept included an entirely impractical feature: an internal pond, circulating through the house.[50]

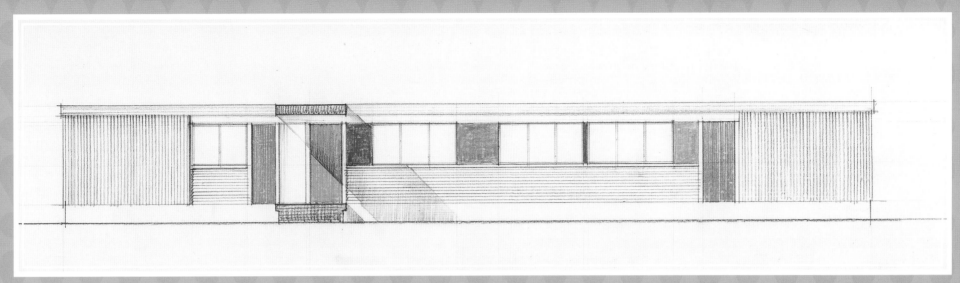

152. Alexander Girard, design drawing for the Jackson house (not built), Lothrop Road, Grosse Pointe, MI, circa 1949. Note the treatment of the façade with brightly colored plywood panels. Colored pencil on paper. Courtesy Alexander Girard Estate, Vitra Design Museum. MAR-17167-34.

153. View of the Fletcher Motel, Alpena, MI, circa 1949. Architect: Alexander Girard. Note the brightly colored plywood panels. The interior spaces were furnished by Knoll Inc. © 2017 Girard Studio LLC. All Rights Reserved.

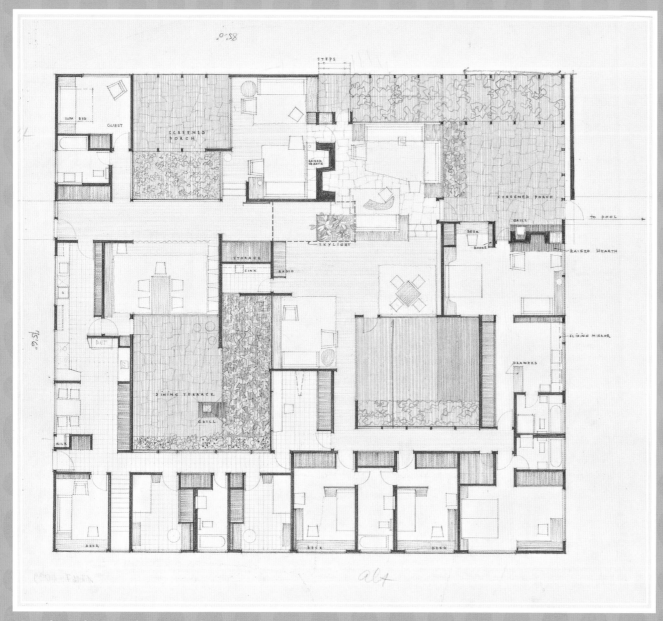

154. Alexander Girard, concept sketch for the Jackson house floor plan, Lothrop Road, Grosse Pointe, MI. Note the elevated living room with double-sided hearth and multiple interior courtyards. Colored pencil on paper. Courtesy Alexander Girard Estate, Vitra Design Museum.

155. Alexander Girard, site-plan concept drawing for the Jackson house and carport. Colored pencil on paper. Note the prominent placement of the carport in the front of the house and the "bridge" to the entrance. Courtesy Alexander Girard Estate, Vitra Design Museum. MAR-17167-04.

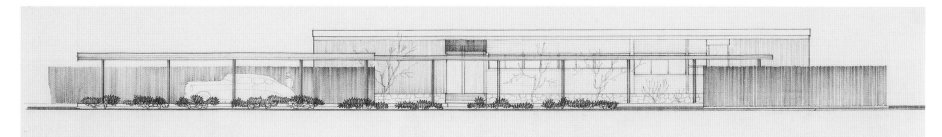

156. Alexander Girard, detail of elevation drawing for the Jackson house, Lothrop Road, Grosse Pointe, MI. Note the prominent placement of the carport at the front of the house, with a recognizable 1949 Hudson Commodore. Courtesy Alexander Girard Estate, Vitra Design Museum. MAR-17167-02.

Most Room! Best Ride! Safest!
"The New Step-Down Ride"

Available only in Hudson because
Hudson is built differently

Best ride? Yes! Free-flowing, low-built design quickly tells you that the New Hudson has the lowest center of gravity in any American automobile—and this right along with full road clearance! As a result, you know instinctively that this thrilling motor car hugs the road more tenaciously than any other automobile, and is therefore America's best-riding and safest car! Hudson dealers everywhere invite you to try "The New Step-Down Ride" and experience these wonders firsthand!

Safest? Absolutely! Hudson's low center of gravity makes it a steady, sure-handling car. And for even greater safety, Hudson's Monobilt body-and-frame*, an all-welded, all-steel single unit of construction, rides you down within a base frame (shown in red above) with box-section steel girders completely encircling and protecting the passenger compartment—even outside the rear wheels!   *Trade-mark and patents pending.

Most room in any car at any price, and with all this you get, in Hudson, America's best-riding, safest car!
Your very first glance inside the New Hudson shows you that the seats are positioned not only ahead of the rear axle, but entirely ahead of the rear wheels.
This permits full use of body width, and as a result, the sensational New Hudson of normal exterior width brings you seat cushions that are *up to 12 inches wider* than those in cars of greater outside dimensions! Even the door controls and arm rests in Hudson are set in recessed door panels so that they do not interfere with passenger room.

You'll see, too, that Hudson's exclusive "step-down" design, with its recessed floor, brings vital space into the passenger compartment, instead of wasting it under the floor and between frame members as is the case in all other cars!
This provides, in Hudson, more head room than in any mass-produced car built today.
But Hudson's fabulous room is only part of the story. We invite you to read, to the left, why "The New Step-Down Ride" is America's best and safest ride—then see your Hudson dealer—soon! Hudson Motor Car Company, Detroit 14.

HUDSON

NOW ... 3 GREAT SERIES

Lower-Priced Pacemaker   Famous Super   Custom Commodore

MOST ROOM! ... BEST RIDE! ... SAFEST!

ONLY HUDSON, THE CAR WITH "THE NEW STEP-DOWN RIDE", BRINGS YOU THESE ADDITIONAL FEATURES ... Chrome-alloy motor blocks which minimize wear and reduce upkeep costs • *Triple-Safe Brakes*—finest hydraulic system with reserve mechanical system on same pedal, plus finger-tip-release parking brake • *Fluid-Cushioned Clutch* • *Wide-arc vision* with Curved Full-View windshield and rear window • *Weather-Control*—Hudson's heater-conditioned-air system • *Super-Cushion tires* • *Safety-Type wide rims* • *Center-Point Steering* and more than 20 other high-performance, long-life features that help make "step-down" designed Hudsons leaders in resale value, coast to coast, as is shown by Official Used Car Guide Books! †Optional at extra cost.

157. Advertisement for Hudson Motor Car Company, 1949. Courtesy FCA. Hudson is a registered trademark of FCA USA LLC.

The Jackson house design included another unique feature not shown in any of Girard's other house designs: a prominent garage/carport at the front of the house. As shown in several site-plan concept drawings (fig. 155), visitors would have walked over a "bridge" and past the carport (which included space for three cars) in order to get to the front door. Inspired by the client's position as vice president of Hudson Motor Car Company, one Girard elevation drawing for the Jackson house (fig. 156) shows a car in the carport. Significantly, the sloping contours of the car clearly identify it as a 1949 Hudson Commodore (fig. 157).[51] Within the interior of the house, Girard experimented—as in 222 Lothrop—with varying levels. Girard's plan, elevation, and interior drawings for the Jackson house (fig. 154) include two elevated living areas, joined by a central, double-sided hearth. A Girard concept drawing (fig. 158) shows an elevated living-room area, with seating and tables clustered around the (double-sided?) fireplace. The concept is the inverse of the sunken "conversation pit" that Girard conceived soon afterward for the Rieveschl house (figs. 246 and 248) and then perfected in the Miller house (fig. 254). Sadly, the Jackson house was never completed. However, many of the ideas explored in the Jackson house drawings came to fruition in another project: the McLucas house.

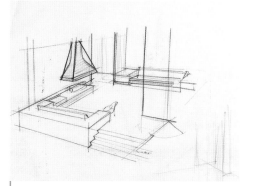

158. Alexander Girard, concept drawing for the living room of the Jackson house. Here the living room, with its cove-like seating area, is elevated. Colored pencil on paper. Courtesy Alexander Girard Estate, Vitra Design Museum. MAR-17167-03.

159. View of the McLucas house, Grosse Pointe, MI, from the backyard. Architect: Alexander Girard. Photographer: James Haefner.

Culmination

The John and Kathleen McLucas House

It would seem that the Girard approach matures real
architecture, . . . architecture not only as art but as the
great fundamental art, as the enhancement of life.

—Edgar Kaufmann Jr.

An article in the *Detroit Free Press*, dated August 6, 1950, provides a tantalizing reference to
a new Girard design in Grosse Pointe: the house commissioned by Mr. and Mrs. John N.
McLucas on 55 Vendome (fig. 159). The article, titled "Christmas Present," announces
the expected date of occupancy by the McLucas family. More importantly, it also alludes
to the modernist aesthetic of the house, which is described as a "straight-forward American contemporary design." However, despite its description as "straight-forward,"
there is no doubt that in 1950, the McLucas house—a single-story, minimalist-style
home, "all done in wood and glass"—contrasted sharply with its traditional neighbors on Vendome.[1] The impact would have been maximized by its location: not the
Pine Woods of Lothrop Road but prime real estate: a prominent corner lot at the
intersection of Vendome Road and Grosse Pointe Boulevard.

Patrons

The bold site and style of the McLucas house reflected the extraordinary life story
of its patrons, John and Kathleen McLucas, who were not native to Grosse Pointe.
John Nichols ("Jack") McLucas (fig. 160) came to Detroit from Kansas City in 1945 to
accept a position as vice president of the National Bank of Detroit (NBD), after serving in
the US Army Air Transport Command during World War II.[2] The move was likely dictated
by his father, Walter S. McLucas, who had been called to Detroit from Kansas City in 1933

160. John N. McLucas. Photographer: Moffett Studio. Courtesy Burton Historical Collection, Detroit Public Library, with permission from W. Scott McLucas.

162. Kathleen McLucas. Photographer: Blackstone Studios.

161. Walter Scott McLucas addressing the employees of National Bank of Detroit, December 20, 1941. Photographers: Spencer and Wyckoff. Courtesy W. Scott McLucas.

to lead NBD, newly created with funding from General Motors to stabilize Detroit's banking system.[3] A photograph showing Walter McLucas addressing NBD employees on December 20, 1941 (fig. 161), illustrates his larger-than-life stature at NBD and in Detroit, a heritage that he hoped to pass down to his only son. In 1926, Jack McLucas had married Hamilton Simpson ("Hammie"), a Kansas City socialite, with whom he had a son, named Walter Scott after his grandfather. Jack and Hammie divorced in May 1945. By August 1946, Jack McLucas had met and married Kathleen Smith and adopted her daughter, Virginia.[4] However, Kathleen McLucas (fig. 162) was far from a typical Grosse Pointe banker's wife. Although she was an American citizen, Kathleen had lived in Shanghai, China, from the age of six and had traveled extensively in China and Japan, where she had spent many summers.[5] On December 23, 1933, "Elsie" Kathleen Smith had married Sydney Montague Carlisle, a deputy commissioner in the Chinese Maritime Customs office.[6] Their daughter, Virginia, was born on December 18, 1938, in Shanghai.[7] These were "halcyon days" in Shanghai, which was the financial, political, cultural, and industrial capital of China and home to settlements of wealthy expatriates from many nations.[8] The Carlisle family, part of this privileged class, lived a lavish lifestyle, which included travel within Asia but also to Europe and the United States. Kathleen later recalled, "The world had been going to the devil outside my bailiwick and I had cavorted gaily . . . and paid no never mind."[9]

After Pearl Harbor, Kathleen and seven-year-old Virginia were separated from Sydney and endured the Japanese occupation of Shanghai with rare courage and aplomb. Kathleen later described how she evaded capture by the Japanese secret police with the help of fake documents, contraband chocolate wafers, and the sheer force of her personal charm.[10] However, by April 1943, Sydney, Kathleen (listed as "Elsie Kathleen"), and Virginia (nicknamed "Ginka") were among the roughly fourteen thousand Allied nationals who were sent to Japanese internment camps in Shanghai. All three are listed as internees in the Lunghwa camp in Shanghai (fig. 163), the same camp popularized in the J. G. Ballard novel and film *Empire of the Sun*.[11] Kathleen and Virginia spent six months in the camp, facing deprivation and dengue fever. However, given their status as American citizens, they were eligible in September 1943 for repatriation, a covert exchange of war prisoners brokered by the American and Japanese governments.[12] In September 1943, Kathleen, Virginia, and more than one thousand other repatriates sailed from Shanghai, arriving (after a prisoner exchange in Singapore) in New York on December 1, 1943.[13] Sydney (a South African citizen) remained in the Lunghwa camp for the duration of the

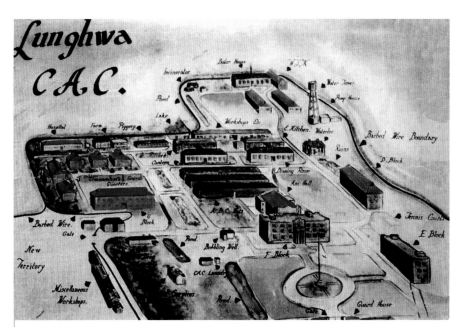

163. Bird's-eye view of Lunghwa camp, Shanghai, China, during World War II. Artist: unknown. Courtesy Greg Leck.

war; the family never reunited.[14] Kathleen recounted her life story—including the harrowing six-month internment experience and repatriation journey—in vivid detail in a 1945 memoir, *The Rampant Refugee*.[15]

By 1945, Kathleen and Virginia were staying with Kathleen's sister and brother-in-law, Dorothy ("Dot") and Henry ("Hank") Kelly, in Santa Fe, New Mexico. According to one account, it was here that she met the recently divorced Jack McLucas.[16] By July 1946, Mr. and Mrs. John N. McLucas were married and living with Virginia in Detroit at the Whittier.[17] By one account, Walter McLucas did not approve of his new, unconventional daughter-in-law.[18] Nevertheless, by the end of the year, the McLucas family had moved to Grosse Pointe, where all three fit seamlessly into the upper echelons of society, centered on memberships in prominent clubs such as the Detroit Athletic Club, the Country Club of Detroit, the Turtle Lake Club, the Grosse Pointe Hunt Club, and the Junior League of Detroit. Fittingly, Kathleen and Virginia adopted nicknames that corresponded with their new environment: "Elsie" (Kathleen) became "Kitty," and "Ginka" (Virginia) became "Jinx."

The official entrée of Mr. and Mrs. John N. McLucas into Grosse Pointe society came in 1947, when they were listed in the exclusive social registry, the *Social Secretary of*

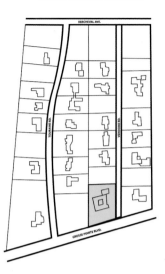

164. Plan of Vendome Road, circa 1950. Artwork by Rachel Goad. Based on "1945 Sanborn Fire Safety" map, Sanborn Map Collection.

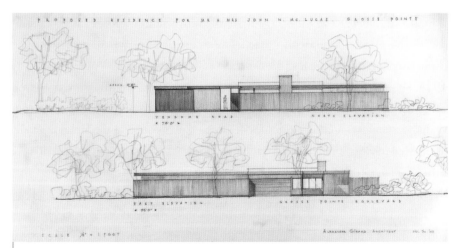

165. Alexander Girard, proposed residence for Mr. and Mrs. John N. McLucas, Grosse Pointe, MI, December 20, 1949. North elevation (Vendome Road) and east elevation (Grosse Pointe Boulevard). Colored pencil on paper. Courtesy Alexander Girard Estate, Vitra Design Museum. MAR-17240-05.

Detroit.[19] More importantly, however, the address listed in the registry (455 Lakeland) placed them just down the street from Mr. and Mrs. Alexander Girard (380 Lakeland). While one can only speculate how and when Jack and Kitty McLucas met Sandro and Susan Girard, they were certainly connected socially. As a member of the Turtle Lake hunting and fishing club, Jack McLucas would have known Richard Jackson, Girard's friend and client.[20] Jack and Kitty McLucas were also good friends with Ralph and Mary Fletcher, who in 1949 commissioned Girard to design their Alpena motel. No doubt, Susan and Sandro Girard would have appreciated the "lovely jade figurines and Chinese screens" collected by Kathleen and referenced in the aforementioned "Christmas Present" article. Susan and Sandro Girard certainly visited the McLucas home on Lakeland in November 1950, when they attended a party to celebrate the publication of a book, *Dancing Diplomats*, written

These Men Take Bank Directorates and Executive Posts

BEN R. MARSH   JAMES B. WEBBER, JR.   HENRY FORD II   JAMES W. PARKER

DONALD F. VALLEY   BEN E. YOUNG   HENRY T. BODMAN   JOHN N. McLUCAS

166. "These Men Take Bank Directorates and Executive Posts," article in the Detroit News, January 11, 1950, celebrating the elevation of John N. McLucas to general vice president at NBD Bank. Courtesy Zuma Press.

by Kitty's sister and brother-in-law, Hank and Dot Kelly.[21] More significant, perhaps, is that Jack and Kitty McLucas were connected–through the Kellys–to Santa Fe, New Mexico, where the Girard family moved in 1953.[22]

These factors may have influenced Jack and Kitty's decision on August 17, 1949 to purchase a prominent site (lots 108–15) in the Hamilton Park Subdivision, 55 Vendome (fig. 164) and to hire Alexander Girard to design their new home.[23] Significantly, Girard's earliest proposal drawing for the residence (fig. 165) is dated December 20, 1949 (one month after the close of the *For Modern Living* exhibition at DIA) and signed "Alexander Girard Architect."[24] At midcentury, Vendome Road was home to many prominent Grosse Pointe businessmen, including Wilbur Brucker, former Michigan governor (56 Vendome), and Henry T. Bodman, general vice president of NBD Bank (78 Vendome), all of whom had built or purchased traditional-style homes. On January 11, 1950, Jack McLucas was featured in a *Detroit Free Press* article (fig. 166) celebrating Detroit businessmen newly named to banking directorates and executive posts.[25] The list also included Ford Motor Company president Henry Ford II (named to the board of Manufacturer's Bank), J. L. Hudson vice president and general manager James B. Webber Jr. (named to the board of NBD Bank), and Henry T. Bodman.

167. View of the McLucas house from Vendome Road. Architect: Alexander Girard. Photographer: Robert R. Lubera.

However, while John N. McLucas fit the Vendome standard in his status as NBD general vice president (and son of NBD's chairman, Walter S. McLucas), the architectural style of his house did not.

Architecture: "A New Concept of Beauty"

A glimpse of the McLucas house from Vendome Road (fig. 167) highlights the innovative—and, at times, seemingly contradictory—aspects of its design. Indoor and outdoor spaces blend seamlessly: views *into* the house's interior provide views of *outdoor* spaces. The natural finish of the wood posts and screen wall contrasts—yet coexists—with areas of bold color, both outside and inside. The house is orthogonal in nature, yet it nestles organically into its lushly landscaped site. These elements derive from a variety of design traditions (from Miesian modernism to traditional Japanese architecture), disciplines (from architecture to interior design), and projects (from the General Motors Technical Center to the *For Modern Living* exhibition at the Detroit Institute of Arts).

At the time the McLucas house was designed (1949–50), Girard was collaborating with the modernist innovators Charles Eames, Minoru Yamasaki, and Eero Saarinen on a variety of projects—private, corporate, and institutional—each of which attempted to define "modern" style in postwar America. However, Alexander Girard was not a mere copyist: as noted by Leslie Piña, Girard's "talent was in absorbing, synthesizing and then seemingly inventing new forms."[26] Piña was referring to Girard's "translation" of folk art elements into prints and patterns for Herman Miller, although the statement applies equally to Girard's architecture. MOMA curator Edgar Kaufmann Jr. agreed, identifying in each of Girard's architectural projects a unique, unmistakable "Girard touch."[27] In that sense, Girard's architectural design process, involving the union of diverse design traditions, disciplines, and projects into a unified yet unique whole, may be best described as synergistic. The concept of the sum being greater than the parts was similarly articulated by Girard, Yamasaki, and Saarinen in their November 1948 proposal "Theme for D.I.A. Exhibition 1949," in which they asserted that modern design was composed of certain core design qualities.[28] These included the following:

1. **Freedom**
   a. A new understanding of the quality and use of space
   b. The opening up to sun, air, and sky
   c. Letting the outside in
   d. The breaking down of the "box" house and room
   e. The use of space as form

2. **Honesty**
   a. In the use and expression of materials, as against imitation and camouflage
   b. In manufacturing methods and their expression, as against the imitation of handicraft by the machine
   c. In the expression of function with regard to form and use

3. **Simplicity**
   a. The concept that a simple form as an exact solution to a problem is beautiful, as against the ostentation of overelaboration and over-ornamentation

4. **Lightness**
   a. The effort to use the least amount of material in the solution of a problem, as opposed to massive and excessive weight—in the great tradition of the Gothic cathedrals

5. **Naturalness**
   a. The urge to achieve a natural way of life, as against the outmoded formalities of the past
   b. An emphasis on the enjoyment of the forms and variety of natural objects—in themselves and in their contrasting relation to the geometry of man's creations

Other criteria, referenced elsewhere in exhibition discussions, included the following:
   Free use of color

   New forms due to new technology[29]

The document went on to explain that "the total that results from and embodies these qualities, without effort or intention, generates "A New Concept of Beauty," defined as "an intangible quality that emanates from all this work."[30] The "beauty" of this new modern design encompassed physical and spiritual as well as purely aesthetic aspects, with the ultimate goal of enhancing everyday life in the modern era. These concepts are illustrated perfectly in the McLucas house, which, given its conspicuous setting, its synergistic style, and its timing in the aftermath of the DIA exhibition, represents the culmination of Girard's design work up to 1950. Significantly, it is also the only home designed entirely by Girard during his Detroit period that still survives today.

168. Model for the McLucas house (north elevation). Photographer: Elmer Astelford. Courtesy Alexander Girard Estate, Vitra Design Museum. MAR-04808-02.

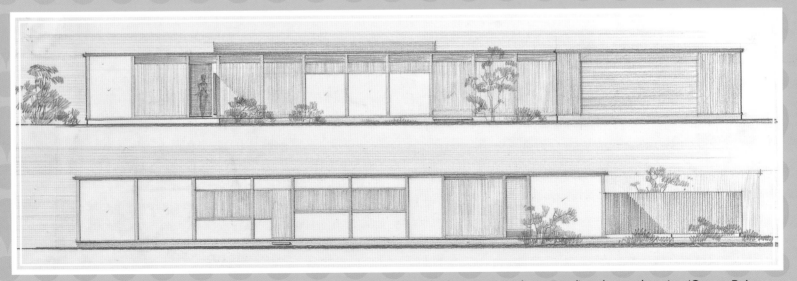

169. Alexander Girard, detail from sketches for McLucas house, showing north elevation (Vendome Road) and east elevation (Grosse Pointe Boulevard). Colored pencil on paper. Courtesy Alexander Girard Estate, Vitra Design Museum. MAR-17240-11.

170. View of the Rietveld Schroeder house, Utrecht, Netherlands, 1924. Architect: Gerrit Rietveld. © Basvb. Wikimedia Commons / CC-BY-SA-3.0 Netherlands.

171. View of the Charles and Ray Eames house (Case Study House #8), Santa Monica, CA, 1949. Architects: Charles and Ray Eames. Photographer: Leslie Schwartz. © 2017 Eames Office, LLC.

Exterior

Traditional Grosse Pointers would have been shocked by the Vendome façade of the McLucas house, best viewed in a Girard model and drawing (figs. 168 and 169). The house would have seemed too simple: all structure and no style. The minimalist, rectilinear form of the house, with its single story, flat roof, and vast expanses of window walls, rejects Grosse Pointe architectural tradition, recalling instead the modernist ideal of Ludwig Mies van der Rohe.[31] Remember that Girard had witnessed the unveiling of Mies's iconic Barcelona Pavilion (fig. 13) in 1929. He would also have been familiar with the architect's design for the Farnsworth house, a domestic adaptation of his Barcelona masterpiece, which was unveiled at MOMA in 1947.[32] Indeed, "simplicity"—a characteristic of Miesian modernism—was one of the core qualities of Girard's "New Concept of Beauty." However, Girard was also inspired by more colorful modernist masterpieces, from the De Stijl–style Rietveld Schroeder house (fig. 170) to those

designed for the iconic Case Study House program, spearheaded by John Entenza, editor of *Arts and Architecture* magazine.[33] These included Case Study House #8, designed by and for Girard's friends Charles and Ray Eames, and Case Study House #9, designed by Charles Eames and Eero Saarinen for John Entenza.[34] Intended to serve as models of mass production for a postwar public, the houses were built of steel and glass, with prefabricated, industrial components. The Eames house (fig. 171) was built according to a modular system with steel bays painted black and in-filled with one of several materials, including plaster, plywood, asbestos, glass, and laminate.[35] The plaster panels—colored black, white, beige, red, and blue—contrast dramatically with the black steel framework.

The December 20, 1949, presentation drawing for the McLucas house (fig. 165) shows a similar combination of geometry and bold color, including blue plywood panels and an orange door.[36] However, there are pronounced differences as well. The McLucas house—unlike the Eames house—features an exposed, wood-framed, post-and-beam structure instead of a steel frame. As in the Jackson house (fig. 152), the McLucas house façade is divided into repeating rectangular bays framed in cedar wood, subdivided

172. Aerial view of the McLucas house model. Photographer: Elmer Astelford. Courtesy Alexander Girard Estate, Vitra Design Museum. MAR-04808-01.

173. View of the McLucas house from Grosse Pointe Boulevard. Architect: Alexander Girard. The dining-room bay, featuring a wide window wall, is visible in the photo at far right. Photographer: Robert R. Lubera.

into smaller rectangular elements and in-filled with painted plywood panels and glass window walls. The result is a masterful, abstract composition of solids and voids and of horizontal and vertical planes. The sense of overall design unity would have been more pronounced in Girard's original plan. The architect's model (fig. 172) shows three rectangular screen walls in cedar wood: one accenting the front entrance and two others (not built) running from the garage toward Vendome Road and from the garage toward the edge of the property line.[37] As in the Goodenough house (fig. 130), these screen walls both provided privacy and reiterated the rectangular geometry and the wood trim of the house, integrating it into the surrounding landscape. Girard employed a similar system of repeating rectangular bays on the Grosse Pointe Boulevard façade (fig. 173), although here he adapted the form to the different function of the spaces beyond. While the dining-room bay features an expansive glass window wall, the service areas feature larger plywood panels and smaller, sliding windows.

The bold geometric design and the prominent use of wood as a structural and a decorative element in the McLucas house suggest the influence of a second aesthetic: traditional Japanese architecture. Clay Lancaster observed the Japanese influence on modern American architecture beginning in the 1930s, inspired by the publication of two books: Jiro Harada's *The Lesson of Japanese Architecture* and Bruno Taut's *Fundamentals of Japanese Architecture*.[38] Harada summarized in his book the basic elements of traditional Japanese architecture and illustrated key examples, such as the Katsura Imperial Villa in Kyoto (fig. 137).[39] The impact of Japanese architectural principles on modern American architecture is evident in the "organic architecture" of Frank Lloyd Wright.[40] Pat Kirkham describes an "overall Japanese feel" in the design of the Eames house.[41] Indeed, one could argue that by midcentury, many "Japanese" elements—that is, wood-frame structure, rectilinear geometric design, integration with nature, and open floor plans, subdivided with screens—had become core components of modern architecture. Elizabeth Smith writes that the Case Study House program—famous for its steel-frame structures—also included post-and-beam, wood-frame houses designed by Julius Ralph Davidson, Richard Neutra, and Rodney Walker, which were "less overtly technological but no less modern."[42]

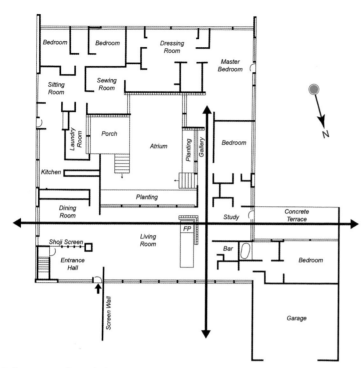

174. Schematic plan of the McLucas house with arrows showing the north-south and east-west axes. Adapted by Rachel Goad from floor plan in Alexander Girard Estate collection, Vitra Design Museum (published in "Girard Editorial").

175. View of the entrance, McLucas house, 55 Vendome, Grosse Pointe Farms, MI. Photographer: Robert R. Lubera.

However, certain aspects of the McLucas house design seem more directly indebted to traditional Japanese architecture. These include the use of cedar wood in combination with white wall surfaces, the crushed-stone border originally around the perimeter of the house, the rare specimens of bamboo in the garden, and the use of *shoji* and *fusuma* screens inside.[43] These elements may reflect Girard's collaboration with Yamasaki, whose designs for the Goodenough and Baker houses were inspired in part by traditional Japanese architecture.[44] However, the "Girard Editorial" in the 1953 *Monthly Bulletin, Michigan Society of Architects*–directly supervised by Girard–referenced his own "profound debt to Japanese architecture and the philosophy behind it."[45] However, it is likely that many of the more overt Japanese references—inside and out—were dictated by Girard's patroness Kitty McLucas, who had traveled extensively in Japan.[46] Indeed, the *Detroit News* article of 1950 stated that the "wood and glass" design of the house would be "a perfect background for the lovely jade figurines and Chinese screens collected by Mrs. McLucas in the Orient."[47]

Interior

Girard's design for the interior spaces of the McLucas house demonstrates perfectly the quality of "freedom" advocated by Girard, Yamasaki, and Saarinen in their "New Concept of Beauty" proposal, defined as "breaking down the 'box' house and room."[48] As shown in the aforementioned model (fig. 172), the house is centered on an open court, allowing for the free flow of space throughout the single story. Public and private areas are disposed around this central court (labeled by Girard as an atrium), with the service areas clustered on the east side of the property (facing Grosse Pointe Boulevard), the public/living and entertaining areas on the north side (facing Vendome), and the private spaces on the south and west sides, facing the backyard. The concept of an open space, enclosed within the house and yet open to the elements, had been explored already by Girard and Yamasaki in the Goodenough house (fig. 139) and more expansively by Girard in the Jackson house (fig. 154). However, one could argue that the McLucas atrium—larger and more fully integrated into the living spaces of the house—is the most successful.

176. Interior view of the McLucas house, showing the screen wall (left), shoji screen (center), and dining room (right). Photographer: Robert R. Lubera.

A schematic plan of the McLucas house (fig. 174) shows the two axes around which the interior spaces are structured. The first is an east-west axis, running from the dining room in the east to the study in the west (and outdoors in both directions); the other, north-south axis runs from the master bedroom down the long corridor, labeled in Girard plans as the "gallery," and down through the west end of the living room and outdoors. The same departure from Grosse Pointe convention is evident in the front entrance (fig. 175), which—rejecting the traditional round arches, triangular pediments, and porches prevalent elsewhere on Vendome Road—consists of a plywood panel, window wall, and door, highlighted subtly with a canopy soffit and header. The window wall frames the entrance hall and its rear *shoji*-like screen, which reiterates on a smaller scale the rectangular nature of the façade. A wooden screen wall, extending down the concrete walkway toward the Vendome approach, both directs the visitor toward the entrance and shields the living room from view. In true Girard fashion, the front door is accented with bold color, providing a hint of the bold color palette inside.[49]

Moving into the house, the entrance hall (fig. 176) is defined by two screening elements. The first—at the rear of the hall, separating it from the dining room—is a modern interpretation of the traditional Japanese *shoji*, a moveable partition wall, constructed of a lightweight wood lattice grid set within a wood frame and covered with *washi* paper.[50] While screen walls were a common feature in modern architecture at midcentury, here the traditional wooden framework is maintained, although in-filled with a modern laminate material instead of paper.[51] The Japanese inspiration is clear in a floor-plan concept drawing dated December 6, 1949 (fig. 177), which identifies two *shoji* screens, one in the dining room and another in the master bedroom.[52] As built, the *shoji* screen in the entrance hall—open at the ends—maintains the flow of space and light between the entrance hall and the dining room, while maximizing privacy from the entrance hall and Vendome Road.

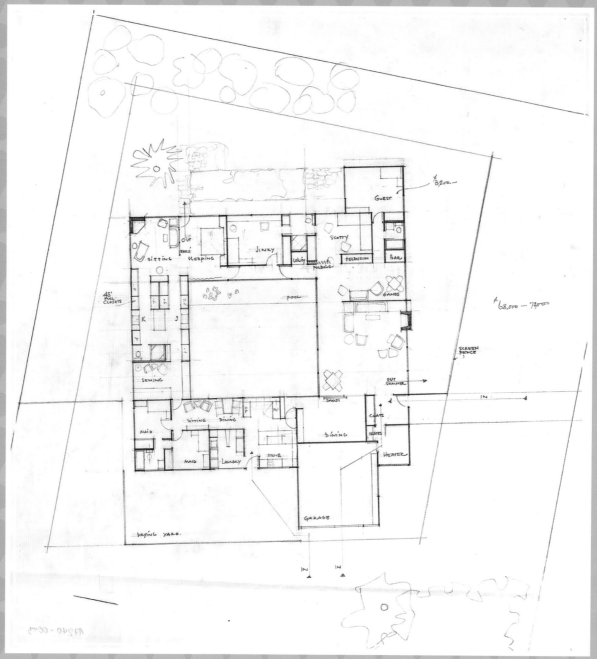

177. Alexander Girard, floor-plan concept drawing for the McLucas house, December 6, 1949. Two shoji screens are indicated: one separating the living room from the dining room and another in the master bedroom. Two sliding glass doors are indicated: one in the living room, adjacent to the entrance screen wall (indicated with an arrow and the words "out summer") and another in the master bedroom (indicated with an arrow and the word "out"). The drawing includes bedrooms for both Jinx ("Jinky") and Scott ("Scotty") McLucas. Courtesy Alexander Girard Estate, Vitra Design Museum.

178. Interior view of the McLucas house living room, looking north (toward Vendome Road) out the window walls. Photographer: Robert R. Lubera.

179. Interior of the McLucas house, view of living room. At left is the view west out to the backyard. At center is the fireplace/hearth. At right, note the furred plaster wall that occupies the three middle bays of the north living-room wall, providing privacy from Vendome Road. Above is the soaring, open-web joist ceiling. Photographer: Robert R. Lubera.

180. Interior view of the McLucas house, dining room. At left is the shoji screen, screening the dining room from the entrance hall. At right are the built-in cabinets and display cases, which divide the dining room from the kitchen. Photographer: Robert R. Lubera.

At right upon entering is a second screening element: a cedar-wood partition wall, which—as in Girard's own house—extends from the entrance into the hall, directing the viewer into the expansive living room. Here we see another aspect of the "freedom" advocated by Girard, Yamasaki, and Saarinen: the "openness to sun, air and sky, letting the outside in."[53] The integration of interior and exterior space is immediately apparent in the view out the two window walls (fig. 178) of the living room's north wall (facing Vendome Road). Here the wooden screen wall extends visually "through" the wall from the outside walkway into the entrance hall. The December 1949 floor-plan concept drawing (fig. 177)—which includes a sliding door adjacent to the screen wall—would have allowed for a physical (as well as a visual) inside-outside connection. In the next three bays, adjacent to the two aforementioned window walls, a furred plaster wall (fig. 179), echoing the three plywood panel bays on the exterior of the house, creates a zone of privacy from Vendome Road. Aluminum clerestory windows above the wall provide light and ventilation and invite the outside in. Three additional window walls on the garage side of the living room connect the living room again to the outdoors, although privacy is maintained by the screen wall near the entrance, the garage wall, and the extensive landscaping.

Turning toward the east, the dining room (fig. 180) offers uninterrupted views outside through an eight-foot-wide window wall and a full-height-operable louvered window section. Privacy from street views is ensured, however, by slots for draperies, by

182. Interior view of the McLucas house, showing fusuma doors, located between the living room and the dining room. Photographer: Robert R. Lubera.

181. Interior of the Katsura Imperial Villa, Kyoto, Japan. Inside the Shokin-tei Pavilion with sliding fusuma doors. Photographer: Raphael Azevedo Franca.

183. Interior of the Katsura Imperial Villa, Kyoto, Japan. View of a storage room in the New Goten, with open and closed shelves. From Arthur Drexler, Architecture of Japan, with permission of the Estate of Arthur Drexler.

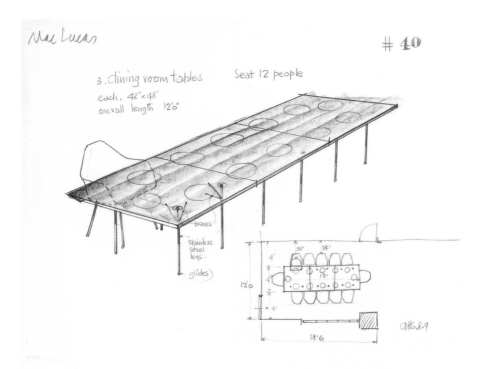

184. Alexander Girard, drawing for the McLucas house dining-room table, showing sectional dining table and Eames dining chair. Courtesy Alexander Girard Estate, Vitra Design Museum.

landscaping along Grosse Pointe Boulevard, and by the aforementioned freestanding *shoji* screen. The open flow of space between the living and dining rooms can be subdivided through the use of another screening element derived from Japanese architectural tradition: the *fusuma*. *Fusuma*, as shown in the Katsura Imperial Villa (fig. 181), differ from *shoji* in that they are sliding screens and are opaque, providing more privacy.[54] Girard's *fusuma* (fig. 182) relate directly to Japanese tradition, including the ornamental door pull; however, Girard's doors are solid and were originally covered with grass cloth instead of the traditional *washi* paper.[55] Floor-to-ceiling cabinets for storage and display divide the dining room from the kitchen, while providing access (for food) through a sliding panel and (for people) through a door (fig. 180). Girard's use of built-in storage with sliding panels, promoted at midcentury by Nelson and others, also derives from Japanese tradition.[56] The glassed-in display cases in the McLucas dining room are reminiscent of the *tokonoma*, a decorative alcove found in traditional Japanese homes. Given that Girard had expressed a "profound debt" to Japanese architecture, he would no

185. Eames molded armchair. © 2017 Eames Office LLC.

doubt have been familiar with Japanese exemplars at the Katsura Imperial Villa (fig. 183) and elsewhere.[57]

However, while Japanese built-ins were usually white, the storage doors in the McLucas dining room were painted in bold primary colors (evident in the background of another McLucas-era photo, figure 202).[58] Girard's incorporation of color relates his built-ins more closely to other midcentury examples, including George Nelson's Storagewall (fig. 70) and the boldly colored storage units displayed in the Eames room (fig. 71) at the *For Modern Living* exhibition the previous year. A Girard drawing provides detailed dimensions for the dining-room table (fig. 184), which was custom designed and complemented by Eames chairs (fig. 185). As in Girard's own home, the dining-room table consisted of a series of smaller tables (in this case, three tables each measuring forty-eight inches square), which could be reconfigured easily for maximum flexibility.[59]

186. Interior of the McLucas house, view of the living room looking west. At left is the open-air atrium. Photographer: Robert R. Lubera

As in many of Girard's residential designs, the living room—the nucleus of the modern, multifunctional home—features a dramatic, sloping ceiling (fig. 186). Consistent with Girard's interest in multilevel designs, the height of the living room ceiling (rising to ten feet and three inches at its apex) contrasts sharply with the lower ceiling heights in the entrance hall and dining room. Of particular interest is the open-web steel-joist structure. The use of standardized, industrial materials in a "direct and honest" manner was a common feature of midcentury modern architecture and a philosophy promoted by Girard in his foreword to the DIA *For Modern Living* catalogue.[60] Similar trusses—albeit of three-dimensional design to provide more stability—were used in Eero Saarinen's design for the GM Technical Center (fig. 31). Remember that Girard was collaborating with Saarinen at the time on the *For Modern Living* exhibition and possibly already serving as color consultant for the GMTC. A surviving design drawing for the living room

(fig. 187) demonstrates that Girard viewed the exposed joists as integral to the design of the room. Indeed, Girard and many midcentury architects viewed the ceiling as a new design element, "a fifth wall," intended to "communicate seamlessly with the rest of the interior."[61] A similar exposed steel joist appears in the living room of the Eames house (fig. 188), designed by Girard's friends Charles and Ray Eames.[62] Girard's ceiling joists make a bolder visual statement in a concept drawing for the McLucas living room, in which they are shown as red (fig. 189). While there is no evidence that the joists were ever painted red, the color would have matched the painted steel legs of the magazine rack that Girard designed for the living room.

The other focal point of the living room is the fireplace, which sits on a low stone hearth and abuts an L-shaped brick wall. A plan drawing, dated February 10, 1950 (fig. 190), shows the fireplace as a freestanding element, centered at the west end of the

187. Alexander Girard, design drawing for the McLucas house living room. Courtesy Alexander Girard Estate, Vitra Design Museum.

188. Interior of the Eames house, Santa Monica, CA. This view of the living room shows the exposed steel joists. Photographer: Tim Street-Porter.

living room. However, notations on a revised floor plan in the Vitra Design Museum, revised April 8, 1950 (fig. 191), indicate that Girard had moved the fireplace (marked with an x) off center, added the L-shaped enclosure (likely the one shown in figs. 187 and 189), and extended the hearth across the living room. As in Girard's own home, the hearth serves both to provide storage for wood and to subdivide the large room. There is no traditional mantle; instead, the low height of the stone hearth (which opens eight feet wide) encourages views into the spaces beyond.

The aforementioned Girard living-room drawing (fig. 187)—likely done after the April 1950 revision—documents his intent to use the hearth and a grouping of couches, chairs, and tables both to define the main living area and to reiterate the rectilinear lines of the house. Here—as in Girard's drawing for the Jackson house living room (fig. 158)—the clustered seating and fireplace complex anticipates the conversation pit, conceived for the Rieveschl house (fig. 246). The design and placement of the furniture in the living room also reflects Girard's quest for a "continuum of design," in which "architecture and each element within the interior design of the building were intertwined."[63] This was a common concept at midcentury, when many of the leading furniture designers were also architects. The placement of the couches corresponds with the architectural sight lines, and their dimensions reflect an overall design unity as well.

Girard's design for the living room demonstrates his desire to create a functional, beautiful space for modern living: the "reintegration of art with life" advocated by Girard, Yamasaki, and Saarinen in the DIA exhibition of the previous year.[64] This meant spaces and furniture enlivened through a variety of textures and employing a "free use of color," a term used by Charles Eames in reference to his exhibition room.[65]

189. Alexander Girard, drawing for the McLucas house hearth and furniture. Note the variety of colors and texture, including bricks, textiles, wood, plants, and steel joists, which are shown here as red. Courtesy Alexander Girard Estate, Vitra Design Museum.

Demonstrating this concept, Girard uses two types of brick around the fireplace: a tan brick (matching the fireplace hood) on the brick wall that surrounds the fireplace, facing the entrance, and a bold, yellow glazed brick on the walls facing the atrium and the rear of the house.[66] The Girard drawing of the hearth (fig. 189) shows the yellow glazed-brick wall, accented by pink and blue sofas. Stacked wood, plants, and custom-designed tables in black-and-white Formica would have provided additional contrasts of colors and textures.

Girard's drawings for the McLucas house furnishings demonstrate another key aspect of modern design, promoted by Girard and others at the time: "new forms due to new material." New technologies such as Formica, a melamine resin that resisted heat and was available in many colors, were essential to this "New Concept of Beauty." Formica

furniture (fig. 192) was both visually appealing and easy to care for, resulting in less housework.[67] This would have appealed to Girard's Grosse Pointe clients—even though all of them had live-in maids. Girard drawings (figs. 193–95) provide detailed instructions for the construction of a magazine rack, side table, and coffee table, made from birch plywood and black-and-white Formica. The drawings capture perfectly the correspondence between modern design and modern life. Given that some drawings are initialed and stamped with Girard's seal as a registered architect (fig. 196), they may also illustrate Girard's ideal synthesis of structure and interior in architecture.

Like the advertisements of the era (created by advertising executives such as Girard's friend and the *For Modern Living* exhibition public-relations director William Laurie), Girard's drawings paint a vivid picture of life in the "mad men" era of the 1950s. Girard

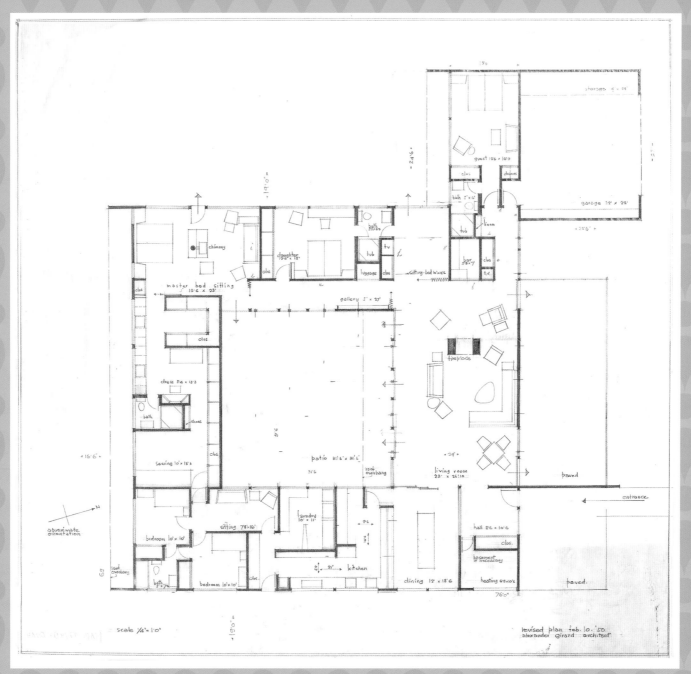

190. Alexander Girard, floor-plan concept drawing for the McLucas house, February 10, 1950. Note that the here the fireplace is centered on the west end of the living room. Girard has added a fusuma between the living and dining rooms. The arrows pointing from indoors to outdoors, noted on the north wall of the living room, in the study, and in the atrium, indicate the presence of sliding glass doors, allowing indoor-outdoor access. Here Girard shows the area outside the living room as paved. Courtesy Alexander Girard Estate, Vitra Design Museum.

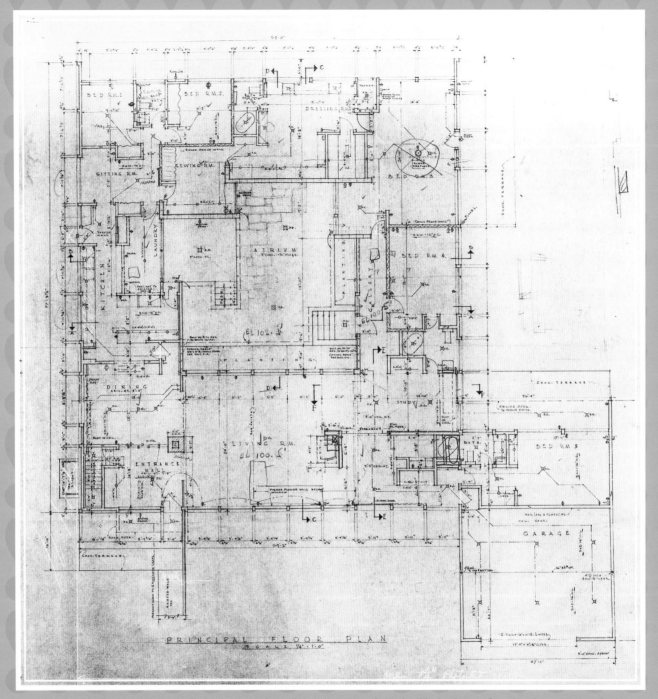

191. Floor plan for the McLucas house, revised April 8, 1950. Pencil marks (likely done after April 8, 1950) indicate a change to the design of the hearth and the rejection of the fireplace in the master bedroom. Courtesy Alexander Girard Estate, Vitra Design Museum.

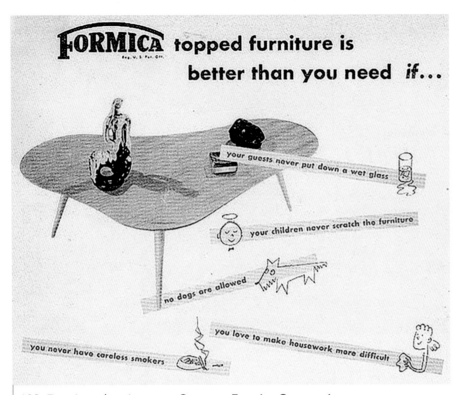

192. Formica advertisement. Courtesy Formica Corporation.

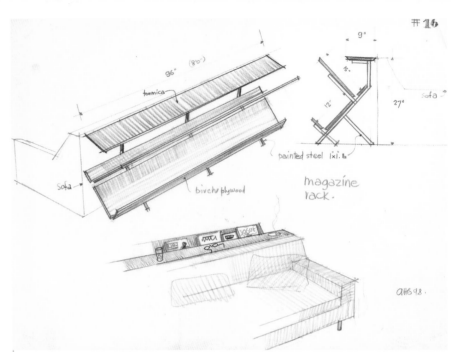

193. Alexander Girard, drawing with specifications for McLucas house magazine rack. Colored pencil on paper. Courtesy Alexander Girard Estate, Vitra Design Museum.

194. Alexander Girard, drawing with specifications for McLucas house white Formica table. Colored pencil on paper. Courtesy Alexander Girard Estate, Vitra Design Museum.

likely knew about his patrons' penchant for parties, referenced vividly in Kitty's memoir, *The Rampant Refugee*. Indeed, the west end of the living room featured a full bar (fig. 197), complete with a sink, a refrigerator, and built-in storage for glasses and more than one hundred bottles of alcohol. While a plan concept sketch from December 6, 1949 (fig. 177), includes a small bar, by February 1950 (fig. 190), Girard had expanded it, substituting the bar in place of the planned bedroom for Scott ("Scotty") McLucas, Jack's son from his first marriage.[68] The black-and-white Formica tables in Girard's drawings (figs. 194 and 195) leave ample room for the essentials of 1950s entertaining, including lit cigarettes, martini shakers, and stuffed-olive appetizers. These images were living proof of the innate Americanness of modern design, a major contention of the DIA *For Modern Living* exhibition.

A McLucas-era photo (fig. 198) shows the magazine rack—identical to one in Girard's own house—stocked with *Life*, *Vogue*, *Time*, and *U.S. News* magazines, ready to be browsed. In 1956, the rack would have included the January 23, 1956, issue of *Sports Illustrated*, which featured seventeen-year-old Jinx McLucas, modeling après-ski wear

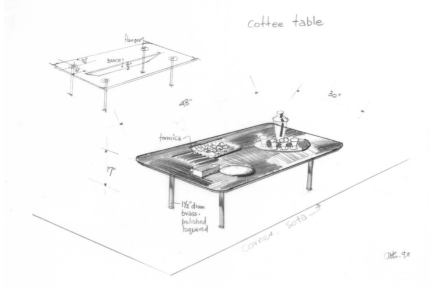

coffee table

195. Alexander Girard, drawing with specifications for McLucas house black Formica table. Colored pencil on paper. Courtesy Alexander Girard Estate, Vitra Design Museum.

196. Detail of fig. 195. Note that the drawing includes Girard's initials and his raised seal as registered architect in the state of Michigan.

197. Interior of the McLucas house, bar. Photographer: Robert R. Lubera.

while on a spring-break ski trip in the Swiss Alps.[69] Jinx had been a fixture in Grosse Pointe society news since her arrival in Grosse Pointe. At ten, she was featured in a *Detroit Free Press* story, which recounted her journey "from . . . prison camp to show ring."[70] By the time she reached her teens, Jinx's birthday parties made local news, and at nineteen, a *Detroit Free Press* article, "Cream of Young Society," dubbed her "queen of the debs [debutantes]."[71] The accompanying photo shows Jinx—then attending Foxcroft boarding school—in the McLucas home (figs. 199 and 200). Another *Detroit Free Press* article, of June 24, 1957, titled "Debs Light the Sky," captured Jack, Kitty, and Jinx McLucas at Jinx's debutante entrance at the Country Club of Detroit, which included geranium trees and a "lush red carpet" (fig. 201).

The black Formica table—as completed—is shown in a McLucas-era photo (fig. 202), taken from the more intimate space on the opposite side of the hearth. This area was set apart from the larger living-room space by its by its lower ceiling height (seven feet and five inches) and by its narrow proportions. The space, complete with built-in shelves for a television and a record player, was intended as an entertainment area. However, the yellow-brick wall (which wraps around and behind the fireplace) was used to display the McLucases' collection of folk art (evident in fig. 202), likely inspired not only by Girard but also by Jack and Kitty's time in Santa Fe with Dot and Hank Kelly. This space inter-

198. View of the McLucas house, living room from entrance looking west, circa 1960. Note the Girard custom-designed magazine rack in the foreground, stocked with magazines. Photographer: Carl Sultzman.

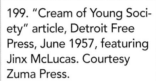

199. "Cream of Young Society" article, Detroit Free Press, June 1957, featuring Jinx McLucas. Courtesy Zuma Press.

200. Jinx McLucas in the McLucas house, from "Cream of Young Society" article, Detroit Free Press, June 1957. Courtesy Zuma Press.

201. John and Kathleen McLucas at the Country Club of Detroit, from "Debs Light the Sky" article, Detroit Free Press, June 1957. Courtesy Zuma Press.

sects a corridor on the north side of the house, leading to the garage and a guest room. It also connects visually to the outdoors through the three window walls on the north side of the living room.

Girard's specifications, noted in construction drawings for the living-room windows on the north side of the house, further demonstrate his intent to maximize the livability of his spaces—through technology and design. The window walls here are identified in construction drawings as "twindows" or thermal windows, measuring one and a quarter inch thick, no doubt to minimize heat loss in winter; all the other window walls in the house are specified as a quarter inch thick.[72] In the "Index to Trades," a detailed list of instructions for contractors, Girard specifies that "extreme care" be used in the placement of posts, to allow "windows and double glass" to be properly framed into openings.[73] Furthermore, the orientation of the living room enhances its livability: during the winter months, sun exposure in the living room (through the south-facing atrium windows) is maximized, whereas in the summer months, it is minimized.[74] Given that Girard had adapted his own house—through skylights and a swinging garage door—for similar functional concerns, there is no doubt that the orientation was deliberate.[75]

On the western end of the main living area—and of the east-west axis—is the study. As in the dining room, a foldable partition—here an accordion-like sliding wall—allows for further subdivision of the interior space. The study ends in a window wall and a door, which opens onto a concrete terrace providing direct access to the backyard. Standing in the study at the intersection of the north-south and east-west axes, one can see "through" the house to the outside in both directions: looking west through the study to the backyard and looking east (fig. 203) through the dining room toward Grosse Pointe Boulevard.

202. View of the McLucas house living room toward the entrance, circa 1960. This photo shows (at center) the black Formica coffee table designed by Girard in the living room. The view of the dining room in the distance offers a glimpse of the custom-designed dining table and the multicolored cabinet doors. On the yellow glazed-brick wall at right are kachina dolls, indicating an interest in folk art. Photographer: Carl Sultzman.

203. Interior of the McLucas house, living room, view from the study looking east toward the dining room and outside to Grosse Pointe Boulevard. Photographer: James Haefner.

Standing at the same point but looking south down the other north-south axis and toward the central atrium (fig. 204), the walls virtually disappear. Five window-wall panels, each topped by a header and clerestory windows and framed in cedar wood, afford full view into the central atrium. Here (fig. 205) the steel joists extend literally through the window-wall wood posts to the outside, where they support the roof overhang, enlarging visually the already expansive living room.

The serene privacy of the atrium is contested, however, by the glazed-brick walls in bold, primary colors: yellow, blue, and red. A Girard drawing (fig. 206) shows that the bold color of the atrium walls was originally conceived as brightly colored plywood, as adopted by Girard in his own home, the Jackson house (fig. 152), and the Fletcher Motel (fig. 153).[76] Indeed, the "Index to Trades" document includes a specification that exterior plywood be painted with "bright primary colors, as directed."[77] However, in the end, the plywood was replaced with glazed brick, which was applied to three walls of the atrium

204. Interior of the McLucas house, living room, looking south toward the atrium (center) and down the gallery toward the master bedroom (far right). Photographer: Robert R. Lubera.

205. View of the McLucas house atrium from the living room. Note how the steel joists extend from the living-room ceiling through the wood posts to the outside, supporting the roof overhang. Photographer: Robert R. Lubera.

(evident in fig. 205). Significantly, two of the glazed-brick walls extend from outside to inside spaces (fig. 207).

There is no documentation specifying exactly when or why the plywood was replaced with glazed brick. However, there is little doubt concerning the source of the glazed bricks, then a new technology. The "Girard Editorial" from the 1953 *Monthly Bulletin, Michigan Society of Architects* connects the brick—lemon yellow, royal blue, and scarlet red—with that developed for the General Motors Technical Center complex.[78] Both the color palette and the "hand-crafted aesthetic" of the glazed bricks (fig. 208) demonstrate a direct link to the GMTC project.[79] Their identification as GMTC bricks has been determined a likely conclusion by Susan Skarsgard, manager of the General Motors Design Archive & Special Collections and foremost expert on the Technical Center.[80] This opinion is based both on Girard's involvement as a design and color consultant to the GMTC project and on a visual, on-site inspection of the bricks. The

206. Alexander Girard, design drawing for the McLucas house atrium. Colored pencil on paper. Note that the boldly colored atrium walls in this sketch appear to be plywood panels and not glazed bricks. Courtesy Alexander Girard Estate, Vitra Design Museum.

208. Detail of red glazed-brick wall in the gallery of the McLucas house. The color, texture, and Claycraft logo (on the reverse) of the bricks connect them with the GMTC project. Photographer: Robert R. Lubera.

207. View of the McLucas house looking south down the gallery and toward the master bedroom. Note the inside-outside red glazed-brick wall at left. In the distance, one can see the yellow glazed-brick wall in the master bedroom. Photographer: James Haefner.

209. Interior and exterior glazed brick, Central Restaurant Building, General Motors Technical Center, Warren, MI, January 13, 2017. Courtesy GM Design Archive & Special Collections.

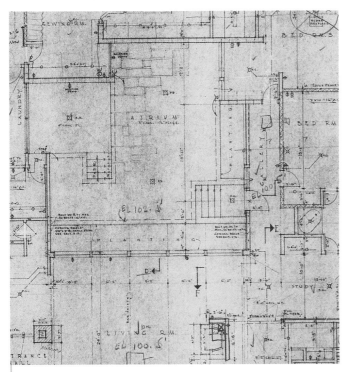

210. Detail of fig. 191, floor plan of McLucas house, revised April 1950. This detail shows the atrium, which—for the first time—indicates inside-outside walls. The door swings indicate the two access points (one from the kitchen and another from the gallery) into the atrium. The main, higher level of the atrium is accessed by steps. Courtesy Alexander Girard Estate, Vitra Design Museum.

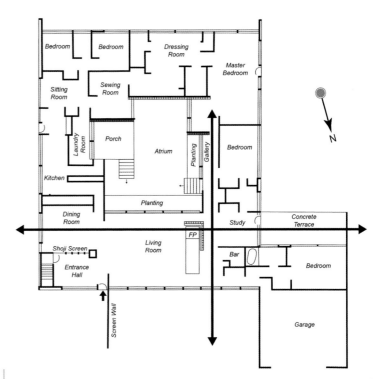

211. Schematic plan of the McLucas house, showing the location of the glazed-brick walls. Adapted by Rachel Goad from floor plan in Alexander Girard Estate collection, Vitra Design Museum (published in "Girard Editorial").

connection with the GMTC is reinforced by the Claycraft logo visible on the reverse of one of the bricks.[81]

Girard's use of the bricks in walls extending from exterior to interior spaces—evident both in the gallery (figs. 207 and 208) and in the master bedroom—demonstrates another link to the GMTC project. Eero Saarinen's use of glazed-brick walls, which often linked indoor and outdoor spaces (fig. 209), has been characterized as an "architecture of interspaces."[82] The use of glazed bricks in exterior and interior spaces—along with other GMTC innovations such as modular building components, moveable partition walls, suspended spiral staircases, and bold colors—was actively promoted for domestic use after the opening of the GMTC in May 1956.[83] However, Girard's incorporation of

glazed-brick walls in the McLucas house's atrium dates much earlier, likely to the spring of 1950. There is no sign of the inside-outside walls in Girard's December 6, 1949, plan drawing (fig. 177), which shows a rectangular atrium with a reflecting pool, an element likely derived from traditional Japanese and Chinese gardens. In the February 1950 plan drawing (fig. 190), Girard's experiments with inside-outside connections take the form of sliding glass doors (note the arrows indicating outside access). It is in the revised floor plan, dated April 1950 (fig. 191 and detail in fig. 210), that the inside-outside walls first appear, projecting from the atrium into the sewing room, the master bedroom, and the gallery.[84] As indicated on the McLucas schematic plan (fig. 211), these are the same walls that would later be decorated with glazed brick. The change both in the design of

212. Alexander Girard, concept sketch for the Great Hall and exhibition rooms, *For Modern Living* exhibition, Detroit Institute of Arts, Detroit, MI, 1949. This bold, multicolor concept for the Great Hall was never executed. Courtesy Alexander Girard Estate, Vitra Design Museum. MAR-17168-05.

213. Exterior, General Motors Technical Center, Warren, MI, 1946–56. Note the bright, multicolor glazed-brick walls. Photographer: Balthasar Korab. Courtesy Library of Congress.

the atrium and in the materials used as color accents (glazed bricks in "bright, primary colors" instead of plywood) suggests that Girard got access to GMTC bricks sometime between February and April 1950.[85]

It is interesting to note that Girard's change in the design of the living-room hearth–also decorated with glazed brick–appears in the same revised floor plan, dated April 1950 (fig. 191). Given that the GMTC campus was not open to the press until the summer of 1951, Girard's access to GMTC bricks and design concepts in the spring of 1950 must have come through his relationship with Eero Saarinen.[86] In the spring of 1950, Girard had just finished one collaboration with Saarinen (the *For Modern Living* exhibition) and may have begun another (color consultant for the GMTC).[87] The striking similarity between the bold color schemes proposed for the *For Modern Living* exhibition (fig. 212), the GMTC (fig. 213), and the McLucas house atrium (fig. 214)–all conceived in the years 1948–50–demonstrates clearly the cross-pollination of ideas between Girard and Saarinen. During the same time frame, Girard and Saarinen had also started a new architectural collaboration: the design of the Miller Cottage in Muskoka, Ontario.[88] The patrons, J. Irwin and Xenia Miller, later hired Saarinen and Girard to design their home in Columbus, Indiana.[89]

The bold color of the brick walls would have been more prominent in the atrium as originally designed, which featured–as in Girard's own house and in the Jackson house–a multilevel concept. As the April 1950 floor plan (fig. 210) shows, the two entrance points into the atrium–a concrete patio / screened porch accessed from the kitchen and a doorway accessed from the gallery–were on ground level. However, the floor of the atrium itself was elevated and accessed by steps. A Girard concept drawing (fig. 215) showing a section of the living room and atrium looking east (the figure at right is standing inside the atrium) showcases the intended multilevel concept.

Girard's interest in capturing visual interest through multilevel, interconnected spaces is best showcased in the master bedroom. Here (fig. 216) the yellow glazed-brick wall clearly extends from the sewing room through the atrium and into the master bedroom, blurring the line between outside and inside. The lower edge of the glazed-brick wall evident today clearly indicates the original, higher floor level of the atrium.[90] A Girard drawing for a custom-designed, built-in desk and lamp in the same space (fig. 217) demonstrates even more clearly the multilevel effect intended by Girard. The unique, conical desk chair shown in the drawing and in a McLucas-era photo (fig. 218) is the

214. View of the McLucas house atrium from the living room, showing the blue, yellow, and red glazed-brick walls. Photographer: James Haefner.

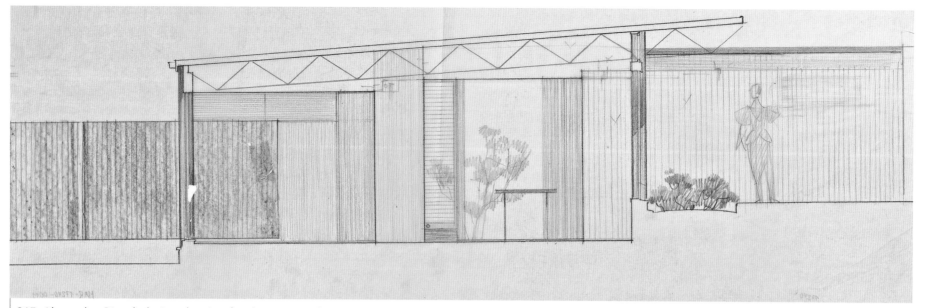

215. Alexander Girard, design drawing for the McLucas house atrium. This section drawing (looking east) demonstrates the multilevel effect of Girard's design. At left is the screen wall, extending from the concrete walk "through" the wall into the entrance hall. At center is the dining room, and at right is the atrium (the figure at far right is inside the raised atrium). Colored pencil on paper. Courtesy Alexander Girard Estate, Vitra Design Museum.

216. View of McLucas house interior, master bedroom. Note the inside-outside yellow glazed-brick wall that extends from the sewing room through the atrium and to the master bedroom. Photographer: James Haefner.

model 132 chair, designed by Don Knorr in 1946 and manufactured by Knoll beginning in 1950.[91]

In keeping with the "free use of color" promoted in the *For Modern Living* exhibition (then just recently completed), the yellow glazed brick was intensified by equally bold pink carpeting and pink-and-yellow-print draperies. Kitty McLucas must have shared the "color courage" referenced by one of the exhibition enthusiasts in the *Detroit News*.[92] A Grosse Pointe society columnist agreed, stating, "I know a gal, who when she wants to describe the most heavenly shade of pink . . . does it this way: It's exactly the same shade as the rug in Mrs. John McLucas' bedroom."[93] The photograph (fig. 218) shows that the bedroom was accented with additional colors and textures, including (at left) an Eames storage unit and (on the walls) grass-cloth wallpaper. The display case in the same photo may also show the jade figurines referenced in the August 1950 *Detroit Free Press* article.[94]

The view of the living room from the atrium (fig. 219) demonstrates another of Girard's modernist criteria: "naturalness," defined as "an emphasis on the enjoyment of the forms and variety of natural objects—in themselves and in their contrasting relation to the geometry of man's creation."[95] Indeed, while the McLucas family—unlike the

217. Alexander Girard, drawing for the built-in desk and lamp in the master bedroom. This drawing illustrates the multilevel effect of Girard's design: the atrium floor is clearly elevated above that of the house. Colored pencil on paper. Courtesy Alexander Girard Estate, Vitra Design Museum.

218. View of the McLucas house, master bedroom, circa 1960. The photo shows (at left) the Don Knorr model 132 chair and an Eames storage unit and (at right) the built-in bookcase and display wall. Courtesy Carl Sultzman.

Goodenoughs and the Rieveschls—did not live in the Pine Woods of Lothrop, Girard succeeded in creating an atmosphere of serenity and seclusion. This phenomenon is illustrated clearly in an aerial photograph of the house, shot by James Haefner with the aid of a drone (fig. 220): here Girard's geometric structure is fully enveloped by its organic surroundings.

The integration of structure and nature is also evident in Girard's design for the master bedroom, which changed considerably over time. In the December 1949 plan (fig. 177), the room was divided into sleeping and sitting quarters by a *shoji* screen. The February 1950 plan (fig. 190) maintained the division of the large room, although the *shoji* screen was replaced by a fireplace. The "Index to Trades" document specifies an Acorn House Inc. fireplace in "Chinese red."[96] However, the revised plan of April 1950 (fig. 191) includes several modifications, including the elimination of the fireplace in the master bedroom.[97] The final design for the master bedroom features two wide window

walls, framed in cedar wood and separated by a door and a plaster wall with a window. The result is a masterpiece of Girard's "naturalness": one can barely distinguish where the house ends and the backyard begins (fig. 221). The transparency of the house is demonstrated fully in a view from the backyard through the master bedroom and into the atrium (fig. 222). Even more spectacular is the view through the house at night (fig. 223).

Perhaps nowhere was Girard's innovative adaptation of architecture for modern living more on display than in his design for the master bathroom / dressing room (figs. 224 and 225). As in his own home, the space was multifunctional and high tech, featuring built-in storage with a multitude of drawers, plastic laminate countertops with a metal backsplash, pull-out towel bars, and his and her sinks. Special features included a walk-in closet (then a rarity) and a full-length, tripartite mirror, lit with custom bulbs. However, Girard's love of bold color and pattern was best showcased on the floor. Here Girard used vivid pink and white vinyl-composite tile in a harlequin motif, creating a

219. View of the McLucas house from the atrium, looking toward the living room. Photographer: Robert R. Lubera.

221. View of the master bedroom of the McLucas house toward the backyard. Photographer: Robert R. Lubera.

220. Aerial view of the McLucas house. Photographer: James Haefner.

222. View of the master bedroom and backyard of the McLucas house through the window wall. This photo showcases the transparency of the house: here one can see through the window wall of the master bedroom into the atrium. Photographer: Robert R. Lubera.

223. Night view of the McLucas house from the backyard. Photographer: Robert R. Lubera.

224. View of the master bathroom of the McLucas house toward the master bedroom, showing the built-in cabinets and original flooring. Note the bold pink and white, harlequin-patterned floor tile and built-in cabinetry. Photographer: Robert R. Lubera.

surface that was functional, decorative, and expressive (remember that pink was Kitty's favorite color). As shown in figure 218, the tile floor extended into the master bedroom, accented there by Kitty's pink rug. The flow of space continued from the master bedroom/bathroom into the service wing, consisting of the sewing room, sitting room, laundry room, two bedrooms, and the kitchen. As in Girard's own house, the kitchen featured cupboards with sliding, black Masonite doors, for maximum work space and storage. However, having live-in servants, the McLucas family would not have spent much time here.

The McLucas family continued to live at 55 Vendome until 1960. By that time, Kitty McLucas had reached her social peak, serving in 1952–53 as president of the Junior League of Detroit. Jack McLucas, featured in a 1958 *Detroit Free Press* article, titled "The Men behind It All," had been promoted to senior vice president at NBD.[98] On September 4, 1958, the society page of the *Grosse Pointe News* covered the engagement of Virginia Montague McLucas to Gregory Baldwin, heir to the Ulupalakua Ranch, located on forty thousand acres of land on the island of Maui.[99] Once Jinx moved to Hawaii, Kitty and Jack did too. Jack retired from NBD in February 1961, and while the 1961 *Social Secretary of Detroit* lists two addresses for Mr. and Mrs. John N. McLucas—55 Vendome and a winter home in Honolulu, Hawaii—in 1962, there is no listing at all.[100] One could say that Grosse Pointe had served them—including Girard—surprisingly well. MOMA curator Edgar Kaufmann Jr. wrote in his essay on Girard's architecture, "Girard seems to be reaching artistic mastery. His core concept of architecture is symphonic—relationships to site, to materials, to structure, to the flow of use in and around the building, to the modulation of light, to accentuating color, all these are conceived and integrated in a full rich entity."[101] His comments apply directly to the McLucas house, as does his conclusion that Girard's architecture serves "not only as art but . . . as the enhancement of life."[102] After completing the McLucas house, Girard had one final architectural experiment in Grosse Pointe: the Rieveschl house.

225. View of the master bathroom of the McLucas house toward the sewing room. Photographer: Robert R. Lubera.

226. Jan Rieveschl in the Rieveschl house "conversation pit," circa 1951. Photographer: Charles Eames. © 2017 Eames Office LLC.

Radical Iteration

The George and Betty Rieveschl House

As far as I am concerned, the greatest compliment
one can receive in this racket is "You know, I didn't
get a chance to see it properly." That means there
is enough color, detail and quality to make it
almost incomprehensible, to see beyond the
initial shot, the initial look.

—Alexander Girard

Even though Jan Rieveschl was only four at the time, he recalls
clearly the day that that he moved into his family's new home in
the Pine Woods of Lothrop. The Rieveschl family had moved
from Cincinnati to Detroit in 1943, when George started work
at Parke-Davis, then the nation's largest drug manufacturer. The
focus was the development of his own discovery: an antihistamine,
later marketed and sold by Parke-Davis as Benadryl.[1] By 1951, the
family had lived in Grosse Pointe for more than seven years, but in
a modest, traditional two-story house on Vernier Road. When they
arrived at their new home on 232 Lothrop, Jan—whose tiny stature is
captured in a Charles Eames photo (fig. 226), where he stands ankle deep
in the family-room bear-skin rug—was "frightened that he would get lost."[2]
He had good reason: the new house was an anomaly, composed of four separate

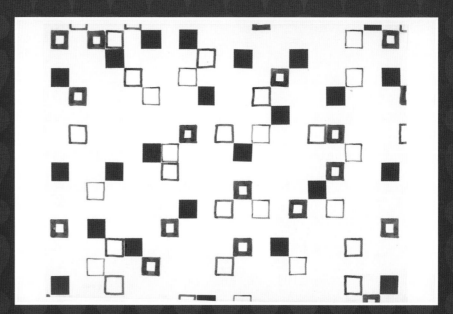

228. Alexander Girard, drawing and collage, design for Herman Miller Textile, "Small Squares," 1952. Brush and ink, gouache on wove paper, mounted on white tracing paper, 37 × 50 cm. Gift of Alexander H. Girard. Photo credit: Cooper Hewitt, Smithsonian Design Museum / Art Resource, NY.

George Nelson–industrial designer, architect, author, director of design for Herman Miller. Leaving for a month's visit to Germany at the invitation of the German Government.

Charles Eames–designer, architect, film maker. Invited to visit Japan by the Japanese Government. Currently off to Germany under the auspices of the German Foreign Office.

Alexander Girard–architect, interior designer, creator of Herman Miller's fabric collection. Leaving for India to collect material for a new show at New York's Museum of Modern Art.

The extraordinary number and variety of distinctions heaped on Herman Miller's team of designers is probably unique in U.S. industry. We at Herman Miller would like to think that these are due, in part at least, to their remarkable performance in connection with the company's continuing program of research and design in furniture and fabrics.

herman **M**iller, zeeland, mich.

227. "Traveling Men" advertisement for Herman Miller, showing (left to right) George Nelson, Charles Eames, and Alexander Girard. Courtesy Herman Miller.

229. George and Betty Rieveschl, circa 1950s. Courtesy Jan Rieveschl.

wings–service, living/dining, sleeping, and guestroom/studio–linked together by long passageways that sloped up and down with the changing contours of the surrounding site. As one author wrote, "Far from completely understanding the house at first glance, you walk around, or down passageways, to hit pavilions that turn out unexpectedly large and elaborate."[3] Jan soon came to love the house, stating, "There is no place that I return to in my dreams more than the house at 232 Lothrop."[4] A writer for *House and Home* magazine agreed, calling a visit to the house a trip "through Girard's Wonderland."[5]

Indeed, if the McLucas house represented the culmination of Girard's conceptions about modern design up to 1950, the Rieveschl house, completed in 1951, represented a new direction, a "radical iteration" of his earlier design ideas.[6] This was fueled by the expansion of Girard's reputation as a designer beyond Detroit, including his subsequent involvement in MOMA's "Good Design" competition at the Merchandise Mart in Chicago. In October 1951, Girard signed a contract with Herman Miller to "assemble and coordinate" a line of fabrics for the company, a move that culminated in the 1952 creation of the Herman Miller Textile Division.[7] Girard became part of the Herman Miller "dream team," already consisting of George Nelson and Charles Eames (fig. 227). Leslie Piña explains that Girard's initial goal at Herman Miller was to "establish a fabric collection based on his architectural training."[8] As a result, Girard's first fabric designs, which included "Small Squares" (fig. 228), consisted of geometric prints incorporating stripes, circles, and triangles. Piña called them a "refreshing addition to a rather dull market."[9] Girard also wanted to maximize consumer choices, allowing people to "express themselves through their environments."[10] One could say that Girard's last Grosse Pointe residence, the Rieveschl house–a bold experiment in geometry, color, pattern, and texture–demonstrates many of the same concerns evident in his fabric designs but translated into 3-D form.

Art historians have questioned how Girard "convinced the [Rieveschl] family to accept" the "delightfully off-kilter" house that he had designed for them.[11] However, the answer is clear: his patrons, George and Betty Rieveschl (fig. 229), not only embraced but actively helped to shape Girard's creation. While George Rieveschl, a chemical engineer, is best known for inventing the antihistamine Benadryl, he had originally wanted to become a commercial artist. He later told the *Cincinnati Post*, "If I had found an art job back in the 30s, I would have taken it."[12] Indeed, while Gary Rieveschl recalls his father's status as a "mover and shaker" in Detroit, Gary's brother, Jan, recalls that family life was shaped not by his father's work but instead by music, literature, and art.[13] These passions, shared by both George and Betty Rieveschl, were manifested in the design of their house. While it is not known how they met Girard, George and Clara Bettina ("Betty") Rieveschl clearly recognized in Girard a kindred spirit, who could make their dream house–funded in part by Benadryl royalties–a reality.[14] Jan and Gary Rieveschl characterize their parents as Girard's "coconspirators," complicit in "turning him loose" to create his boldest architectural experiment.[15]

On June 30, 1950, George and Betty Rieveschl bought lots 55b and 55c/56a (fig. 230) at the dead end of Lothrop Road.[16] Their property, 232 Lothrop (fig. 231) formed the last part of the Pine Woods enclave already occupied by the Goodenough and Girard houses. On September 5, 1950, Alexander Girard applied for a building permit, estimating a $55,000 cost for the wood-frame house.[17] A Girard sketch (fig. 232) shows that he envisioned the house as an organic entity, spreading out like "fingers" into the sprawling Pine Woods landscape.[18] Girard's intent to merge structure and site is evident in a topographical plan drawing (fig. 233), which shows the elevation of the proposed house relative to the surrounding landscape. Here Girard took his fascination with changing levels–evident in the Girard, Jackson, and McLucas houses–to a new extreme. Because the drawing has no key or date, it is difficult to interpret with complete accuracy. However, Girard's intent is clear: the adaptation of the house to the rolling contours of its Pine Woods site. The floor levels of the service and living/dining areas rise highest (plus thirty inches), corresponding with the high point of the site, then slope down with the terrain to the living room's lower level (plus twelve inches) and to the bedroom (minus twelve inches) and the guest/playroom (minus six inches) wings on the lowest areas of the site.

The numbers also indicate the downward trajectory of the passageways between the four wings of the house. As noted in the drawing, the passage leading from the central living-room wing to the bedroom wing slopes downward twelve inches (from plus six to minus six inches). The dramatic differential is evident in a Charles Eames photograph (fig. 234), which shows an aerial view of the house, taken from the roof of the nearby pavilion. Conversely, in the areas marked "fill" on the drawing, Girard sculpted the terrain–as in his own home–to match his architectural vision. The resulting, organic interrelationship between the house and landscape is evident in another Eames photograph, which shows a pine tree growing literally through the kitchen-roof overhang (fig. 235). However, paradoxically, Girard's design for the Rieveschl house was also rooted in geometry, consisting of a series of square and rectangular units.

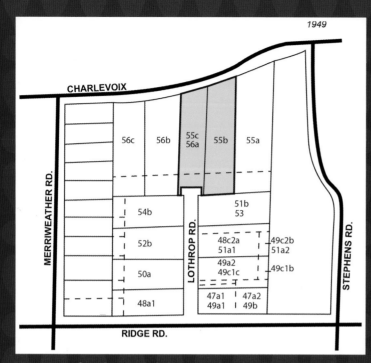

1949

CHARLEVOIX

56c | 56b | 55c/56a | 55b | 55a

54b | 51b / 53
52b | 48c2a / 51a1 | 49c2b / 51a2
50a | 49a2 / 49c1c | 49c1b
48a1 | 47a1 / 49a1 | 47a2 / 49b

MERRIWEATHER RD.
LOTHROP RD.
STEPHENS RD.

RIDGE RD.

230. Map of Lothrop's Subdivision, showing lots 55b and 55c/56a (232 Lothrop), purchased by George and Betty Rieveschl. Artwork by Rachel Goad, based on the "1969 Grosse Pointe, Michigan Area Plat Book," Grosse Pointe Historical Society Archives.

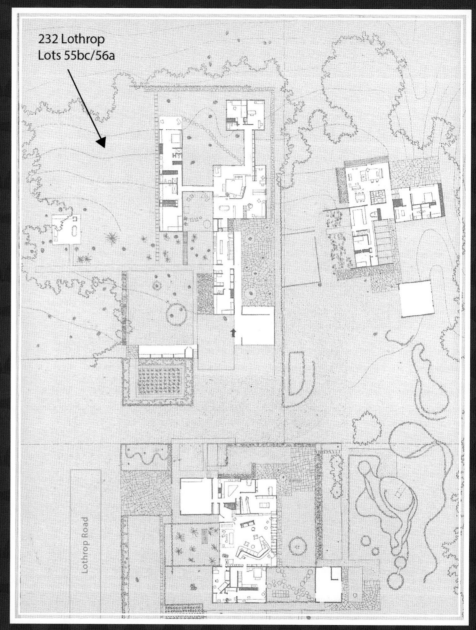

232 Lothrop
Lots 55bc/56a

Lothrop Road

231. Plan of the Pine Woods houses on Lothrop designed by Girard and Yamasaki (1949–51). Highlighted area shows 232 Lothrop (Rieveschl house). Adapted by Rachel Goad from "1949 Lothrop Road Plan," Alexander Girard Estate, Vitra Design Museum (published in "Serendipity in the Woods"). MAR-04799-01.

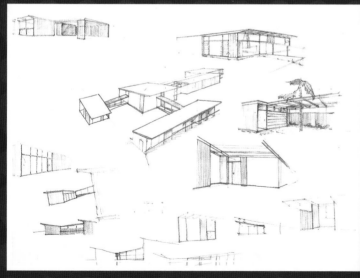

232. Alexander Girard, concept sketches for the Rieveschl house, Grosse Pointe, MI. Pencil on paper. Courtesy Alexander Girard Estate, Vitra Design Museum. MAR-17243-02.

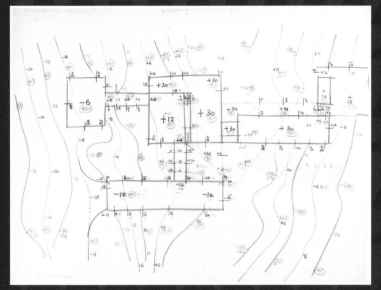

233. Alexander Girard, topographical/plan sketch for the Rieveschl house, Grosse Pointe, MI. This drawing illustrates clearly Girard's multilevel concept and the extent to which Girard adapted the house to the rolling contours of its site. Colored pencil on paper. Courtesy Alexander Girard Estate, Vitra Design Museum. MAR-17243-04.

234. Exterior of the Rieveschl house from the garden pavilion. Architect: Alexander Girard. In the background, one can see the central (tallest) living/dining-room wing and the corridor sloping down to the bedroom wing in the foreground. Photographer: Charles Eames. © 2017 Eames Office LLC.

235. Aerial view of the Rieveschl house, showing exterior patios. This photo was taken from the roof of the bedroom wing, looking toward the living/dining-room wing. Note (at center) the glassed-in corridor connecting the living/dining and bedroom wings and (in the distance) the pine tree growing through the roof overhang of the service wing. Photographer: Charles Eames. © 2017 Eames Office LLC.

236. Alexander Girard, 1951 Christmas card for the Rieveschl family, showing sketch of the Rieveschl house. Courtesy Rieveschl family.

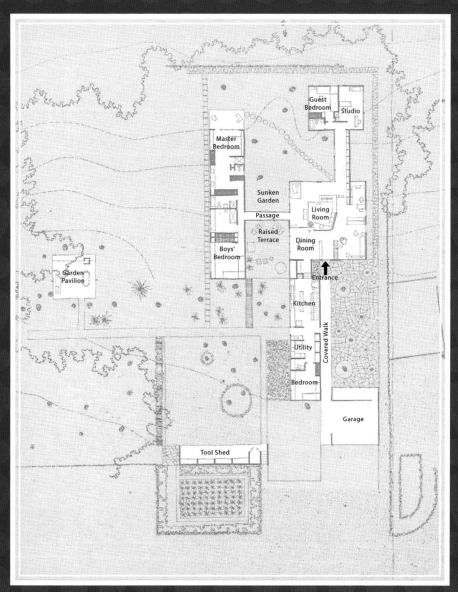

237. Floor plan of the Rieveschl house. Adapted by Rachel Goad from "1949 Lothrop Road Plan," Alexander Girard Estate, Vitra Design Museum (published in "Serendipity in the Woods"). MAR-04799-01.

238. View of the Rieveschl house, covered walk to entrance, Grosse Pointe, MI. Architect: Alexander Girard. Note the overhead skylight. Photographer: Charles Eames. © 2017 Eames Office LLC.

239. Exterior view of the Rieveschl house at night, showing outdoor patio, living/dining-room wing, and (at center) the glassed-in passageway between living/dining-room and bedroom wings. Grosse Pointe, MI. Photographer: Charles Eames. © 2017 Eames Office, LLC.

Reiterating the textile metaphor, one author wrote, "the architecture superimposes an orderly pattern" on the landscape, resulting in a checkerboard-like pattern of outdoor courts and terraces, matched by indoor enclosures.[19] Girard illustrated this concept clearly in a drawing (fig. 236) for the Rieveschl 1951 family Christmas card.

While many architectural elements drew on Girard's past architectural experience, here they were stretched to their limits, as demonstrated in the floor plan of the house (fig. 237). As in the Goodenough house (fig. 139), the covered walk leading from the garage to the front entrance is flanked by a flagstone terrace, pierced with trees. However, here the roof is cut away by an overhead skylight and dramatically lit at night by floodlights (fig. 238). Other passageways, such as that leading from the central living/dining-room wing to the bedroom wing (fig. 239), were glassed in on both sides, creating the impression of actually being outside. A Charles Eames photograph (fig. 240) demonstrates how Girard accentuated the changing level of this downward-sloping corridor and of the ter-

rain outside by creating an "off balance treatment" in the plaster siding.[20] In this photo, the viewer is in the living room, looking down the corridor toward the bedroom wing. On the east side of the corridor (at left in the photo), the siding rises upward to match the level of the raised terrace outside; on the west side (at right in the photo), it tapers downward to showcase a sunken garden. It was for this passageway that Girard designed a magnificent runner—executed by V'Soske—characterized by bold color and geometry (fig. 241). Girard's unique synthesis of the geometric and the organic is evident in a cautionary note on his design drawing (fig. 242), which reads, "all lines slightly off parallel are intentionally so and are part of this design." Jan Rieveschl remembers traversing the carpet "twenty times a day" and even rolling it up so that he and his brother could roll their "Rube Goldberg constructions," activated via marbles, down the rolling slope from the living room to the bedroom wing.[21]

As in all of Girard's houses, the heart of the Rieveschl residence was the living room, which was divided into five subspaces, including a central hearth area with built-in seating, a dining area, and areas for quiet reading and even for watching television and movies. As shown in a floor-plan drawing labeled "Furniture Layout" (fig. 243), many spaces included furniture (green dot), cabinetry (red dot), and textiles (yellow dot), custom designed by Girard. The passage leading to the studio/guest wing was lined with Girard's trademark floor-to-ceiling, glass-shelved bookcases. As indicated on the aforementioned topographical/plan drawing (fig. 233), the living/dining-room wing was multilevel in conception. Highest were the dining and entertainment areas closest to the main entrance. Two steps down was the second level, which included spaces connecting to the bedroom and studio/guest-room wing passageways. Lowest was the fur-carpeted sanctum near the fireplace.

While the living/dining wing—as indicated on the topographical/plan drawing—was located on the highest point of the site, it was also the tallest. Girard concept sketches for the Rieveschl house indicate that he considered using an exposed steel-joist ceiling (fig. 244) and a glazed-brick wall in bold primary colors (fig. 245), as in the McLucas house (then recently completed). However, in the end, he combined elements from his previous residential designs to create a unique concept: a dramatic ceiling composed of exposed pine beams that slope upward toward (and through) towering, transparent window walls, topped by clerestory windows. At the center of the living room was an entirely new creation: a sunken, fur-carpeted seating area, later dubbed a "conversation pit" (fig. 246).[22] As in Girard's own home, the seating area included built-in couches, a radio,

240. Interior view of the Rieveschl house, showing conversation pit and view down glassed-in corridor from living/dining-room wing to bedroom wing, Grosse Pointe, MI. Photographer: Charles Eames. © 2017 Eames Office, LLC.

241. Alexander Girard in his 222 Lothrop home with the Rieveschl house runner. Courtesy Alexander Girard Estate, Vitra Design Museum.

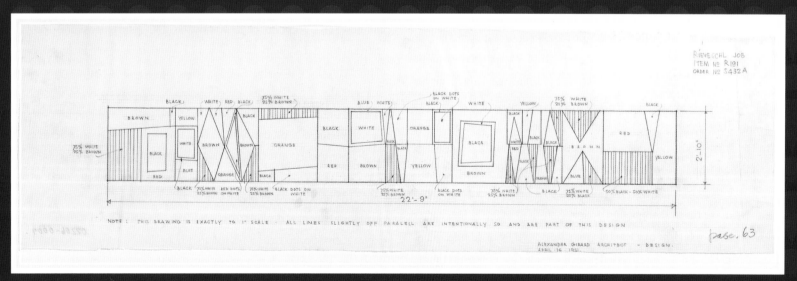

242. Alexander Girard, drawing for the Rieveschl house runner, with notes. Pencil on paper. Courtesy Alexander Girard Estate, Vitra Design Museum. MAR-02206-01.

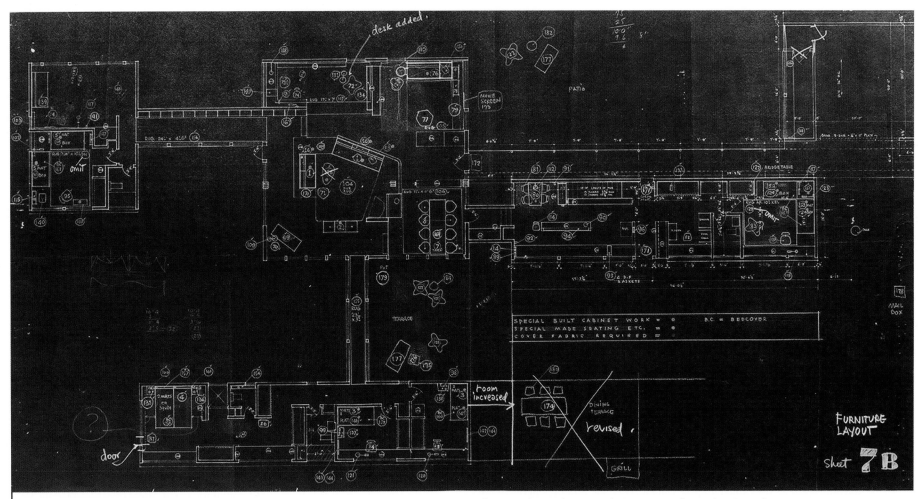

243. Construction drawings for the Rieveschl house, sheet 7B, "Furniture Layout." Architect: Alexander Girard. Courtesy Alexander Girard Estate, Vitra Design Museum. MAR-02206-02.

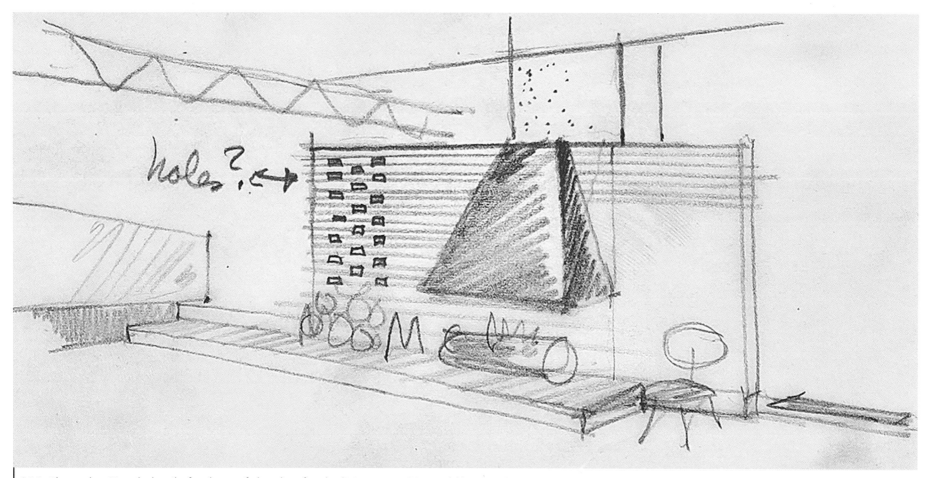

244. Alexander Girard, detail of a sheet of sketches for the living room, Rieveschl house, Grosse Pointe, MI. Note the indication of steel ceiling joists and the unique cut-away design in the hearth wall. Pencil on paper. Courtesy Alexander Girard Estate, Vitra Design Museum. Detail of MAR-17243-06.

and a plaster partition wall. However, here all were clustered snugly around—instead of across from—the fireplace. A transparent curtain provided a subtle barrier between the living and dining zones; additional lighting came from a new product: an overhead, acrylic skylight called a Wascolite Skydome.[23]

What does not come across in the surviving photos (primarily black and white) is the profusion of colors, textures, forms, and cultures assembled within the house, reflecting the tastes of both Girard, the designer, and Betty and George Rieveschl, his clients. An early cross-section drawing of the living room (fig. 247) shows a living plant (seen

against a bamboo backdrop), juxtaposed with the glazed bricks of the proposed fireplace, and a sheer fabric panel. Visible at left are the floor-to-ceiling bookshelves that lined the passageway to the studio/guest-room wing. The bold visual impact of the conversation pit, accented with plants and bright Thaibok silk pillows, was best captured in a color photograph shot by Balthasar Korab after a later William Kessler renovation (fig. 248). In characteristic Girard fashion, bold color was integral to the design of architectural as well as decorative elements. Doors were accented in bold, "conspicuous" colors such as "dark maroon, blue or sepia," granting them both an aesthetic and a functional

245. Alexander Girard, study for the living room of the Rieveschl house, Grosse Pointe, MI. Note the proposed use—as in the McLucas house—of a yellow glazed-brick wall. Colored pencil on paper. Courtesy Alexander Girard Estate, Vitra Design Museum. MAR-17243-01.

246. Living room of the Rieveschl house, Grosse Pointe, MI. Architect: Alexander Girard. This Charles Eames photograph documents the original design of the living room, with the bear-skin rug in the conversation pit. Photographer: Charles Eames. © 2017 Eames Office LLC.

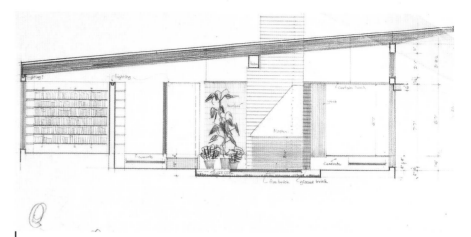

247. Alexander Girard, design drawing for the Rieveschl house, Grosse Pointe, MI, showing the multilevel effect. Colored pencil on paper. Courtesy Alexander Girard Estate, Vitra Design Museum. MAR-17243-03.

purpose.[24] One author detected a deeper meaning in the proliferation of doorways and passageways throughout the house, noting that Girard conceived them as "symbols of, as well as instruments for, movement and unrestraint."[25]

The bold visual and textural effect of Girard's creations were amplified by the Rieveschls' eclectic art collection, which ranged from folk art discovered during trips to Guatemala (with Sandro and Susan Girard) to German expressionist paintings.[26] One author, writing for *House and Home* magazine, characterized the aesthetic—shared by Girard and the Rieveschls—as a "consistency of confusion."[27] He stated, "you look up and find yourself facing a hand-sculptured, asbestos plastered and gourd-shaped fireplace, and there are more free-form screens, tables, lamps, and *objets d'art* than even a Freud might have dreamed up."[28] However, the author clearly intended the comment as a compliment. He later described Girard's radical approach as "collage

architecture," clarifying that the diverse elements coalesced under the "unifying personality of the designer"—aided in this case by the parallel wishes of the patrons.[29] Gary Rieveschl recalls that his family's house "attracted serious gawker attention," requiring them to put up a high fence to maintain their privacy.[30] It is interesting to note that George Rieveschl was one of three "prominent Grosse Pointe Farms men" referenced in a June 5, 1952, *Detroit Free Press* article as charged with building fences above the six-foot maximum.[31] The other two men were Girard's other Grosse Pointe clients: John N. McLucas and Daniel Goodenough. Evidently, a tall fence was one "price" for building modern in Grosse Pointe.

248. Living room of the Kieveschi house, Grosse Pointe, MI. Architects. Alexander Girard and William Kessler. This photo shows the living room after the renovation by William Kessler. Photographer: Balthasar Korab. Courtesy Archives of Michigan.

249. Alexander and Susan Girard in the living room of their Santa Fe, NM, home, 1960s. Photograph: Charles Eames. © 2017 Eames Office, LLC.

onclusion
Girard from Detroit to Santa Fe

We should sincerely create that which is utterly contemporary and practical and in perfect harmony with the aesthetic and spiritual tradition of our people.

—Alexander Girard

If Grosse Pointers thought that Alexander Girard had gone too far in his architecture and interior designs, it was clear to him that he had not gone far enough. In the spring of 1953, he advertised a sale of interior décor, in preparation for his family's departure for Santa Fe, New Mexico, in June.[1] The decision to move was likely spurred by several factors. Girard did not—as one might have initially expected—leave Grosse Pointe for lack of work. Through his independent and collaborative projects, Girard had played a major role in cultivating modern design in Detroit—and had even dented the aesthetic armor of its most traditional suburb, Grosse Pointe. However, by 1953, Girard, then forty-six years old, had clearly expanded his horizons beyond Detroit, professionally as well as geographically. The incredible breadth of Girard's design work at the time was captured in a March 1, 1953, *Detroit Free Press* article, titled "Girard: The Man Who Is Five Different People" (fig. 250). The four-page feature celebrated Girard's work as "a registered architect, a color consultant, a large-scale collector, an artist, and a designer of exhibitions, interiors, landscapes, sculpture, furniture, textiles . . . , radio cabinets, and toys."[2] The article—one of several published about Girard between 1952 and 1953—was both a summation of Girard's past work and a preview of future projects, many of which evolved from ideas incubated in Detroit.[3]

GIRARD
The Man Who Is Five Different People

Alexander Girard of Grosse Pointe has many identities. He's a registered architect, a color consultant, a large-scale collector, an artist, and a designer of exhibitions, interiors, landscapes, sculpture, furniture, textiles, lamps, ceramics, clocks, radio cabinets and toys.

In an age of specialization this needs explaining.

"When you practice in all fields of design, each field benefits from your experience in the others," Girard says. "And all design is related, whether houses, gardens, furniture or women's clothes."

Born in Florence, Girard studied and worked in Italy, Spain, France, Germany, Sweden and England. The European regard for craftsmanship probably accounts for his interest in carrying out his designs with his own hands—in wood, plastic, paper and paint. A small tool shop is as much a part of his professional equipment as a drafting board.

The fact that Girard was enlisted to create a setting for the 1953 "Good Design" Exhibit in Chicago recalls his association with the first such exhibit when it was launched at the Detroit Institute of Arts.

Dr. E. P. Richardson, director of the Art Institute, characterizes his colleague this way:

"Girard is a fellow of brilliant talents and varied interests which he hides behind an air of morose gloom. You look at him and think the poor chap has lost his last friend and his lunch was terrible. Don't worry; all it means is that he has just thought of some brilliant design idea that will presently delight you."

Free Press Photo by ANDY PLOPCHAN

250. "Girard: The Man Who Is Five Different People," article in the Detroit Free Press, March 1, 1953. Courtesy Zuma Press.

Page 1 of the article referenced Girard's role as exhibition designer for the 1953 *Good Design* show at the Merchandise Mart of Chicago, the fourth in a series organized by MOMA's Edgar Kaufmann Jr. These shows, held biannually at the Chicago Merchandise Mart (in January and June to coincide with the home-furnishing market), with an additional showing at MOMA in November, represented a new merger of art and commerce.[4] In 1950, Girard had served as a juror for the first *Good Design* show, which was designed by Charles and Ray Eames; by 1953, he had been selected as a designer (fig. 251).[5] Building on his work for the 1949 DIA exhibition, Girard's 1953 *Good Design* installation included a unique system of display (fig. 252), merging the grid-like structure of the Hall of Objects "jungle gym" with the Storagewall concept pioneered by

251. Alexander Girard with Charles and Ray Eames setting up the Good Design exhibition at the Merchandise Mart, Chicago, IL, 1953. © 2017 Girard Studio LLC. All rights reserved.

252. Installation view of the exhibition Good Design, June 1953, the Merchandise Mart, Chicago, IL, organized and shown at the Museum of Modern Art. Gelatin silver print. Photographer: Carl Ulrich. Museum of Modern Art Exhibition Records, 542.13, Museum of Modern Art Archives, New York. Digital Image © The Museum of Modern Art / Licensed by SCALA / Art Resource, NY.

From the collection
of fabrics and wallpapers
designed by Alexander Girard
for Herman Miller.

253. Alexander Girard, swatch showing fabric and wallpaper designs for Herman Miller. Courtesy Herman Miller.

254. Conversation pit in the living room, Miller house, Columbus, IN, 1953–57. Architect: Eero Saarinen and Associates. Note the fifty-foot rosewood storage wall and the conversation pit designed by Alexander Girard. IMA Photography. Courtesy Indianapolis Museum of Art.

George Nelson. Contrary to Girard's standard practice, however, the displays were all in black and white.[6] The objects—the sole source of color—were displayed in shelving units and on large, plastic platform displays, which were brilliantly lit and set against a dark background, creating a "chiaroscuro" effect that was both "dramatic and theatrical."[7] Girard continued to design visually stunning installations and exhibitions for Herman Miller and other clients throughout his career.

Page 3 of the *Detroit Free Press* article, subtitled "He Shocks You with Color," referenced Girard's new status as director of Herman Miller's new Fabric Division. In June 1952, Girard had launched a line of woven and printed fabrics for Herman Miller.[8] Susan Brown characterizes the collection—available in more than thirty patterns and 120 colorways, in eight bright colors and six neutral colors—as a "toolbox for architects and interior designers" (fig. 253).[9] Girard's creative reservoir was seemingly bottomless. Indeed, Brown writes that Girard's "pure, cohesive and highly personal vision was the sole creative force behind the Herman Miller Fabric Division for twenty years."[10] Later in Girard's career, his work at Herman Miller expanded from textile design to other

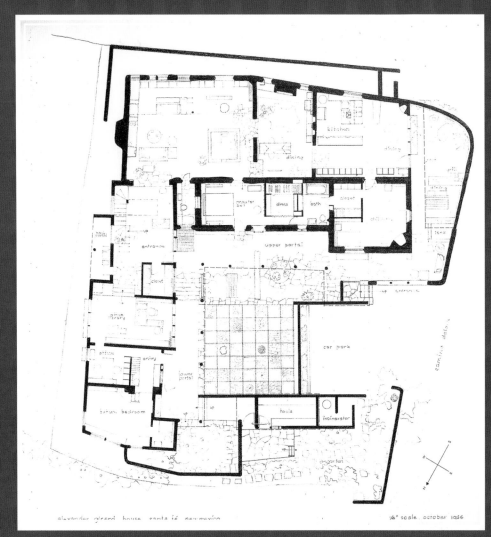

255. Floor plan of the Girard house, Santa Fe, NM, October 1956. Courtesy Alexander Girard Estate, Vitra Design Museum. MAR-04901-01.

256. Girard house, Santa Fe, NM, with view of the exterior courtyard. © 2017 Girard Studio LLC.

257. Living room of the Girard house, Santa Fe, NM. Note the bold, colorful wall mural and display. © 2017 Girard Studio LLC.

fields of design. These included the design of the Herman Miller showroom in San Francisco (1958) and in 1961 the design of a unique design store, the Textiles & Objects ("T&O") shop, intended to promote the sale of Herman Miller textiles and related decorative objects.[11]

The rest of the *Detroit News* article focused on Girard's architecture and interior design work, focusing primarily on the Girard family home on Lothrop. However, by 1953, Girard's textiles were showcased in a new, collaborative project with Eero Saarinen: the design of the Irwin and Xenia Miller house in Columbus, Indiana, completed in 1957.[12] While the design of the steel, glass, and marble structure is credited to Eero Saarinen, it is the interior spaces (fig. 254), designed by the "interior architect" Girard, that set the house apart from any other. These included the fifteen-square-foot "conversation pit" and the fifty-foot-long rosewood storage wall (dubbed a "three-dimensional mural"), running the length of the entrance hall.[13] Both were accented with brilliantly colored textiles and collectibles from across the world—in deliberate, dramatic contrast with the white-stone floors and walls.[14] Both evolved from designs conceived during Girard's Detroit period, from the colorful "jungle gym" display units of the *For Modern Living* exhibition to the sunken seating area and wall-to-wall bookshelf display units of the Rieveschl house.[15]

Given Girard's incredible productivity during the years 1952–53, it is no wonder he commented that he went to Santa Fe to "have the luxury of not being interrupted."[16] However, he also clearly wanted to escape from the restrictive nature of Grosse Pointe to a new cultural and geographical landscape, one that placed no limits on his creativity. By 1953, the Pine Woods of Lothrop was no longer a "hinterland," and Sandro and Susan had already set their sights on a more remote, exotic setting: Santa Fe, New Mexico. At the time, New Mexico was an increasingly popular tourist destination and a mecca for artists, including Georgia O'Keefe.[17] In a letter dated October 29, 1953, Girard described his new home to his Grosse Pointe friends Bill and Thayer Laurie as "the most ultra fantastically beautiful place," including mountains, pine forests, ruins, processions, and "sunsets better than any postcard."[18]

However, while Susan and Sandro had left Grosse Pointe behind, it is interesting to note that they retained their revisionary outlook. Indeed, as they had done in 1947, Susan and Sandro Girard purchased a home in Santa Fe consisting of preexisting adobe structures (some up to two hundred years, some up to seventy-five years, and others as recent as five years old), which they renovated into a unique, new creation.[19] Girard

later commented on why they had chosen the house: "because it afforded a lot of interior space which was adaptable to all the experimenting we like to do."[20] As in New York and Grosse Pointe, the new, hybrid home (fig. 255) included space for Girard's office. However, here typical Girardian forms were transformed with vernacular touches: exposed, timber beams, a conversation pit of plastered cinder block (fig. 249), adobe-sculpted built-in furniture, and elaborate succulent gardens (fig. 256). Whereas Girard had sculpted the landscape in Grosse Pointe, here he sculpted the walls themselves, cutting them away in areas to create niches and to frame exterior and interior vistas. White adobe walls and ceilings provided a "unified arena for . . . many visual events," including a multicolored interior wall, bedecked with candles and folk art (fig. 257).[21]

In Santa Fe, the Storagewall concept pioneered by George Nelson evolved into a wall-sized "altar" (fig. 258) for the Girards' ever-increasing collection of folk art, which by 1961 had grown to over seventy thousand objects.[22] These objects, frequently rearranged by Girard, were valued less for their historical than for their humanistic and aesthetic value, "as nourishment for the creative spirit of the present."[23] Girard transformed the Santa Fe house throughout the four decades that he lived there. These changes were documented through photographs by Charles Eames and featured in national and international design publications, from the *New York Times* to *Vogue*.[24] As Jochen Eisenbrand noted, "Thanks to Girard, Santa Fe took a place next to Los Angeles and New York as the third epicenter of American design."[25] The Santa Fe house, in its various permutations, embodied Girard's all-encompassing definition of architecture, integrating not only structure and interior but art and life. Although the landscape had changed, the mind of the master had not: Girard's artistic genius, incubated during his time in Detroit, continued to evolve until his death in Santa Fe on January 31, 1993. He never lost his belief in the power of design—whether architecture, furnishings, textiles, toys, or art installations—to transform humanity. As he once stated, "'Tutto il mondo è paese,' The whole world must know about itself. . . . The colors vary, their languages vary, but their spirits and aspirations are interwoven into one incredibly rich humanity."[26]

258. Girard house, Santa Fe, NM, with view of Alcoa storage wall designed by Alexander Girard. The storage wall shown here was used in an advertisement in the Saturday Evening Post, July 27, 1957. Photographer: Charles Eames. © 2017 Eames Office LLC.

Appendix: Alexander Girard Design Sites in Grosse Pointe, circa 1950

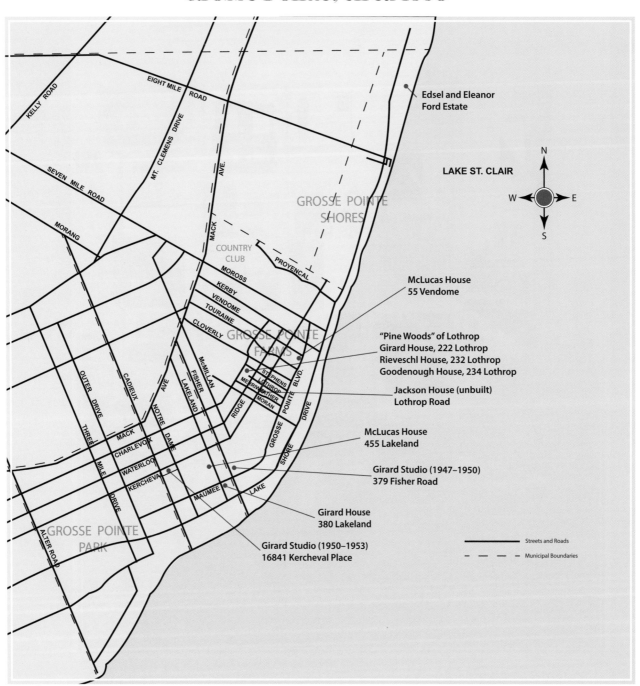

Edsel and Eleanor
Ford Estate

LAKE ST. CLAIR

N
W   E
S

GROSSE POINTE
SHORES

McLucas House
55 Vendome

"Pine Woods" of Lothrop
Girard House, 222 Lothrop
Rieveschl House, 232 Lothrop
Goodenough House, 234 Lothrop

Jackson House (unbuilt)
Lothrop Road

McLucas House
455 Lakeland

Girard Studio (1947–1950)
379 Fisher Road

Girard House
380 Lakeland

Girard Studio (1950–1953)
16841 Kercheval Place

———— Streets and Roads

– – – – Municipal Boundaries

259. Artwork: Rachel Goad.

cknowledgments

This book would not have been possible without help from many individuals and institutions. These include the following:

Architects and professors of architecture John Comazzi, Mónica Ponce de León, Greg Saldana, and Christopher Rawlins, Rudolph Architects, and architectural historian Dale Gyure.

Artists/designers Alexander Fedirko and Christina Liedtke and special mention to artist John Sauve for his advice on the publication process and for my introduction to Wayne State University Press.

At AIA Michigan, Evelyn Dougherty, Events/Documents.

Clem Chargot and Three C's Landscaping for always going above and beyond to keep the McLucas house beautiful year-round.

At Cranbrook Academy of Art, Christopher Scoates, Director of Cranbrook Academy of Art and Art Museum; Scott Winter, Director of Development; Judy Dyki, Director of Library and Academic Resources.

At Cranbrook Art Museum, Andrew Blauvelt, Director; Christine McNulty, Registrar; Steffi Duarte, Jeanne and Ralph Graham Collections Fellow.

At the Cranbrook Center for Collections and Research, Director Greg Wittkopp, Head Archivist Leslie Edwards, Archivist Gina Tecos, Special Projects Archivist Cheri Gay, and Associate Archivist Belinda Krencicki.

At the Detroit Institute of Arts, Salvador Salort-Pons, Director; Alan Darr, Walter B. Ford II Curator of European Sculpture and Decorative Arts; James Hanks, Archivist, Research Library & Archives; Maria Ketchum, Head Librarian, Research Library and Archives; Jessica Herczeg-Konecny, Digital Asset Manager; and Laurel Sicklesteel-Patterson, Director of Development Operations.

Detroit Free Press reporter and columnist John Gallagher.

At Docomomo USA/MI, Chapter President Deborah Goldstein.

At the Eames Foundation, the Eames family members, Eames and Llisa Demetrios, Byron Atwood, Carla Hartman and Lucia Atwood, and at the Eames Office, LLC, David Hertsgaard, Archivist; Genevieve Fong, Manager, Permissions and Licensing; and Daniel Ostroff, for their help in securing epigraphs and images for the book.

For securing permission from the Estate of Minoru Yamasaki, Taro Yamasaki.

For securing permission from the Estate of Arthur Drexler, Joan Carol Drexler.

At Esto, Christine Cordazzo and Caroline Hirsch.

Express Photo for help in scanning blueprints and photographs.

At FCA, Danielle Szostak, Historical Services.

At Formica, Stephanie Lang, Senior Communications/PR Specialist.

Friends Laurelyn Head, Brian and Missy Sullivan, and Mary Bartek, Kathy Donigan, and Jan Torno have listened to the evolving story of the book, as have colleagues Elisabeth Thoburn, Chris Seguin, Robin Ward, Clara DeGalan, Selina Christin, Cathy Andonian, and Djennin Cassab. Rachel Head and Emmett Burns stepped in to help with citations and other key last-minute tasks.

The Fundacio Mies van der Rohe and photographer Pepo Segura.

At the George N. Fletcher Public Library in Alpena, Michigan, Special Collections Librarians Robert Lyngos and Marlo Broad.

Graphic designer Rachel Goad, who worked tirelessly on the maps and diagrams for the book, which are indispensable for the understanding of Girard's architecture.

Greg Leck for his research on Japanese internment camps in China.

Benjamin Gravel and Katie Doelle for sharing their expertise on Grosse Pointe architecture.

At the General Motors Design Archive and Special Collections, Design Manager Susan Skarsgard for her insights on the McLucas house bricks and on GMTC history, for her help in securing photographs of the GMTC bricks, and for several tours of the magnificent General Motors Technical Center; Lead Archivist and Curator Natalie Morath and Larry Kinsel, Researcher, for documentation and photographs relating to Girard's role at the GMTC.

Girard scholars Monica Obniski, Alexandra Lange, and Keira Coffee.

At the Grosse Pointe Historical Society, Director of Education Izzy Donnelly and Researcher Pam Scanlon.

At the Grosse Pointe Farms City Offices, City Manager Shane Reeside.

Grosse Pointe residents, present and past, who provided information on Girard, Girard's clients, and on Grosse Pointe and Detroit at midcentury: special mention goes to Doris Brucker, Abby Peck, Fred Ollison III, Gerald and Susan White, Joan Micou, Katherine Duff Rines, Robert Robinson, and Krystn Rollins for providing information on the McLucas family; Elizabeth Goodenough, who dedicated so much time to searching her personal archives, reading my manuscript, and connecting me with so many people who knew the Girards and grew up in the Pine Woods of Lothrop, including Dan Goodenough and Pixie Goodenough Dodge, Richard Jackson Jr., Linda Jackson Roecklin, David Laurie, Duncan Laurie, Ann Mesritz, Gary Rieveschl, Jan Rieveschl, and Sandy Weiner. Special thanks to Tim and Ann Kay.

Greg Hamme, an artisan of great talent who immediately recognized the historical significance of the McLucas house restoration. His years of effort in the refurbishment of the original cedar wood was instrumental in bringing the McLucas house back to its midcentury glory.

At Herman Miller, Max De Pree, CEO; Ben Watson, Executive Creative Director; Sam Grawe, Global Brand Director; Amy Auschermann, Corporate Archivist, for their help in illuminating Girard's role at Herman Miller and in securing images for the book.

At the Huntington Library, Jenny Watts, Curator of Photographs; David Zeidberg, Director; Mona Shulman; Stephanie Arias.

At the Indianapolis Museum of Art and the Miller House Archives, Shelley Selim, Associate Curator of Design and Decorative Arts, Archivists Samantha Norling and Anne Young.

Daniel T. "Budd" Kelly Jr. for memories of Santa Fe, the Girards, and the Kelly family.

At Knoll Inc., Archivists David Bright and Maya Sorabjee.

Extended McLucas family members, including W. Scott McLucas for his remembrances of his grandfather Walter McLucas and his father, John McLucas; Sibyl Baldwin and Claire Bird for their remembrances of their mother, Jinx McLucas. Susan Brandenburg for helping to secure permissions for images of the McLucas family.

At Meadowbrook Hall, Madelyn Rzadkowolski, Director of Curatorial Services.

At the Michigan History Center, Archivists Andrea Gleitzen, Jessica Harden, and Mark Harvey.

At the Michigan State Historic Preservation Office, State Historic Preservation Officer Brian Conway and Preservation Planner Amy Arnold.

At Todd Oldham Studio, designer Todd Oldham and Tony Longoria.

At Palm Springs Modernism Week, Treasurer Mark Davis.

John Parnell Jr. for finding documentation on the building permits, deeds, and lawsuits relating to the Girard-designed houses in Grosse Pointe.

Photographers Tim Street-Porter, James Haefner, and Robert R. Lubera for the amazing images, especially the previously unpublished photographs of the McLucas house.

At PPG, Catie Landis, Associate Marketing Manager.

Realtor Dennis Andrus for sharing photographs of and information on Girard houses in Grosse Pointe.

At Scala / Art Resource, Robbi Siegel.

Shelley and John Schoenherr for sharing their expertise and enthusiasm for Yamasaki.

The late Jim Smith and Shirley Smith Rooney for remembrances of the Girards and Lothrop Road during the midcentury period. Thanks also to the Rowe family and the Koch family.

At Smith Group JJR, Susan Arneson, Vice President of Marketing & Communications.

At the Saul Steinberg Foundation, Sheila Schwartz, Research & Archives Director.

At the University of Michigan Art, Architecture & Engineering Library, Rebecca Price, Architecture, Urban Planning & Visual Resources Librarian.

At the Vitra Design Museum, Chief Curator Jochen Eisenbrand and Archivists Andreas Nutz and Matthias Pühl for their help in locating, shooting, and sending high-res images of original Girard drawings and other materials from the Alexander Girard Estate collection at the Vitra Design Museum for use in this book.

At the Walker Art Center, Jill Vuchetich, Archivist, Head of Archives and Library.

At the Walter P. Reuther Library, Mary Wallace, AV Permissions Archivist.

At Wayne State University Press, Kathryn Wildfong, Director; Annie Martin, Editor in Chief; Kristin Harpster, Editorial Design and Production Manager; Rachel Ross, Senior Designer; Emily Nowak, Marketing and Sales Manager; Ceylan Akturk, Assistant Editor, Rights and Permissions; Kristina Stonehill, Promotions Manager; Jamie Jones, Advertising and Exhibits Manager; and copyeditor Andrew Katz.

At Zuma Press, Florence Combes, Licensing Manager.

Several individuals deserve special acknowledgment.

The Girard family and Girard Studio LLC, including Alexander Girard's son, Marshall Girard (and his wife, Alexis Girard), and grandchildren, Alexander Kori Girard and Aleishall Girard Maxon, provided support in the form of valuable information, photographs, and enthusiasm for the project.

Architect Marc Pagani and interior/project designer Alexis Kim read the manuscript and toured the McLucas house with me, providing invaluable commentary on architectural structure, materials, and terminology.

Ruth Adler Schnee, my dear friend, wrote the foreword to this book. Throughout the past six years, she has shared her fascinating experiences in Detroit during the midcentury period and her personal interactions with midcentury pioneers Alexander Girard, Eero Saarinen, Charles and Ray Eames, Minoru Yamasaki, and others. She also served as design consultant for the McLucas house during its restoration. Her life and work has been an inspiration for me and countless others.

Perhaps most important—there would be no book without them—are the three successive families who owned the McLucas house, which inspired this book.

Thanks to Jack, Kitty, and Jinx McLucas, whose incredible life story led to the creation of the McLucas house. Dr. Carl Sultzman bought the house and preserved it, even after he no longer lived in it. Nancy Sultzman Sutton and the entire Sultzman family loved the house and helped me secure photographs for the book.

The current owners of the McLucas house, Robert and Mary Lubera, have dedicated so much of their time, talent, and resources to the restoration of the house and to the discovery of its history. Their support during every stage of this process has been invaluable. Their willingness to open their house to a seemingly endless succession of visiting architects, scholars, and artists—especially at their annual Arts, Beats, and Eats parties—is the perfect fulfillment of Alexander Girard's desired union of art and life. A special thank-you to my nephew, John, who was only two years old when he moved into 55 Vendome. He has grown up, surrounded by the wonderful world of Alexander Girard. His creative mind has expanded through his interactions with a myriad of visiting architects, scholars, and artists. Only time will tell how Alexander Girard's magic will influence the next generation.

My family has been my rock during this long process. My mom and dad, Elizabeth and Richard Lubera, have supported my work in every way, especially in making it possible to secure the images necessary for publication.

Family members Dave, Katie, Andrew, Stephen, and Becky Lubera, Jennie Wolf, Dolores Kawsky, and the Miller and Spatafora families have followed the progress of the book from day one.

My husband, Paul, and son, Will, have provided insightful comments and critical IT and emotional support from start to finish. My daughter, Sarah, served as my prime reader, critic, and enthusiast through every stage of writing and revising. Teddie has been my faithful companion through many long hours of writing. I could not have completed this book without you all, and I owe you a huge debt of gratitude.

Notes

Introduction

Epigraph: Richardson, introduction to *Exhibition for Modern Living*, 8.

1. E. P. Richardson, draft of the introduction to *Exhibition for Modern Living* catalogue, June 7, 1949, Box 67, Folder 10, Edgar P. Richardson Records, 1930–62 (hereafter RCH).

2. Ibid.

3. "What Is Modern?," *Pathfinder News Magazine*, October 5, 1949, 42.

4. The attendance numbers are referenced in letters to James Webber Jr. and to Girard: E. P. Richardson to J. Webber, November 22, 1949, RCH 67/9; and E. P. Richardson to A. Girard, November 28 1949, RCH 67/9.

5. Sugrue, "Motor City."

6. Ibid. The term "arsenal of democracy" comes from a Fireside Chat given by President FDR on December 29, 1940. Detroit's auto companies responded, repurposing auto factories for the production of jeeps, M-5 tanks, and B-24 bombers. For more on this subject, see Baime, *Arsenal of Democracy*.

7 .Richardson, introduction to *Exhibition for Modern Living*, 7–8.

8. Ibid., 8.

9 .E. P. Richardson to J. Webber Jr., November 15, 1949, RCH 67/9.

10. Defenbacher, "Editorial Note," 14.

11. Eisenbrand, introduction to *Alexander Girard*, 13. Eisenbrand attributes the phenomenon both to the scholarly neglect of interior design as a discipline and to the fact that many of Girard's masterpieces no longer survive.

12. Kaufmann, "Alexander Girard's Architecture," 20.

13. "Biography," in Eisenbrand and Kries, *Alexander Girard*, 330–31.

14. Eisenbrand, "Whole World a Village," 143–45. Eisenbrand's essay discusses the influence of Girard's family's background in antiques on his later career.

Kaufmann's characterization of Girard as a "Renaissance man" ("Alexander Girard's Architecture," 19) reflects the diversity of Girard's design background and influences as well as his expertise in a variety of design fields.

15. Eisenbrand, "Whole World a Village," 147. The term "fantastic universe" was coined by Eisenbrand, who viewed the Republic of Fife as a precursor to Girard's later interest in folk art.

16. Kaufmann, "Alexander Girard's Architecture," 19. Kaufmann notes a common denominator in Girard's designs: "a leaven of playfulness–even the houses and gardens . . . have some qualities of toys."

17. "Biography," 330–38.

18. Kaufmann, "Alexander Girard's Architecture," 19. Kaufmann's essay addresses the variety of influences on Girard at the time, from the Neo-Rococo theaters of Kaufmann to the "playful handcrafts that flourished then in Milan, Vienna and Paris."

19. Oldham and Coffee, *Alexander Girard*, 380. Oldham and Coffee cite a *Detroit News* article, which called the apartment "the first example of modern decoration in Florence." As noted in the "Girard editorial," 22, Girard's use of metal tubes related to Brener's "chromium tube experiments" and preceded those of Le Corbusier.

20. For more on the Barcelona pavilion and its significance, see "Pavilion." The original pavilion, which also featured the Mies van der Rohe–designed *Barcelona Chair*, was disassembled in 1930 but reconstructed on the same site in 1983–86. Girard contributed to the exhibition in the Italian Pavilion of the exposition.

21. Oldham and Coffee, *Alexander Girard*, 384. As noted by Oldham and Coffee, Girard's description of his own style as "aesthetic functionalism" signified an integration of traditional minimalist modern form with a "richness of design" that integrated decoration in the form of curves, color, and texture.

22. "Biography," 331.

23. For the influence of Girard's father in securing his commissions in New York City, see ibid., 339; and Kaufmann, "Alexander Girard's Architecture," 19.

24. Oldham and Coffee, *Alexander Girard*, 80. Oldham and Coffee discuss Girard's New York City commissions.

25. "Biography," 338. Girard became a registered architect in Connecticut and Michigan in 1937.

26. Ibid. The social status of the family is demonstrated by the fact that the wedding was held in St. Patrick's Cathedral and was published in the *New York Times*: "Susan W. Needham Wed to Architect." According to the Girard family, Sandro met Susan during her time studying abroad in Florence.

27. For more information on the Girards' New York City apartment, which also served as a model for potential interior design clients, see "List of Works," in Eisenbrand and Kries, *Alexander Girard*, 374–75.

28. Oldham and Coffee, *Alexander Girard*, 20, describe Susan as "the liaison between Girard and the world," writing that she "dealt with clients, she cared if Girard got press or credit," allowing her husband to stay "focused on his designs." The fact that Susan came from a wealthy and well-connected Scarsdale family certainly aided in securing social and business contacts; it likely provided a financial safety net for the Girards as well.

29. Conversation with the author, March 2016.

30. For the origin of the Sansusi joint name and symbol, see "Biography," 338. The logo is also an ancient symbol for infinity.

31. For more on the Girards' move to Detroit, see "Biography," 339; and Obniski, "Theatrical Art," 202–5. Obniski states that the Girards' apartment on 1461 East Jefferson Avenue in Detroit became "an official branch of the [Esling] studio" (202).

32. For more on Girard's design studios in Grosse Pointe, see chapter 2.

33. Kahn's innovative industrial projects include the Packard Motor Car Company Plant (1905), the Ford Motor Company Highland Park (1909), and River Rouge (1917–28) plants. For more on Kahn's work in Detroit, see the upcoming book *Building the Modern World: Albert Kahn in Detroit* by Michael Hodges.

34. For more on the Edsel and Eleanor Clay Ford estate and traditional architecture in Grosse Pointe, see chapter 3.

Chapter 1. Connections

Epigraph: Charles Eames, "Making Connections," Aspen Design Conference, June 1978 (unpublished papers), from the Charles and Ray Eames Papers, 1850–1989, Manuscripts Division, Library of Congress, © 2017 Eames Office, LLC.

1. Girard also redesigned the cafeteria and other company office and public spaces. For Girard's designs at Detrola, see Oldham and Coffee, *Alexander Girard*, 90–107; "List of Works," in Eisenbrand and Kries, *Alexander Girard*, 378–89, and "Factory Cafeteria."

2. "Factory Cafeteria," 150.

3. The quote is referenced in Oldham and Coffee, *Alexander Girard*, 90; and in "Biography," in Eisenbrand and Kries, *Alexander Girard*, 346. Three Girard-designed radios were featured in the inaugural exhibition of the Walker Art Center's new Gallery of Everyday Art as examples of "ideas for better living." As noted in the Girard exhibition catalogue ("List of Works," 422), Girard designed tabletop radios, console radios, and portable record players. Most housings were made of wood, plywood, and plastic, although some were covered in a new material, Lumite, developed by Dow Chemical.

4. "Both Fish and Fowl," 41. The article, widely attributed to George Nelson, distinguished between "art industries" such as ceramics and textiles" and "formerly artless industries" such as clocks and refrigerators (98).

5. Arnold and Conway, "Introduction," 21. Brian Conway, state historic preservation officer and manager for the Michigan Modern Project, has actively promoted Michigan's role in the development of modernism. For a history of the Michigan Modern Project, which encompassed two exhibitions and symposia, see Conway, "Acknowledgments."

6. Hess, foreword to *Michigan Modern*. Hess argues that histories of modernism "overplay the role of Europeans in introducing Modern ideas to the United States in the 1930s, while underplaying Michigan's role."

7. Arnold and Conway, "Introduction," 21.

8. Ibid.

9. Eisenbrand, introduction to *Alexander Girard*, 13. Eisenbrand notes that Girard is the last unknown within the group.

10. The reference to Cranbrook as a "tripartite institution" was made by Neil Harris in "North by Midwest," 18. For the history of Cranbrook's founding, see Taragin, "History of the Cranbrook Community."

11. For the history of Cranbrook House and Gardens, see Cranbrook House and Gardens, "Our History."

12. Taragin, "History of the Cranbrook Community," 38. George Booth got his start in the newspaper industry from his father-in-law, James E. Scripps, who was an early supporter of the Detroit Museum of Art. Taragin details Booth's role in founding both the Detroit Society of Arts and Crafts and the Detroit School of Design. Booth ran his father-in-law's *Evening News* (later the *Detroit News*) and founded the Booth Newspapers chain.

13. Clark, "Cranbrook and the Search for Twentieth-Century Form," 24–25. Clark writes that the American Academy in Rome served as an early inspiration for Cranbrook.

14. Taragin, "History of the Cranbrook Community," 38. Taragin notes that it was Henry Scripps Booth, an architecture student at the University of Michigan, who facilitated the introduction to Eliel Saarinen. In conversation with the author, Leslie Edwards noted that Booth and Saarinen met in December of 1923.

15. For the development of Cranbrook Academy of Art in the 1930s, see Wittkopp, "Cranbrook Academy of Art."

16. Edwards, "Competition, Collaboration, and Connection," 162.

17. Taragin, "History of the Cranbrook Community," 44. Evidently, the designer Harry Weese aptly referred to Cranbrook as a "Scandinavian Bauhaus" for its role as a magnet for many iconic northern European instructors, including Milles, Strengell, and Grotell. For the evolution of the ceramics program at Cranbrook and Grotell's acceptance of the Cranbrook position (1938), see Eidelberg, "Ceramics."

18. R. Miller, "Interior Design and Furniture," 91. Miller writes that the first generation of Cranbrook designers, represented by Eliel Saarinen and his son Eero, was European, whereas the second wave included midwesterners such as Charles Eames, Florence Knoll, and others.

19. Edwards, "Competition, Collaboration, and Connection," 164–65, describes visits to Cranbrook by Alvar Aalto in 1938 and Walter Gropius in 1940.

20. For more on the competition, see Noyes, *Organic Design in Home Furnishings*.

21. McCoy, "Charles and Ray Eames," 21. McCoy calls the entry "the first version of the most famous chair of the century." While molded plywood itself was not new, its intended mass production was. However, McCoy states that after the MOMA show, Eames discovered that the mass production of molded plywood chairs was not as cost-effective as he had believed ($75 in an era when "only 10% of the population made over $10,000 a year").

22. The Entenza House, CSH #9, was built adjacent to the Eameses' own house, CSH #8. For more on the Case Study House project, conceived by John Entenza in 1945, see Smith, *Case Study Houses*; and Smith, Gossel, and Schulman, *Case Study Houses*.

23. For a complete discussion of Saarinen's model 70 "Womb" chair and the model 72 side chair, which have been hailed as the "first mass produced plastic chairs," see Lutz and Kroloff, *Knoll*.

24. Albert Christ-Janer to Alexander Girard, April 6, 1946, Cranbrook Art Museum Exhibition Records. Christ-Janer's letter references Girard abstract sculptures exhibited at the DIA, likely in the *Origins of Modern Sculpture* exhibition, which ran from January 22 through March 3, 1946.

25. Albert Christ-Janer to Alexander Girard, August 9, 1946, Cranbrook Art Museum Exhibition Records.

26. Albert Christ-Janer to Alexander Girard, November 22, 1946, Cranbrook Art Museum Exhibition Records. In the letter, Christ-Janer references the visit, stating, "It was a pleasure to see people living with such imagination." In a letter dated December 14, 1946, Christ-Janer references the works already on display in the gallery and asks "to pick up a few more pieces for the exhibition."

27. Albert Christ-Janer to Alexander Girard, January 29, 1947, Cranbrook Art Museum Exhibition Records. According to the letter, Girard was paid $50 for the painting.

28. For a discussion of the *For Modern Living* exhibition, see chapter 2.

29. *Fourth Biennial Exhibition of Textiles and Ceramics*, February 14–March 15, 1953, Cranbrook Art Museum Exhibition Records.

30. Caplan, *Design of Herman Miller*, 26.

31. Ibid., 24.

32. Ibid., 27.

33. The accumulation of talent by Nelson was made possible by the support of the De Pree family. As Herman Miller CEO Max De Pree once stated, "There are two ways of competing in this business—you can nickel and dime the competition to death or you can take giant steps that distinguish you from them. But the only way to take giant steps is to have giants" (quoted in Caplan, *Design of Herman Miller*, 18).

34. Wright and Nelson, *Tomorrow's House*. According to the authors, "design" included not just the "trimmings around the front door and fireplace" but also the "basic scheme of the house" (2).

35. The book also critiqued the inefficiency of most traditional American home design. As Wright and Nelson note, "Less honest thought goes into the design of the average middle-class house than into the fender of a cheap automobile" (ibid.).

36. The Storagewall concept was published in *Life* magazine on January 22, 1945. The Storagewall concept was marketed and sold by Herman Miller beginning in 1946.

37. For Nelson's discussion of modern design at Herman Miller as a moralistic crusade, see Nelson, introduction to "Nelson/Eames/Girard/Propst," 7.

38. The timeline of the Eameses' work at Herman Miller is taken from Piña, *Alexander Girard*, 179–80. According to Kirkham, *Charles and Ray Eames*, 222n58, Ray Eames created graphics and advertising for Herman Miller, a relationship that continued after Charles's death.

39. Caplan, *Design of Herman Miller*, 43–44. Charles Eames had been working with plywood since 1938, first with Eero Saarinen and then with Ray Eames. In 1942, the new Molded Plywood Division of Evans Products produced plywood leg splints, designed by Charles and Ray, for the US Navy; they later produced plywood furniture. In 1947, Evans Products negotiated an arrangement with Herman Miller: the Eameses would design plywood furniture, to be produced by Evans and then marketed and distributed by Herman Miller. In 1949, Herman Miller acquired exclusive market and distribution rights for Eames molded plywood furniture.

40. Kirkham, *Charles and Ray Eames*, 226.

41. For a timeline of Girard's work at Herman Miller, see Piña, *Alexander Girard*, 180–81. Girard's draft contract, written in an October 3, 1951, letter from D. J. De Pree to Alexander Girard, is referenced by Susan Brown in "Alexander Girard," 180.

42. Piña, *Alexander Girard*, 17.

43. Ibid., 5.

44. Brown, "Alexander Girard," 170.

45. Ibid.

46. Girard's innovative role in the design and production of a unified fabric line at Herman Miller is addressed extensively by Brown, "Alexander Girard"; and Piña, *Alexander Girard*.

47. Larsen, "Alexander Girard," 35.

48. The artifacts that the Girards purchased in their travels around the world, including Mexico, India, Poland, Hungary, Russia, Brazil, and Africa, were donated to the International Folk Art Museum in Santa Fe in 1978.

49. Alexander Girard, "Mr. Girard Answers His Critics." For a discussion of Girard's large-scale, fabric environmental enrichment panels, see Piña, *Alexander Girard*, 143–78. The panels were designed to correspond with Herman Miller Action Office 2 components.

50. In 1945, Robert Swanson, Eliel's son-in-law, was a partner in the firm, although he left in 1947 after a disagreement with Eero. For a complete timeline of Eero Saarinen's career, see "Chronology," in Pelkonen and Albrecht, *Eero Saarinen*, 322–39.

51. For the timeline of the project, see Skarsgard, "Where Today Meets Tomorrow." Susan Skarsgard is the author and designer of an original book on the GMTC, which shares the same title as the aforementioned essay in *Michigan Modern: Design That Shaped America*.

52. Prior to the construction of the Tech Center, General Motors product development was concentrated in the Argonaut Building (1928–30), located across the street from the GM headquarters, the General Motors Building. Both structures were designed by Albert Kahn. For more, see Hill and Gallagher, *AIA Detroit*, 176.

53. Skarsgard, "Where Today Meets Tomorrow," 106.

54. Ibid., 106–7. Skarsgard attributes the delay to a UAW strike and to "changing post-war market conditions." For a comparison between the 1945 and the 1948 concepts, see Cooperman, "Challenge to the Future." The selection of Eero was recommended by Harley Earl.

55. Skarsgard, "Where Today Meets Tomorrow," 111.

56. For more on this innovative, collaborative approach, see Fletcher, "General Motors Technical Center."

57. For the new technologies implemented at the GMTC, see ibid.; and Cooperman, "Challenge to the Future," 250. Many of the new technologies developed for the GMTC are also discussed by Hastings, "Case Study of Sandwich Panel Design and Experience."

58. Fletcher, "General Motors Technical Center," 233.

59. Cooperman, "Challenge to the Future," 252. Cooperman views Saarinen's use of "vivid, shiny, yet visibly variable and thus seemingly handcrafted color" in the bricks as essential to his "Americanizing" of Mies's "modernist vocabulary." Skarsgard, "Where Today Meets Tomorrow," 110, views the "handcrafted aesthetic" of the bricks as a "symbolic celebration of the enduring human force in industrial society."

60. Joseph Lacy Memoirs, n.d. Lacy attributes the bold red color to Eliel Saarinen, who wanted the building to be "red like the red in the American flag." In an interview, Grotell describes the evolution of—and her frustration with—the project. She states, "I came out from the studio on a Sunday morning. There I met Mr. Eliel Saarinen. . . . I had given him one of these bowls with this red glaze inside. And he said, 'Can you glaze bricks with that color?' . . . That's how it started. Then, they brought me bricks and bricks, . . . and I had to glaze them all in the colors they wanted. . . . I did not work on the final glaze. But I showed it could be glazed on brick." Schlanger and Takaezu, *Maija Grotell*, 27–29.

61. Skarsgard, "Where Today Meets Tomorrow," 110, references the "handcrafted aesthetic" of the bricks. Fletcher, "General Motors Technical Center," 234, notes the disconnect between the "Arts and Crafts tradition" that inspired the bricks and the "larger network of ideas and expertise" that ensured their production.

62. Joseph Lacy in his memoirs references the colors of the bricks. Fletcher ("General Motors Technical Center," 234) publishes a photo of a mock-up wall, composed of glazed bricks, set up (likely during the winter of 1950–51) to test the resilience of the glazes under cold temperatures.

63. Schlanger and Takaezu, *Maija Grotell*, 29. According to Grotell, only one color had to be replaced. The color palette of the bricks is referenced in Skarsgard, "Where Today Meets Tomorrow," 110.

64. For a timeline of the GMTC construction, see "A History of the Development & Construction of the GM Technical Center," Box 2, General Motors Technical Center Research Collection. The Engineering buildings were featured in "Eero Saarinen's Masterpiece." The phrase "industrial Versailles" appeared in the title of an *Architectural Forum* article, dated May 1956 ("GM's Industrial Versailles").

65. "Biography," 346.

66. Lipstadt, "Gateway Arch." According to Lipstadt, the winning team consisted of Eero Saarinen, designer; J. Henderson Barr, associate designer; Dan Kiley, landscape architect; Lilian Swann Saarinen, sculptor; and Alexander Girard, painter.

67. "List of Works," 382, 384.

68. Girard's role as color consultant for the GMTC is published in "Girard Editorial," 26. This issue of the *Monthly Bulletin, Michigan Society of Architects Bulletin* was supervised by Girard.

69. George Moon, "An American Versailles: Eero Saarinen and the General Motors Technical Center–A Privilege Remembered," George Moon Collection, 343. Moon recalls that Aline Saarinen, Eero's wife, credited Girard with the "fanciful color scheme used in the plant." He also writes that Girard frequented Saarinen's office "as a friend, as an advisor, and as a man hired to do a specific job" (343). Thank you to Natalie Morath for the reference.

70. "List of Works," 382.

71. Moon, "American Versailles," 346. Moon explains that the bold color scheme of the Power Plant was functional as well as decorative: "Contrary to legend, the color scheme was not done capriciously. While some color was used for décor, the primary functions are color coded to standards: air–blue, electrical–black, gas–yellow, feed water–orange, steam–silver. The colors were picked by Girard, but he did follow codes."

72. For more on Girard's collaborations with Eero Saarinen on the *For Modern Living* exhibition at the DIA (1948–49), see chapter 2. For more on Girard's incorporation of GMTC bricks into his own architectural projects, see chapter 5.

73. For a discussion of Yamasaki's work in Detroit, see Gallagher, *Yamasaki in Detroit*. For a discussion of Yamasaki at SH&G, see Holleman and Gallagher, *Smith, Hinchman & Grylls*, 147–57.

74. For the history of SH&G's projects in the 1920s, see Holleman and Gallagher, *Smith, Hinchman & Grylls*, 97–129. For the Guardian Building, see Tottis, *Guardian Building*.

75. Holleman and Gallagher, *Smith, Hinchman & Grylls*, 147. Yamasaki was originally from Seattle but had been working in New York City. He was hired by SH&G in 1945.

76. Ibid. In W. Hawkins Ferry's seminal text *The Buildings of Detroit*, 365–66, the author notes that the Federal Reserve Bank addition "ushered in a new era of commercial architecture in downtown Detroit."

77. For more on the role of SH&G in the GMTC project, see Holleman and Gallagher, *Smith, Hinchman & Gryllst*, 148–54. Saarinen, Saarinen & Associates were named the design architects; SH&G were named the coarchitects and engineers.

78. Ibid., 148.

79. Ibid.

80. Ibid., 149. One of Yamasaki's complaints with SH&G was that he was never permitted to meet with clients directly and that younger executives at the firm were not allowed to buy stock in the company.

81. Dale Gyure, in conversation with the author, 2017. Gyure, author of the forthcoming book *Minoru Yamasaki: Humanist Architecture for a Modernist World*, states that the partnerships originated in July 1949 and ended in June 1955. However, after 1955, the Detroit office became Yamasaki, Leinweber & Associates and the St. Louis office became Hellmuth, Obata & Kassebaum.

82. The residence in Greenwich, Connecticut, was published in "House Hidden in the Woods."

83. For more on the *For Modern Living* exhibition, see chapter 2.

84. Contract between A. H. Girard and Minoru Yamasaki, Box 3, Folder 2, Minoru Yamasaki Papers.

85. Ibid.

86. For an overview of Girard's 1949 projects, see "List of Works," 382–84. For more on the Goodenough house, see chapter 4.

87. "List of Works," 382. According to this source, a model of the house was exhibited in the 1949 *For Modern Living* exhibition at the DIA.

88. Yamasaki, *Life in Architecture*, 23.

89. Ibid. "I tried either to buy or rent one [a house] in Birmingham, Bloomfield Hills, or Grosse Pointe. I became friendly with the realtor who was helping us. He told me in confidence that it was hopeless to buy a house in one of those areas. . . . He would be driven out of the real estate association if he did so." Thank you to John Gallagher for the reference. This theory is reinforced by the deed restriction of the Lothrop Pines subdivision, which specified, "Caucasian race only."

90. Ibid. Yamasaki notes that "from the beginnings" of his partnerships with Hellmuth and Leinweber, he commuted between the two offices in Detroit and in St. Louis, working up to seven days a week and thirteen hours a day.

Chapter 2. Promotion

Epigraph: "What Is Modern?," 42.

1. "Offices and Showroom," 94.

2. "Little Shop Grows Up."

3. Nicholson, *Contemporary Shops in the United States*, 78–80.

4. *Social Secretary of Detroit: 1941 Edition*, 83. Sandro and Susan (Mr. and Mrs. Alexander Girard) are listed on 380 Lakeland Avenue in Grosse Pointe.

5. The sale was advertised in the *Grosse Pointe News*, May 4, 1944, 6. For more photos and a discussion of the Girards' Lakeland Avenue home, see Oldham and Coffee, *Alexander Girard*, 394–99; "Biography," in Eisenbrand and Kries, *Alexander Girard*, 378–80; and "List of Works," in Eisenbrand and Kries, *Alexander Girard*, 422–24.

6. For the "room without a name," see Wright and Nelson, *Tomorrow's House*, 10–15, 76–80. Girard's design for Harley Earl's office at the GMTC also included a curving partition wall.

7. The evolution of Girard's early design studios in Grosse Pointe are discussed in Obniski, "Theatrical Art," 202–4.

8. Obniski, "Theatrical Art," 204.

9. For more on Thayer and William Laurie Jr., see Maraniss, *Once in a Great City*, 112–16. Thayer Hutchinson, the daughter of B. E. Hutchinson, treasurer of Chrysler Corporation, was prominent in Grosse Pointe social circles. William Laurie Jr., described by Maraniss as the "quintessential Mad Men account executive" and a "power player in Detroit" (112), started his career at Maxon Inc. before moving to the J. Walter Thompson firm in 1957. The Lauries were also instrumental in bringing the Girards to Grosse Pointe. As noted by David Laurie (in conversation with the author, 2017), the Girard home on 380 Lakeland Avenue was the carriage house of 372 Lakeland Avenue, the home of Thayer Laurie's parents, Mr. and Mrs. B. E. Hutchinson. Thank you to Izzy Donnelly at the Grosse Pointe Historical Society Archives for confirming this fact.

10. The Lauries' living room is discussed in Oldham and Coffee, *Alexander Girard*, 330–31; and in "List of Works," 378–79. The photo shows several avant-garde art books on the ledge, including the catalogue of the 1941 MOMA furniture show and Sidney Janis's 1944 book *Abstract and Surrealist Art in America*.

11. In conversation with the author, the Lauries' son Duncan Laurie stated that the guitar and typewriter reference William Laurie, while the bust represents Thayer Laurie; the poodle was a family pet.

12. The quote comes from a flyer prepared by Girard to advertise the opening on January 13, 1947, part of the Alexander Girard Estate collection.

13. "Offices and Showroom," 94–96. The stand was vacated when its former owner, Lena Checkeroff, moved to California. According to the article, Girard converted the hamburger stand to a studio for only $2,000, having been "foiled in his efforts to rent suitable office space in Detroit's swank suburb Grosse Pointe."

14. Ibid.

15. Oldham and Coffee, *Alexander Girard*, 294, provides a list of Girard's 1947 exhibition schedule.

16. "Offices and Showroom," 94. A January 16, 1947, article, "Nostalgia and Curiosity Produce Identical Results," in the *Grosse Pointe News* records a run-in between Susan Girard and some local boys, curious and/or harboring negative feelings about the new shop. Another article, "Rough Drinker," in the *Grosse Pointe News*, dated January 30, 1947, reports that a beer bottle was thrown through the plate glass window of the shop on January 26.

17. "Where to Buy Well Designed Objects," 3. The other Midwest shop featured was Baldwin Kingrey in Chicago.

18. The anecdote is referenced by Piña, *Alexander Girard*, 8; and in the review of the exhibition ("What Is Modern?") published in *Pathfinder News Magazine* on October 5, 1949. This is a credible scenario, given that Girard was connected socially to Webber. Webber's cousin Richard Jackson was one of Girard's good friends, and both Jackson and Webber were members of the Turtle Lake Club in Hillman, Michigan. Girard designed a house for Jackson near the Turtle Club Lake Lodge (referenced hereafter as Jackson Lodge) in 1945.

19. E. P. Richardson, memo to the Arts Commission, July 16, 1948, RCH 67/8. In "Museum Tells Plans for Modern Home Show," in the *Detroit News*, Webber reiterated the educational aspect of the show, stating, "the things on display won't come from our store."

20. E. P. Richardson to R. Ryding, July 9, 1948, RCH 67/8. It is important to note that Richardson had already mounted two key design-related exhibitions at the DIA: *Built in USA: The Exhibition of American Architecture since 1932* (October 6–November 4, 1945) and *Industrial Design* (March 9–April 2, 1947). In 1954, he cofounded the Archives of American Art with the Detroit businessman Lawrence Fleischman.

21. Obniski, "Theatrical Art," 211n18. These included MOMA's *Useful Objects* exhibitions (1938–47) and the Walker Art Center's *Gallery of Everyday Art* (1946), *Idea House I* (1941), and *Idea House II* (1947), all of which included price lists.

22. E. P. Richardson, "Memorandum to Mr. Reuben Ryding on the Detroit Institute of Arts Exhibit," July 28, 1948, RCH 67/8. While Girard was not officially hired until October 1948, Richardson stated in his July 28 letter, "One person will be responsible for putting their [the steering committee's] ideas together . . . and working out all of the design, color scheme and general setting of the exhibition. This one person will be Mr. Alexander Girard."

23. J. Webber to A. Girard, October 5, 1948, RCH 67/8. This letter constituted the contract between J. L. Hudson and Girard for the project.

24. For the complete breakdown of expenses, see "Tentative Budget D.I.A. Exhibition '49," RCH 67/8.

25. A committee of advisers included modernist luminaries from various design fields, including D. J. De Pree, Harley Earl, Edgar Kauffman Jr., Charles Eames, and Florence Knoll.

26. "D.I.A. Exhibit '49 Outline of Organization," September 22, 1948, RCH 67/8.

27. In a press release dated June 12, 1949, Richardson stated, "We all know there exists good design and bad design claiming to be modern design. We expect this exhibition to demonstrate what is the good design." E. P. Richardson, press release, June 12, 1949, RCH 67/10.

28. W. Laurie Jr. to A. Girard, July 27, 1948, RCH 67/10.

29. "Museum Tells Plans for Modern Home Show."

30. Richardson, introduction to *Exhibition for Modern Living*, 7.

31. Ibid., 8.

32. E. P. Richardson to R. Ryding, July 29, 1948, RCH 67/8. Richardson references three options, stating the name would be "something like (1) Five Hundred Answers to Your Questions about 'Modern,' (2) Why Modern? [and] (3) The 'How' and 'Why' of Modern Furniture." "DIA Exhibition Memorandum #2," November 5, 1948, RCH 67/8, lists meetings during the month of October with Girard, Saarinen, Richardson, George Nelson, Edgar Kaufman, and others during the month of October, to discuss the theme, referenced as "Modern Living." However, it is interesting to note that the last bullet point from the memorandum indicates that the "Modern Living" theme had been rejected.

33. The timeline of the meetings and the topics discussed are detailed in "Memorandum #3," December 8, 1948, RCH 67/11. The concept for the new theme is described in "Theme for D.I.A. Exhibition 1949: A New Concept of Beauty," November 10, 1948, RCH 67/8.

34. "Theme for D.I.A. Exhibition 1949."

35. Ibid.

36. E. P. Richardson to A. Girard, November 12, 1948, RCH 67/11. In his letter, Richardson stated, "What I would like to see you and Saarinen and Yamasaki do is an . . . effective demonstration of your 'new ideal of beauty,' keeping it always a positive and vital thing educationally. . . . Setting up a straw man of a 'Victorian room' to knock down is not the way to do it." The rejection of the "Victorian Room" theme and the approval of the "For Modern Living" theme is detailed in "Memorandum #3."

37. "Theme for D.I.A. Exhibition 1949."

38. The source of these design qualities and definitions is the "Theme for D.I.A. Exhibition 1949" document, titled "A New Concept of Beauty" but also referenced as the "Victorian Room."

39. The "free use of color" is referenced in "The Exhibition Rooms," in Girard and Laurie, *Exhibition for Modern Living*, 81. A press release, dated June 12, 1949, RCH 67/10, advertised the "new materials" and technologies to be exhibited "in their own right such as plastics, plywoods, metals and various compositions or any and all materials which will suggest new and interesting solutions to the . . . varied problems of modern living."

40. "Theme for D.I.A. Exhibition 1949."

41. Girard, "For Modern Living." Tom Oldham and Kiera Coffee, in *Alexander Girard*, 272–74, discuss Girard's checklist of the criteria for "modern" objects.

42. The page of exhibition notes is located in the Alexander Girard Estate collection.

43. Oldham and Coffee, *Alexander Girard*, 274.

44. Richardson, press release, June 12, 1949.

45. A. Girard to E. P Richardson, November 12, 1948, RCH 67/11. In a letter dated December 2, 1948 (RCH 67/11), Richardson invited Kaufmann to participate.

46. For the full list of the committee of advisers, see Girard and Laurie, *Exhibition for Modern Living*, 3.

47. The Saul Steinberg drawing was originally published in the *New Yorker* on October 11, 1946.

48. A. Girard to S. Steinberg, July 8, 1949, Saul Steinberg Foundation Archives. In this letter, Girard suggested that the chair be an actual Eames chair. The Steinberg drawing for the back cover of the catalogue did feature an Eames chair, although—in a humorous mixture of modern with outmoded tradition—the modern chair is covered with an antimacassar, a feature of traditional, upholstered furniture.

49. According to the "What Is Modern?" article in *Pathfinder News Magazine*, the exhibition demonstrated that "modern is not what some people consider it: simply streamlining or monotonous uniformity. Neither is it anything long-haired or foreign."

50. In an interview with Joy Hakanson, "Girard Talks about Modern Living Show," Girard stated, "People think that modern is something cooked up by long-haired nuts and radicals across the Atlantic. That isn't true—its roots are deep in independent American life." As noted by Obniski, "Theatrical Art," 214, the American character of the exhibition was reiterated by the bold red, white, and blue palette of its banner.

51. Obniski, "Theatrical Art," 218n38. Obniski notes correctly that "Ludwig Mies van der Rohe's chair did not, however, derive from a mower seat."

52. S. Steinberg to A. Girard, January 26, 1949, Saul Steinberg Foundation Archives.

53. Kouwenhoven, "Background of Modern Design" 21.

54. Kaufmann, "Modern Design in America Now," 27.

55. Kaufmann, introduction to "Selected Objects," 40. "What Is Modern?," 43, states that Girard spent a year collecting some six thousand objects for the show, from which he chose two thousand.

56. "Selected Objects in the Exhibition," in Girard and Laurie, *Exhibition for Modern Living*, 41–71. The catalogue includes photos of a "scant hundred" of the objects, presented by Kaufmann as "symbols of a good life" (introduction to "Selected Objects," 40).

57. "What Is Modern?" According to the article, "all but about 10% [of the objects] were made in America and by machine."

58. C. Eames to M. Grotell, March 23, 1950, Maija Grotell Papers. The pot shown here (fig. 63) is strikingly similar to the one illustrated in the catalogue but is likely not the same one.

59. "Selected Objects in the Exhibition," 46. Both hand-made and machine-made products were included in the 1938 MOMA exhibition *Useful Objects under $5*, as noted by Kauffmann, "Hand-Made and Machine-Made Art." However, in Kaufmann's MOMA exhibition, machine-made objects were hung horizontally, and hand-made objects were hung vertically.

60. Obniski, "Accumulating Things,"133.

61. The term "Jungle Jim (Gym?)" was used by Richardson in a letter to Girard dated April 12, 1949, RCH 67/12, in which he discussed the necessity of acquiring "specially designed cases" and hardware, stating, "our cases simply will not look right in the setting you have designed." The term "jungle gym" was widely used later in reference to the system of display in the Hall of Objects.

62. "Selected Objects in the Exhibition."

63. Kaufmann, introduction to "Exhibition Rooms," 72.

64. Obniski, "Accumulating Things," 142.

65. "The Exhibition Rooms," in Girard and Laurie, *Exhibition for Modern Living*, 78.

66. Ibid., 77.

67. Ibid., 82.

68. Ibid., 83.

69. Ibid.

70. The Eames storage units were produced by Herman Miller beginning in 1950. The DCM chair was also produced by Herman Miller. La Chaise, composed of two bonded fiberglass shells, a chromed base, and natural oak feet, was created for MOMA's 1948 "International Competition for Low-Cost Furniture Design." However, it was not produced until 1996 (by Vitra International), due to cost concerns.

71. "Exhibition Rooms," 80–81. These passages, published in the exhibition catalogue, derived from statements by the artists.

72. Ibid., 81.

73. W. Bostick to K. Prothman, October 19, 1949, Folder 15, William A. Bostick Papers (hereafter referred to as BOS); W. Bostick to A. Girard, January 17, 1950, BOS 15. Bostick's letter to Girard references the black-and-white photographs taken by Elmer Astelford and Kodachrome (color) slides shot by Konrad Prothman; only one color slide has been found. The color advertisement was discovered by DIA archivist James Hanks.

74. "Exhibition Rooms," 81.

75. Hakanson, "Public Reacts."

76. Defenbacher, "Editorial Note."

77. Kaufmann, "For Modern Living."

78. E. P. Richardson to A. Girard, November 28, 1949, RCH 67/9.

79. E. P. Richardson to A. Girard, November 15, 1949, RCH 67/9.

80. E. P. Richardson to J. Webber, November 22, 1949, RCH 67/9.

81. A. Girard to E. P. Richardson, November 18, 1949, RCH 67/9. Girard had actually broached the idea of retaining "some of the show permanently at the DIA" in a letter to E. P. Richardson, dated January 24, 1949 (RCH 67/11).

82. W. Bostick to G. Whitney, November 21, 1940, BOS 15. A letter written by George Whitney, public-relations manager for Hudson's, to Bostick on November 29, 1949 (BOS 15), indicates that the request had been approved.

83. Hakanson, "Museum Reveals Plans."

84. Ibid.

85. E. P. Richardson to J. Webber, November 22, 1949, RCH 67/9.

86. "Department Store Plugs Modern Design," 188. Obniski, "Accumulating Things," 141, writes that the "modern" section at Hudson's featured a "conservative modernism" when compared with that on display at the exhibition.

87. Girard's quote, published in Oldham and Coffee, *Alexander Girard*, 274, referenced the sale of Eames chairs in J. L. Hudson stores. However, Girard did add that "the people from General Motors and various other big corporations came around and looked at all these things."

88. Index of Exhibitors, A. H. Girard and W. D. Laurie Jr. eds., *Exhibition for Modern Living*, 95.

89. For more on the life and career of Ruth Adler Schnee and the evolution of the Adler-Schnee showrooms and studios, see Whitney, *Ruth Adler Schnee*; and Eisenbach and Frisone, *Ruth Adler Schnee*. Adler Schnee's personal account of her life, designs, and studios is captured in an oral history interview, conducted by her daughter, Anita Schnee, November 24–30, 2002, for the Archives of American Art.

90. In conversation with the author, 2017.

91. Crumb, "Young Artist Converts Coach House."

92. In discussion with the author, 2016, Ruth recalled that she and Eddie could not afford to stock catalogues of merchandise. The aforementioned *Detroit News* article explained, "Instead of having all models to show the variations in a piece of furniture, Miss Adler has drawn on the wall, in black and white, the styles in which this cabinet is made." Crumb, "Young Artist Converts Coach House."

93. For an in-depth discussion of these *Good Design* shows sponsored by the MOMA, see Riley and Eigen, "Between the Museum and the Marketplace." The fifty-three-hundred-square-foot space for the first *Good Design* exhibition (1950) was curated by Charles and Ray Eames.

94. "Alexander Girard, Grosse Pointe, Michigan," 104. The article included photographs of the exterior and interior of the design studio.

95. The exhibition is discussed in "Biography," 347.

Chapter 3. Tradition and Innovation

Epigraph: Alexander Girard, notes on modern design for the *For Modern Living* exhibition, Alexander Girard Estate collection, Vitra Design Museum.

1. "Detroit Architect Builds One House."

2. A 1915 brochure promotes the area as "eight miles from the City Hall and the center of Detroit" but yet "far from the hurry and dust of the city." H. A. Jones Real Estate Co., "Grosse Pointe Colony," 1915, 4–5, 8.

3. The phrase comes from Holleman and Gallagher, *Smith, Hinchman & Grylls*, 117.

4. Ibid.

5. Ferry, *Buildings of Detroit*, 299. Albert Kahn designed factories for the Packard, Ford, and Dodge motor companies. These innovative steel, glass, and concrete factories, made possible through Kahn's innovative use of steel-reinforced concrete, influenced European developments in modern architecture. For more on Kahn's innovation and impact, see Carter, "Kahn's Industry."

6. For the tumultuous history of the Dodge brothers, see Hyde, *Dodge Brothers*.

7. Ferry, *Buildings of Detroit*, 297–98, called Rose Terrace "the fulfillment of the dreams of Horace Dodge." The Albert Kahn–designed Rose Terrace should not be confused with the second Rose Terrace, designed for Mrs. Dodge in 1934 (after the death of Horace Dodge) by the Philadelphia architect Horace Trumbauer. The Louis XV style of the home was a fitting site for Mrs. Dodge's collection of French eighteenth-century art. For more on Rose Terrace II, which was demolished in 1976, see ibid., 229.

8. Holleman and Gallagher, *Smith, Hinchman & Grylls*, 117–18. In 1906, John Dodge had hired SH&G to build him a home in Detroit on Boston Boulevard.

9. Holleman and Gallagher, *Smith, Hinchman & Grylls*, 118.

10. Ferry, *Buildings of Detroit*, 269.

11. Ibid., 270. After the death of John Dodge in 1920, his widow, Matilda, moved to a smaller house, leaving her husband's dream house, Harbor Hill, unfinished. She later married Alfred Wilson and built a house on fourteen hundred acres of land in the nearby suburb of Rochester. The SH&G architect William Kapp designed the mansion, dubbed Meadowbrook.

12. While Edsel Ford succeeded his father, Henry Ford, as president of Ford Motor Company on December 31, 1918, he predeceased him. After Edsel died in 1943, Henry Ford reassumed control of Ford Motor Company, although by 1945, control was turned over to his grandson Henry Ford II; Henry Ford died in 1947. For the history of the Ford family and Ford Motor Company, see Lacey, *Ford*.

13. Ferry, "Suburb in Good Taste."

14. For an in-depth analysis of the evolution of Grosse Pointe architecture, see Ferry, *Buildings of Detroit*.

15. The Grosse Pointe resident who best demonstrates this dichotomy is Edsel Ford. While Ford was forward thinking both in his role as CEO of Ford Motor Company and in his patronage of art (which included his collection of non-Western art and his patronage of Diego Rivera's *Detroit Industry* frescoes at DIA), the Cotswold-cottage-style estate designed for him by Albert Kahn is typical of the historical revival trend in Grosse Pointe.

16. Ferry, *Buildings of Detroit*, 94. Lothrop had a distinguished career, both as a lawyer and as US ambassador to Russia between the years 1885 and 1888.

17. For more on Lothrop's history in Grosse Pointe, see Farmer, *Grosse Pointe on Lake Sainte Clair*.

18. Shaw, "Career of George Lothrop."

19. The *Northwestern Reporter* includes a summation of a Supreme Court of Michigan case (*City of Detroit v. Lothrop Estate Company*) from April 5, 1904. The summary of the case, which relates to a tax dispute, includes a history of the Lothrop Estate Company.

20. Wayne County Register of Deeds, liber 24, 7. A 1904 map of the village of Grosse Pointe Farms in the Grosse Pointe Historical Society Archives shows Lothrop's Subdivision running from Grosse Pointe Boulevard to the short block past Ridge Road.

21. By 1938, John Dodge's widow, Mathilda, had remarried. As a result, the John Dodge estate is labeled "Mrs. Alfred Wilson" in the 1938 *Baist's Real Estate* map (fig. 91).

22. This information comes from real-estate documents in the Grosse Pointe Historical Society Archives. Charles Platt is best known in Grosse Pointe for the Russell Alger residence, now known as the Grosse Pointe War Memorial. For a discussion of the J. Stewart Hudson home, see Doelle, "Historical Architecture."

23. Socia, "House of Hidden History," 8. Socia states that the Detroit restaurateur Al Green held the lease on the house in 1933 when Prohibition was repealed. Notations on real-estate records in the Grosse Pointe Historical Society Archives connect Al Green with the property. However, this association cannot be confirmed, given that the title records predating 1947 are incomplete. Gary Freeman identifies the operator of the speakeasy, the Pines, as Joe Vansinamee ("Bootlegging across the Border," 125).

24. Freeman, "Bootlegging across the Border," 122.

25. Vogel, "Small Area of Pine Woods." According to Vogel, the area had up until 1945 comprised eighty acres and been open to the public. Vogel writes that in 1945, Edward Eichstedt, a Detroit city planner, proposed that the area be preserved, for use as a nature preserve, a Boy Scout campground, and even as the site of a Grosse Pointe war memorial.

26. For the impact of James McMillan and his partner, John S. Newberry, on the industrial growth of Detroit and the residential growth of Grosse Pointe, see Arbaugh, "John S. Newberry and James H. McMillan."

27. Ibid., 78–79. McMillan's home, Lake Terrace, was located farther down the lakeshore, next to that of his friend John S. Newberry.

28. Henry B. Joy is best known for his role as president of Packard Motor Company, for which Albert Kahn designed one of his most innovative factories, the Packard Plant on East Grand Boulevard in Detroit. However, Joy was also president of the Lincoln Highway Association, which built one of the first transcontinental highways in the United States. For more on Henry B. Joy, the Packard Plant, and Fair Acres, see Ferry, *Buildings of Detroit*, 180–82, 190–91.

29. Wayne County Register of Deeds, liber 60, 14.

30. Robert O. Derrick, AIA Membership File. Perhaps Derrick's most famous work is the Henry Ford Museum, commissioned by Henry Ford in 1929.

31. Ibid. The file on Derrick includes a letter written by the architect in 1927, in which he requests letters of introduction to houses and "other interesting buildings" while on a trip with a client to England to study "English Domestic Architecture."

32. The house was completed in 1929, but Walker never moved in, plagued by money problems caused by his wild spending habits, Prohibition, and the onset of the Great Depression.

33. This information comes from real-estate records in the Grosse Pointe Historical Society Archives.

34. The warranty deed, dated June 27, 1947, records the sale of land in Lothrop's Subdivision to Alexander H. Girard and Susan N. Girard. No. D162713, Wayne County Register of Deeds, liber 8692, 201.

35. Building permit (No. 2137), dated August 6, 1947, Building Department, City of Grosse Pointe Farms, MI.

36. Hakanson, "Girard Talks about Modern Living Show."

37. "Detroit Architect Builds One House," 95.

38. Ibid. The construction of Girard's home is discussed in Oldham and Coffee, *Alexander Girard*, 400–419; and in several articles, including "House at Grosse Pointe"; and "Girard's Clever Corners," 109.

39. "Detroit Architect Builds One House," 95.

40. Ibid.

41. Crumb, "Grosse Pointe Architect Designs Own Home."

42. "Girard's Clever Corners," 103.

43. "Year's Work (Residential)."

44. "Tour of Homes Scheduled."

45. Ibid. As noted by Oldham and Coffee, *Alexander Girard*, 336, in 1946, Girard had designed modern furniture for the bedroom of Frederick Ford Jr.

46. "Tour of Homes Scheduled."

47. Eisenbrand, "Whole World a Village," 164.

48. These elements were promoted at the time in postwar housing how-to books such as Wright and Nelson's *Tomorrow's House* and Mock's *If You Want to Build a House*.

49. "Girard Editorial," 24.

50. For Nelson's discussion of the "room without a name," see Wright and Nelson, *Tomorrow's House*, 76–80.

51. The term "moveable collage" was suggested by Elizabeth Goodenough, in discussion with the author, 2016.

52. Crumb, "Grosse Pointe Architect Designs Own Home."

53. For a diagram and description of the door concept, see Fitch, "Like the Girards," 81.

54. In a 2016 discussion with the author, Elizabeth Goodenough (who grew up next door to the Girards) recalls that Sandro Girard gave the tree stump to his friend (her father) Daniel Goodenough when they moved from Grosse Pointe to Santa Fe in 1953. The same tree stump is visible in a photograph of the Goodenough house (fig. 138).

55. Barry, "Girard Secret," 79.

56. This information was noted on the verso of photographs in the Alexander Girard Estate collection.

57. Barry, "Girard Secret," 76–78.

58. Crumb, "Grosse Pointe Architect Designs Own Home."

59. This information was noted on the verso of photographs in the Alexander Girard Estate collection.

60. For more on the Girards' folk art collection, see Nestor, *Multiple Visions*; and Glassie, *Spirit of Folk Art*.

61. Obniski, "Accumulating Things," 345–46. Obniski notes that Sandro and Susan Girard rejected the title "collector." She notes (348) that Girard considered himself a "selector."

62. Ibid., 31. Obniski notes that the connection between indigenous Native American art (Mexico and Central and South America) and modern art was explored in a MOMA exhibition of 1933, titled *American Sources of Modern Art*.

63. Ibid., 35.

64. "House at Grosse Pointe," 249.

65. Fitch, "Like the Girards," 84–85.

66. Ibid.

67. "Girard Story," 86. The article dubbed Girard's aesthetic approach as "the play of free taste."

68. "Girard Editorial," 21.

69. Ibid.

70. Ibid.

71. A. Girard to T. Hughes, September 23, 1952, Archives of the American Institute of

Architects, Michigan. The letter, written by Girard to Talmadge Hughes, then president of the Michigan chapter of the AIA, on the subject of the January 1953 bulletin layout, references a sixteen-page "Girard Editorial."

72. "Here Is How Alexander Girard Goes about Designing a House," 126. The author uses the term "collage architecture" in reference to Girard.

Chapter 4. Collaboration and Experimentation

Epigraph: Ferry, *Buildings of Detroit*, 389.

1. Ferry, "Suburb in Good Taste."

2. Ibid.

3. Other modern homes in Grosse Pointe predating Girard include the Pryor (1936), Wells (1939), and Robinson (1941) residences, designed by Alden Dow; the Koebel residence (1939–40), designed by Eliel and Eero Saarinen; and the Rossetti house, built by the architect himself in 1940.

4. "Detroit Architect Builds One House," 95. Three incidences of damage done to the Girard house during its construction, cited in the *Grosse Pointe News* on January 1, March 18, and April 8, 1948, may reflect negative attitudes about the Girards' new modern house. However, it is also possible that the negativity was related to the perceived intrusion by the Girards into an area previously reserved for recreation.

5. The 1945 plan is based on the illustration of Lothrop Road in vol. 20, sheet 98, of the map "1945 Sanborn Fire Safety," Sanborn Map Collection. The 1949 image is based on an illustration of Lothrop Road in "1969 Grosse Pointe, Michigan Area Plat Book," Grosse Pointe Historical Society Archives.

6. The term "enclave" was used by Gary and Jan Rieveschl to refer to the Goodenough, Rieveschl, and Girard houses, which were clustered together at the dead end of Lothrop.

7. "Serendipity in the Woods," 68. The article refers to 222, 232, and 234 Lothrop as "houses by Alexander Girard," although 234 Lothrop is identified as a collaboration with Yamasaki in the "Girard Editorial," 33.

8. The affidavit was part of a lawsuit, brought on November 22, 2002, by Pine Woods homeowners against the Vernier Woods Development company, which had purchased one of the parcels (232 Lothrop), torn down the house, and attempted to divide the one parcel into two home sites. The case was No. 235601 in Wayne County Circuit Court (LC No. 00-001835-CH).

9. The warranty deed, dated January 15, 1949 (no. D313817, Wayne County Register of Deeds, liber 9640, 575), records the sale of land to Daniel and Margaret Goodenough.

10. Ibid. The comment about the "aesthetics of the neighborhood" comes from George Rieveschl's affidavit. Under the terms of the aforementioned deed restrictions, the designated architect could block construction of any structure "if in the opinion of the architect the structure would otherwise be unsuitable or undesirable."

11. Around the same time, Girard and Yamasaki designed a home for the real estate developer Bernard Edelman, which was part of a planned complex of modern homes in Pontiac, Michigan. For more on this commission, see chapter 1; and "List of Works," in Eisenbrand and Kries, *Alexander Girard*, 382–84

12. Riley, "Radcliffe Tour." The other hostesses are identified as Mrs. William D. Laurie and Mrs. Richard Jackson.

13. "DIA Exhibition Memorandum #2," November 5, 1948, RCH 67/8. The memo indicates that Goodenough had accepted the offer to serve as "official legal advisor to the DIA exhibition" on September 22, 1948. During the fall of 1948, Goodenough attended several meetings with Richardson, Ryding, and others to discuss financial details.

14. Warranty deed, dated January 15, 1949 (no. D313817, Wayne County Register of Deeds, liber 9640, 575), records the sale of land to Daniel W. Goodenough and Margaret B. Goodenough. For more on the Goodenough house, see "List of Works," 382–83. However, the Girard exhibition catalogue incorrectly identifies the address as 379 Fisher Road (the address of Girard's studio) and states that the project was not built.

15. Hubred-Golden, "Lumen Goodenough." Hubred-Golden identified Luman Goodenough as a "new kind of pioneer." For more on Luman Goodenough's estate, Longacres (now the Farmington Community Center), see Spicer, *Luman W. Goodenough and David Gray*.

16. Spicer, *Luman W. Goodenough and David Gray*.

17. For the history of the J. L. Hudson department store and the transference of store ownership from J. L. Hudson to his nephews, Richard H., Oscar, James B., and Joseph L. Webber, see "Retail Trade," 97–98.

18. "Girard Editorial," 33.

19. The building permit (No. 2636) is located in the Building Department, City of Grosse Pointe Farms, MI.

20. Contract between A. H. Girard and Minoru Yamasaki, May 1, 1949, Box 3, Folder 2, Minoru Yamasaki Papers.

21. Ibid.

22. Project number 5003, Box 28, Tray 168, Yamasaki Inc. Architectural Firm Records.

23. Walker, Holderness, and Butler, *State by State Guide*, 908. In accordance with state guidelines, "any plan, plat, drawing, map . . . if prepared by a licensee and required to be submitted to a governmental agency for approval or record must carry the embossed or printed seal of the person in responsible charge."

24. This information is taken from an interview with Margaret Goodenough conducted by Shelley and John Schoenherr, who purchased the Goodenough house in 1986.

25. Coffee and Oldham, *Alexander Girard*, 66.

26. The house is credited to the firm Leinweber, Yamasaki & Hellmuth Architects in the article "House Hidden in the Woods." However, the same article discusses Yamasaki alone as the architect responsible for the design.

27. Ibid. The article references traditional Japanese architecture as the primary source of inspiration for the Baker house. The influence of Japanese architecture on Yamasaki was reiterated in a December 26, 1954, *Detroit Free Press* article, titled "An Architect Sums Up Three Japanese Ideas for Your Next House." As noted in his autobiography, *A Life in Architecture* (18), Yamasaki spent the summer of 1933 in Japan, although he states that he was "not yet qualified to understand the greatness of Japanese art."

28. Ferry, *Buildings of Detroit*, 390.

29. Yamasaki, *Life in Architecture*, 29.

30. In a conversation with the author, 2016, Elizabeth Goodenough shared this story about the friendship between her father, Daniel Goodenough, and Alexander Girard.

31. "Architect Sums Up Three Japanese Ideas," 13.

32. "House Hidden in the Woods."

33. Elizabeth Goodenough, in discussion with the author, 2016. According to Elizabeth Goodenough, her mother's book collection was extensive, encompassing that of her grandfather Walter Brooks, his brothers Al and Stanley, and the Detroit geologist, historian, and civic leader Bela Hubbard.

34. Oldham and Coffee, *Alexander Girard*, 6.

35. Pixie Goodenough Dodge, in discussion with the author, 2016.

36. Yamasaki, *Life in Architecture*, 29. In his chapter "The Aesthetics and Practice of Architecture," Yamasaki (29–30) recalls his visit to Japan in 1954, referencing a building that—to him—represented the "epitome of Japanese architectural tradition" and "the embodiment of the standards of beauty as defined by Emerson."

37. A lot survey map in the Alexander Girard Estate collection indicates that the house was to have been built on lot 24 and the easterly part of lot 26 in the Lothrop's Subdivision.

38. Girard and Laurie, *Exhibition for Modern Living*, 3.

39. For the history of the Hudson Motor Company, see Butler, *History of Hudson*.

40. "Retail Trade," 97–98. Oscar, James B., and Joseph L. Webber were the sons of J. L. Hudson's sister, Mary Hudson Webber.

41. W. Laurie to E. P. Richardson, February 11, 1949, RCH 67/11.

42. "Girard Editorial," 27.

43. Richard Jackson Jr., in discussion with the author, 2016.

44. Ibid. Richard Jackson Jr. explains that membership in the club—which owned twenty-five thousand acres of prime hunting and fishing land in northern Michigan, near Alpena—included the use of a private room in the clubhouse. Those who wanted to bring additional family members would have to negotiate the use of another club member's room. As a result, Richard Jackson commissioned Girard to build a private home (Jackson Lodge) for his family near the existing Turtle Lake clubhouse.

45. "Girard Editorial," 27.

46. For a discussion of the *For Modern Living* exhibition, see chapter 2.

47. The timeline for the project is indicated by original Girard drawings in the Alexander Girard Estate collection. In conversation with the author, 2016, Richard Jackson Jr. recalled that a model of the Jackson house was displayed in the *For Modern Living* exhibition.

48. In conversation with the author, Richard Jackson Jr. stated that the proposed site of the new house was immediately behind the Jacksons' old house on Merriweather Road. A lot survey for the proposed house, dated October 1948, indicates that the property included lot 24 and the easterly part of lot 26.

49. For more on the Fletcher Motel in Alpena (demolished), see Oldham and Coffee, *Alexander Girard*, 114–19; and "List of Works," 382, 384

50. Richard Jackson Jr., in discussion with the author, 2016.

51. The identification of the car in the Girard drawing as a 1949 Hudson Commodore was supported by Mike Cherry, Hudson Motor Car enthusiast, in discussion with the author.

Chapter 5. Culmination

Epigraph: Kaufmann, "Alexander Girard's Architecture," 20.

1. "Christmas Present." According to the article, the term "straight-forward American contemporary design" came from the architect.

2. "John N. McLucas," in Dunbar, *Michigan through the Centuries*, 609.

3. For the history of NBD, see "NBD Bancorp, Inc." The move followed the nationwide banking crisis after the stock-market crash of 1929. On February 14, 1933, Michigan's governor, William Comstock, declared a statewide "banking holiday," followed by a nationwide closure of banks in March by President Franklin D. Roosevelt. The National Bank of Detroit was created by the RFC (Reconstruction Finance Corporation) with the financial support of GM, which purchased the bank's common stock for $12.5 million. It was GM president Alfred P. Sloan who insisted that the new chairman be from the Midwest and not from New York City. Walter S. McLucas served as chairman of NBD from 1938 until his death in February 1953. According to Walter McLucas's grandson Scott, McLucas and Sloan were "like two sides of a coin, each of them American pioneers" (*Lucky Life*, 35).

4. McLucas, *Lucky Life*, 69. Jack and Kathleen are referenced as Mr. and Mrs. John McLucas on a cruise to Bermuda in August of 1946.

5. Carlisle, *Rampant Refugee*. Kathleen recounts in her memoir her early life and her travels in China and Japan.

6. Marriage Reports in State Department Decimal Files, 1910-1949, Record Group 59, General

Records of the Department of State, 1763–2002, Series ARC ID: 2555709, Series MLR Number: A1, Entry 3001, Series Box Number: 527, File Number 133, National Archives and Records Administration, Washington, DC, accessed via ancestry.com. Sydney Montague's position is listed on the nominal rolls of the Lunghwa camp in Leck, *Captives of Empire*, 570.

7. Carlisle, *Rampant Refugee*, 40.

8. The term "halcyon days" was used by Greg Leck in his book *Captives of Empire* (27). The book documents the role of British and American bureaucrats in the administration of Chinese corporations in Shanghai and the lavish lifestyle they lived during the 1920s, '30s, and '40s. However, with the advent of war and the Japanese occupation of Shanghai, many families were taken captive and sent to Japanese internment camps.

9. Carlisle, *Rampant Refugee*, 79.

10. Ibid., 72–78.

11. Leck, *Captives of Empire*, 570. Leck publishes the Lunghwa camp internee lists, which includes the Carlisle family. Author J. G. Ballard, then only fourteen, is also shown in the rolls of the camp. Ballard later wrote an account (somewhat fictionalized) based on his experiences in the camp. The novel, *Empire of the Sun*, was published in 1984; in 1987, Steven Spielberg adapted the novel into a movie by the same name.

12. For more on the issue of Japanese internment camps in Shanghai and the repatriation of Americans in 1943, see Leck, *Captives of Empire*. Because of Kathleen's and Virginia's American citizenship, they were repatriated in September 1943, arriving in New York City in December of that year. Ibid., 570.

13. "Passenger Lists of Vessels Arriving at New York, New York, 1820–1957," National Archives Microfilm Publication T715, 8892 rolls, Records of the Immigration and Naturalization Service, National Archives, Washington, DC, accessed via ancestry.com. Surviving documents show the names of Elsie Kathleen and Virginia Clare Carlisle on the SS *Gripsholm* for the second leg of their trip, departing Mormugao, India, on October 22, 1943, and arriving in New York City on December 1, 1943. Their final destination is listed as Kathleen's aunt, Almyra Rowland, in Raleigh, North Carolina.

14. According to Greg Leck, in conversation with the author in 2012, many marriages did not survive internment and repatriation.

15. Carlisle, *Rampant Refugee*. Kathleen's narration of her experiences ends on VE Day, May 8, 1945.

16. McLucas, *Lucky Life*, 69. Scott McLucas writes that Jack and Kitty met through a mutual friend, Lyle Brush.

17. The death notice of Mrs. Grace McLucas (Jack's mother), dated July 15, 1946, references "the son and his wife" as residents of the Whittier. "Mrs. McLucas Dies on Visit to Missouri." Virginia's wedding announcement indicates that she had changed her name from Virginia Clare Carlisle to Virginia Montague McLucas. "Jinx McLucas to Be Bride." Howev-

er, she retained a connection with her birth father, Sydney Montague Carlisle, through her middle name.

18. McLucas, *Lucky Life*, 69. McLucas references the tension between Walter and Kitty McLucas, adding that Walter's antagonism may have been inspired by his affection for Hamilton Simpson, his son's first wife. However, Scott's comment that his father "begged her [Kitty] to stay [in Detroit]" and that he "spent the rest of his life making it up to her" may have inspired the construction of the McLucas house on Vendome several years later.

19. *Social Secretary of Detroit: 1947 Edition*, 126. In 1947 and 1948, Mr. and Mrs. John N. McLucas are listed under the entry for Jack's father, Walter S. McLucas. They received their own registry entry in 1949.

20. In 1945, Richard Jackson had commissioned Girard to build a house (Jackson Lodge) near his private hunting and fishing club in Hillman, MI. For more on Jackson Lodge, see chapter 4.

21. "Post-Concert Supper Party." Other party guests included Mr. and Mrs. Daniel Goodenough (who had just commissioned Girard and Yamasaki to build their house on Lothrop) and Kitty and Dot's half brother, Linton de Cosier.

22. Dorothy had, like her sister, Kathleen, been repatriated from Shanghai, although a year earlier (1942), due to her job at the American consulate in Shanghai. When she returned to the United States, she was transferred to the American embassy in Lima, Peru, where she met Henry ("Hank") Kelly, who was serving as vice consul there. The couple lived in Peru before returning to Hank's hometown, Santa Fe, in 1945. The Kelly family had a long history in Santa Fe, and Hank's father, Daniel T. Kelly, was a board member of the Santa Fe Museum of International Folk Art. Sadly, Hank Kelly died shooting the rapids of the Rio Grande in 1947. For more on the Kelly family in Santa Fe, see Kelly, *Buffalo Tail*.

23. Warranty deed, dated August 17, 1949 (no. D368162, Wayne County Register of Deeds, liber 9936, 328), records the sale of land in Joy Realty Company's Hamilton Park Subdivision to John N. and Kathleen S. McLucas.

24. Girard filed for a building permit (no. 2963 in Building Department, City of Grosse Pointe Farms, MI) on May 12, 1950.

25. "These Men Take Bank Directorates and Executive Posts."

26. Piña, *Alexander Girard*, 6.

27. Kaufmann, "Alexander Girard's Architecture," 20.

28. "Theme for D.I.A. Exhibition 1949." This proposal was titled "A New Concept of Beauty" but nicknamed "the Victorian Room." For more on the executive committee discussion in November 1948 relating to the theme of the DIA *For Modern Living* exhibition, see chapter 2.

29. About these two criteria, see note 39 to chapter 2.

30. "Theme for D.I.A. Exhibition 1949."

31. For more on Girard's exposure to iconic movements and monuments in architecture, both in Europe and in the United States, see the introduction.

32. For more on the Farnsworth house, see the house's website, www.farnsworthhouse.org. The house was designed in 1945 and was included in an exhibition of Mies's work at MOMA in New York in 1947. However, construction did not begin until 1950, and the house was not completed until 1951.

33. For more on the Case Study House program, see Smith, *Case Study Houses*; and Smith, Gossel, and Shulman, *Case Study Houses*.

34. Kirkham, *Charles and Ray Eames*, 121. Kirkham references a December 1950 article in *Interiors*, which refers to the Entenza house as a "low, flat box." The same description would apply to Philip Johnson's postwar domestic architectural experiments (not built), including his *Ladies Home Journal* project houses of July 1945 and June 1946, named "Simple as that," and "House for a Millionaire with no Servants." Elizabeth Smith writes in her book on the Case Study Houses, that the best-known houses from the postwar Case Study House program, designed by Eames, Ellwood, Koenig, and Soriano, best demonstrate the "rigorous application of [International Style] industrial construction methods and materials to residential architecture" (Smith, *Case Study Houses*, 7).

35. For more on the Eames house, see Smith, *Case Study Houses*, 22–25.

36. Girard's original intent can be discerned from the "Index to Trades" document, prepared by Girard as an instruction manual for the builders. The document, owned by Robert and Mary Lubera, specifies that exterior plywood be painted with "three coats of outside Barreled Sunlight gloss or other approved outside paint in bright primary colors, as directed." There is no indication which plywood walls would have had this colorful treatment, although the drawing demonstrates that Girard's original intent was to create a colorful façade.

37. It was common practice for Girard to build models of his residential projects. Sadly, the models survive only in photographs in the Alexander Girard Estate collection.

38. Lancaster, *Japanese Influence in America*, 166. Both books were published in 1936.

39. Harada, *Lesson of Japanese Architecture*, 46–51.

40. For the influence of Japanese art on Wright, see Nute, *Frank Lloyd Wright and Japan*. Arnold and Conway, "Introduction," 28–29, identify Wright's organic architecture, along with the International Style, as the two predominant architectural styles prevalent in America during the 1930s.

41. Kirkham, *Charles and Ray Eames*, 116. For Kirkham, the "overall Japanese 'feel'" of the Eames house derives from the Eameses' reference to "the lightness, the elegance, the minimalism, and the rectilinear geometric forms of Japanese architecture," their use of "flexible interior partitions, lanterns, and pottery" in their interiors, and the "intimate relationship between exterior and interior."

42. Smith, *Case Study Houses*, 7.

43. Locher, *Traditional Japanese Architecture*. The prominence of unpainted wood, used as both a structural and a decorative element, is a key characteristic of traditional Japanese architecture. Locher also explains that raked gravel beds and stone borders are also commonly found in Japanese architecture (178–98).

44. For a discussion of Yamasaki's work and its connection with traditional Japanese architecture, see chapter 4.

45. "Girard Editorial," 27. Girard's role in supervising the sixteen-page "Girard Editorial" in the July 1953 AIA Michigan bulletin is detailed in a September 23, 1951, letter, written by Girard to AIA Michigan president Talmadge Hughes. A. H. Girard to T. Hughes, September 23, 1952, Archives of the American Institute of Architects Michigan.

46. Kitty discusses her travels in Japan in the aforementioned memoir, *The Rampant Refugee*.

47. "Christmas Present."

48. "Theme for D.I.A. Exhibition 1949."

49. The December 20, 1949, presentation drawing (fig. 165) shows an orange door, although the current dark-red (referenced in the "Index to Trades" document as "Chinese red") is believed to be the original color.

50. Locher, *Traditional Japanese Architecture*, 110.

51. The use of overlapping and intersecting screen walls, allowing for the free flow of space, was famously used in modern architecture by Mies in his Barcelona Pavilion in 1929. The original laminate material was replaced with the current material by Dr. Carl Sultzman, the subsequent owner of the house.

52. While this floor-plan concept drawing (located in the Alexander Girard Estate collection) is not dated, an identical plan (denoted "obsolete") is dated December 6, 1949.

53. "Theme for D.I.A. Exhibition 1949."

54. Locher, *Traditional Japanese Architecture*, 111.

55. Ibid., 141. Locher states that ornamental door pulls were common in traditional Japanese *fusuma*.

56. Illustrations of Japanese homes with built-in storage units similar to that designed by Girard for the McLucas house were published in Harada's *Lesson of Japanese Architecture*, 185, 191.

57. "Girard Editorial," 27.

58. Carl Sultzman, in conversation with the author.

59. As noted in Barry, "Girard Secret," 79, Girard's own dining-room table consisted of tables in three different sizes (eighteen by thirty-six, fifty-four by eighteen, and thirty-six by thirty-six inches), which could be reconfigured in various ways.

60. Girard, foreword to *An Exhibition for Modern Living*, 5.

61. Quinn, *Mid-century Modern*, 48.

62. The use of prefabricated, standardized materials in the Eames house, designed between 1945 and 1949, reflected the goal of the Case Study House program: to build low-cost modern housing in the postwar period. The Eames house employed joists manufactured by Truscon, a company started by Albert and Julius Kahn. In conversation with the author, Ken Charles, managing director of the Steel Joist Institute, suggested that the McLucas joists may have been custom designed.

63. Quinn, *Mid-century Modern*, 80–81. As noted by Quinn, many of the most celebrated midcentury furniture designers–Ludwig Mies van der Rohe, Marcel Bruer, Eero Saarinen, Charles Eames, and George Nelson–were trained as architects.

64. "Theme for D.I.A. Exhibition 1949."

65. "Exhibition Rooms," 81.

66. As noted by Marc Pagani, in discussion with the author in 2016, Girard used the second, clay Roman brick because glazed brick cannot be used against a fire wall.

67. American Cyanamid developed the resin in 1938. The Formica Corporation was the prime supplier of melamine, which was used by the US government during World War II but developed for residential use in the 1950s.

68. By 1949, the entry in the *Social Secretary of Detroit* for Mr. and Mrs. John McLucas listed Mr. Walter Scott McLucas II as a student at Yale University. *Social Secretary of Detroit: 1949 Edition*, 125. In conversation with the author in 2015, Scott McLucas stated that he never lived in the McLucas house.

69. "Defying Frost and Storm," 25. In the photo, Jinx (shown in "after-ski uniform") is identified as a "Mt. Tremblant regular."

70. "Tiny Virginia McLucas Eyes Horse Show Honors."

71. "Jinx's Birthday Party." The author gushes over Jinx's wardrobe: gray Bermuda shorts, a scarlet flannel jacket, and ballet slippers. The other article, "Cream of Young Society," was featured in the June 23, 1957, *Detroit Free Press*.

72. The construction drawings for the McLucas house are owned by Robert and Mary Lubera.

73. "Index to Trades," 13.

74. As noted in "Detroit Architect Builds One House," 97, Girard planned his own home in correspondence to sun exposure. In winter, the northern-facing part of the living room was closed off by an overhead garage door (masked by wood paneling) and lit by overhead skylights; in summer, the same door, serving as sun shade, opened to the garden.

75. For more on Girard's adaptation of his own house to connect with the landscape, see chapter 3.

76. Articles in *Architectural Review* ("House at Grosse Pointe," 249) and *Interiors* ("Girard's Clever Corners") document that Girard used brightly colored, stained-fir plywood (yellow, magenta, blue, and purple) for the second-floor playroom walls and that the exterior vertical boards of the bedroom wing were stained orange, contrasting with a blue door.

77. "Index to Trades," 20.

78. "Girard Editorial," 26.

79. Skarsgard, "Where Today Meet Meets Tomorrow," 110.

80. Susan Skarsgard, in discussion with the author, 2016.

81. Claycraft was the company hired to produce bricks for the GMTC project.

82. Skarsgard, "Where Today Meets Tomorrow," 109. Skarsgard references Eero Saarinen's adherence to his father's conception that architects should "always design a thing by considering it in its next larger context–a chair in a room, a room in a house, a house in an environment, an environment in a city plan." She views Saarinen's design of the GMTC as an example of this "interconnectedness." However, in conversation with the author in 2017, she credited the term "architecture of interspaces" to one of "Eliel Saarinen's design tenants that was employed in the overall design of the campus."

83. "Inspiration from a Grand Design." The article predicted that the "fresh concepts of design and color" created at the GMTC would "in years to come . . . find expression in houses across the United States" (94).

84. The February 1950 plan drawing (fig. 190) shows one inside-outside wall on the south end of the gallery, projecting from the atrium into the master bedroom, corresponding with an access point, likely a sliding glass door, to the atrium.

85. "Index to Trades," 20. This page referenced the painting of the exterior plywood in "bright primary colors."

86. Although there is no definitive timeline for the installation of the brick walls at the GMTC, the timeline referenced here comes from "A History of the Development & Construction of the GM Technical Center," Box 2, General Motors Technical Center Research Collection. The GMTC complex (the opening of the Engineering complex only) was celebrated in an *Architectural Forum* article, "Eero Saarinen's Masterpiece: The G.M. Technical Center," published in November 1951.

87. For more on Girard's role as color consultant at the GMTC, see chapter 1. For the collaboration of Girard and Saarinen on the *For Modern Living* exhibition, see chapter 2.

88. For more on the Miller Cottage commission, which began in the spring of 1950, see W. Miller, "Eero and Irwin," 59–61; and Lange, "Alexander Girard in Columbus," 285–90. The commission must have begun by the spring of 1950, when Lange cites a visit by Saarinen, Girard, and their wives to the Miller family's property in Ontario. According to Lange, Elizabeth Miller recalled that Girard "was as much the architect there" ("Alexander Girard in Columbus," 285).

89. For more on the Miller house, see chapter 4 and the conclusion.

90. The atrium was lowered by the second owner, due to flooding issues.

91. As noted by Lutz and Kroloff, *Knoll*, 130, Knorr completed the initial design while he was a graduate student at Cranbrook. He had won first prize (over Charles and Ray Eames) in

the 1948 "Low-Cost Furniture" competition at MOMA. While the original design had a thermal plastic shell, the Knoll version was made from sheet steel.

92. Hakanson, "Public Reacts."

93. "Who, Where and Whatnot."

94. "Christmas Present."

95. "Theme for D.I.A. Exhibition 1949."

96. "Index to Trades."

97. The elimination of the fireplace, indicated with an *X* seems to have been noted in pencil, therefore dating sometime after April 8, 1950.

98. "Men behind It All."

99. "Jinx McLucas to Be Bride." The story of the Baldwin family is very similar to that of the fictional family in the 2011 film *The Descendants*. Henry Perrine Baldwin, the son of a missionary, made his fortune in the sugar-plantation business, with partner Samuel Thomas Alexander. According to "History of Alexander and Baldwin, Inc." (accessed January 30, 2017, www.alexanderbaldwin.com), his original purchase of twelve acres in Maui for $110 grew into a corporation with $1.4 billion in assets, including more than eighty thousand acres of land.

100. *Social Secretary of Detroit: 1961 Edition*, 147; *Social Secretary of Detroit: 1962 Edition*. The 1961 listing for Mr. and Mrs. John McLucas includes both the 55 Vendome address and a winter home in Honolulu, Hawaii. The listing also includes Jack's son, Walter Scott McLucas (then living in London), and Mr. and Mrs. Gregory Baldwin (Virginia Claire McLucas) at the Ulupalakua Ranch in Maui, Hawaii.

101. Kaufmann, "Alexander Girard's Architecture," 20.

102. Ibid.

Chapter 6. Radical Iteration

Epigraph: Oldham and Coffee, *Alexander Girard*, 404.

1. For more details, see "Benadryl"; "George Rieveschl"; and "Biographical Sketch," George Rieveschl Papers. George Rieveschl, an organic chemist, developed diphenhydramine (DPH) during his time in the Department of Chemical Engineering at the University of Cincinnati. While he was initially researching muscle relaxers, he found that his new product helped allergy sufferers. He went to work for Parke-Davis in 1943 to develop the antihistamine.

2. Jan Rieveschl, in discussion with the author, 2016.

3. Anderson, "Serendipity in the Woods," 68.

4. Jan Rieveschl, in discussion with the author, 2016.

5. "Here Is How Alexander Girard Goes about Designing a House," 125.

6. Oldham and Coffee, *Alexander Girard*, 352. For more on the Rieveschl house, see ibid., 344–53; and "List of Works," in Eisenbrand and Kries, *Alexander Girard*, 385–86.

7. Brown, "Alexander Girard," 180n20. Brown references an October 3, 1951, document, "Outline of Working Arrangements," written by D. J. De Pree to Girard. For the timeline of Girard's involvement with Herman Miller, see Piña, *Alexander Girard*, 179–84.

8. Piña, *Alexander Girard*, 17.

9. Ibid.

10. Ibid.

11. Coffee and Oldham, *Alexander Girard*, 352.

12. "George Rieveschl." The *New York Times* obituary references Rieveschl's comments to the *Cincinnati Post*.

13. Gary and Jan Rieveschl, in discussion with the author, 2016.

14. "Biographical Sketch." After Rieveschl went to work for Parke-Davis in 1943, the company purchased the rights to produce the prescription drug under the name Benadryl. However, Parke-Davis granted Rieveschl 5 percent from the proceeds of the drug sales for the next seventeen years.

15. Jan and Gary Rieveschl, in conversation with the author, 2016.

16. No. D460929, Wayne County Register of Deeds, liber 10432, 399, records the sale of land to George Rieveschl Jr. and Clara Bettina Rieveschl.

17. Permit no. 3140, Building Department, City of Grosse Pointe Farms, MI.

18. The reference to the passageways as "fingers" comes from Anderson, "Serendipity in the Woods," 68.

19. "Here Is How Alexander Girard Goes about Designing a House," 123.

20. Anderson, "Serendipity in the Woods," 73.

21. Jan Rieveschl, in discussion with the author, 2016.

22. Girard is often given credit for inventing the concept, which he used most famously in the Miller house in Columbus, IN, a collaboration with Eero Saarinen. Lange ("Alexander Girard in Columbus," 287) noted that the "cove of built-in seating" in the Miller Cottage (another collaboration between Girard and Saarinen) "anticipates the Millers' famous conversation pit." Saarinen later used a "conversation pit" in his design for the TWA Terminal at Idlewild (later renamed JFK) Airport.

23. Anderson, "Serendipity in the Woods," 72.

24. Ibid., 74.

25. Ibid.

26. Jan Rieveschl, in discussion with the author, 2016.

27. "Here Is How Alexander Girard Goes about Designing a House," 126.

28. Ibid., 125.

29. Ibid., 126.

30. Gary Rieveschl, in discussion with the author, 2016.

31. "Grosse Pointe Asks 'How High the Fence?'"

Conclusion

Epigraph: Oldham and Coffee, *Alexander Girard*, 39.

1. *Grosse Pointe News*, May 14, 1953, 22.

2. Braun, "Girard: The Man Who Is Five Different People."

3. These articles included "Here Is How Alexander Girard Goes about Designing a House"; "Girard Editorial"; "Girard Story"; Barry, "Girard Secret"; Fitch, "Like the Girards"; and "Serendipity in the Woods."

4. The intent of the *Good Design* program is described in a MOMA press release, dated November 10, 1949, which states, "It is the first time that an art museum and wholesale merchandising center have co-operated to present the best examples of modern design in home furnishings." For more on Girard's installation of the 1953 *Good Design* show in Chicago, see Obniski, "Theatrical Art," 227–31; and "Good Design 53."

5. Obniski, "Theatrical Art," 227.

6. For Girard's commentary on the displays, see MOMA, "Press Release."

7. Obniski, "Theatrical Art," 228–29.

8. For a discussion of Girard's early textile designs (pre–Herman Miller), see Brown, "Alexander Girard," 180.

9. Ibid., 182.

10. Ibid.

11. For more on the Herman Miller showroom and the Textiles & Objects shop, see Obniski, "Accumulating Things," 190–245; and "List of Works," in Eisenbrand and Kries, *Alexander Girard*, 414–15. The T&O sold an eclectic mix of objects, from Marilyn Neuhard dolls to folk art objects from across the globe. Sadly, the T&O shop was not a commercial success; it closed in 1967.

12. For more on the Miller house, see Monkhouse, "Miller House"; and Lange, "Alexander Girard in Columbus," 291–99. The book Brooks, *Miller House and Garden*, features photographs by Balthasar Korab and Ezra Stoller.

13. "H&G's Hallmark House No. 3," 58–77.

14. Remarkably, the pillows, slipcovers, and collectibles in the conversation pit–designed and/or selected by Girard, in consultation with Xenia Miller–were changed seasonally.

15. It should be noted that Saarinen had also experimented with the "conversation pit" concept, including a sunken sofa in Case Study House #9, the "Entenza" house (1945–49), and a sunken seating area in the TWA Terminal (1956–62).

16. Coffee and Oldham, *Alexander Girard*, 424.

17. Wilson, *Myth of Santa Fe*.

18. Eisenbrand, "Whole World a Village," 140. Thank you to Jochen Eisenbrand for the text of this letter, part of the Alexander Girard Estate collection.

19. "Alexander Girard: His Santa Fe Home," 88; "List of Works," 388–89. According to "Biography," in Eisenbrand and Kries, *Alexander Girard*, 352, the house had belonged to the painter and color theorist Hilaire Hiler.

20. "Fashions in Living," 181.

21. "Alexander Girard: His Santa Fe Home," 94. The multicolored effect was also applied to exterior walls (fig. 256).

22. For an analysis of the Girard folk art collection, donated in 1961 to the Museum of International Folk Art in Santa Fe, see Glassie, *Spirit of Folk Art*, Eisenbrand, "The Whole World a Village," and Obniski, "Accumulating Things." William T. Kelly Jr. (brother-in-law of Dorothy Kelly and son of William T. Kelly, one of the founders of the Museum of International Folk Art) handled the insurance for the Girard house and folk art collection. Kelly (in conversation with the author in 2017) insisted that the Girards create an inventory of the collection. In the early 1960s, the Girards added an annex to the house, which served as a storage facility. In 1978, the Girards donated their collection–by then encompassing more than one hundred thousand objects–to the State of New Mexico. The year 1982 marked the opening of the Girard Wing of the Museum of International Folk Art in Santa Fe.

23. Girard, *Magic of a People*, 9.

24. The range of articles featuring the Girards' Santa Fe home include "Bric-a-Brac Gets Setting in a Divider" and "Fashions in Living."

25. Eisenbrand, "Whole World a Village," 165.

26. Girard, foreword to *Multiple Visions*, iii.

Bibliography

Archives

Archives of the American Institute of Architects, Michigan. Detroit, MI.

Bostick, William. Papers. Detroit Institute of Arts, Detroit, MI.

Building Department. City of Grosse Pointe Farms, MI.

Burton Historical Collection. Detroit Public Library, Detroit, MI.

Cranbrook Art Museum Exhibition Records. Center for Collections and Research, Cranbrook Archives. Bloomfield Hills, MI.

Eames, Charles and Ray. Papers, 1850–1989. Manuscript Division, Library of Congress, Washington, DC.

General Motors Technical Center Research Collection. General Motors Design Archive and Special Collections, Warren, MI.

Girard, Alexander. Estate. Vitra Design Museum, Weil am Rhein, Germany.

Grosse Pointe Historical Society Archives. Grosse Pointe, MI.

Grotell, Maija. Papers. Center for Collections and Research, Cranbrook Archives, Bloomfield Hills, MI.

Herman Miller Archives. Zeeland, MI.

Korab, Balthasar. Collection. Prints & Photographs Online Catalogue, Library of Congress, Washington, DC.

Lacy, Joseph. Memoirs. Center for Collections and Research, Cranbrook Archives, Bloomfield Hills, MI.

Miller House and Garden Collection (1953–2008). Indianapolis Museum of Art, Indianapolis, IN.

Moon, George. Collection. General Motors Design Archive and Special Collections, Warren, MI.

Parker, Maynard. Negatives, Photographs, and Other Material. Huntington Digital Library, San Marino, CA.

Richardson, Edgar P. Records, 1930–62. Detroit Institute of Arts, Detroit, MI.

Rieveschl, George, Jr. Papers. Lloyd Library and Museum, Cincinnati, OH. http://lloydlibrary.org.

Sanborn Map Collection. Detroit Public Library, Detroit, MI.

Saul Steinberg Foundation Archives. New York, NY.

Schnee, Edward and Ruth Adler. Papers. Center for Collections and Research, Cranbrook Archives. Bloomfield Hills, MI.

Schnee, Ruth Adler. Oral history interview, November 24–30, 2002. Archives of American Art, Smithsonian Institution, Washington, D.C. http://aaa.si.edu.

Wayne County Register of Deeds. Detroit, MI.

Yamasaki, Minoru. Papers. Walter P. Reuther Library, Archives of Labor and Urban Affairs, Wayne State University, Detroit, MI.

Yamasaki Inc. Architectural Firm Records. Photographic Collection, Archives of Michigan, Lansing, MI.

Publications

"Alexander Girard, Grosse Pointe, Michigan." *Interiors*, August 1951.

"Alexander Girard: His Santa Fe Home in Two Native Adobe Shells." *Interiors*, October 1954.

Anderson, John. "Casual Vices for Girard's House." *Interiors*, January 1953.

——. "Serendipity in the Woods," *Interiors*, January 1953.

Arbaugh, Thomas. "John S. Newberry and James H. McMillan: Leaders of Industry and Commerce." In *Tonnancour: Life in Grosse Pointe along the Shores of Lake St. Clair*, vol. 2, edited by Arthur M. Woodford, 72–82. Detroit: Omnigraphics, 1996.

"Architect Sums Up Three Japanese Ideas for Your Next House, An." *Detroit Free Press*, December 26, 1954.

Arnold, Amy L., and Brian D. Conway. "Introduction: Michigan's Role in the Development of Modernism." In *Michigan Modern: Design That Shaped America*, edited by Amy L. Arnold and Brian D. Conway, 21–55. Layton, UT: Gibbs Smith, 2014.

——, eds. *Michigan Modern: Design That Shaped America*. Layton, UT: Gibbs Smith, 2014.

Baime, A. J. *The Arsenal of Democracy: FDR, Detroit, and the Epic Quest to Arm America at War*. New York: Houghton Mifflin Harcourt, 2014.

Baist, William Edward, and Harry Valentine Baist. *Baist's Real Estate Atlas: Surveys of Detroit Suburbs in Three Volumes*. Vol. 1, *Subdivisions to 1938*. Philadelphia: G. Wm. Baist, 1915.

Ballard, J. G. *Empire of the Sun*. New York: Simon and Schuster, 1984.

Barry, Joseph A. "The Girard Secret: Seeing the Possibilities in Everything." *House Beautiful*, February 1953.

"Benadryl." Ohio History Central. Accessed January 25, 2017, www.ohiohistorycentral.org/w/Benadryl.

"Both Fish and Fowl Is the Depression-Weaned Vocation of Industrial Design." *Fortune*, February 1934.

Braun, Lillian Jackson. "Girard: The Man Who Is Five Different People." *Detroit Free Press*, March 1, 1953.

"Bric-a-Brac Gets Setting in a Divider." *New York Times*, December 6, 1958.

Brooks, Bradley C. *Miller House and Garden*. New York: Assouline, 2011.

Brown, Susan. "Alexander Girard: Textile Architect." In *Alexander Girard: A Designer's Universe*, edited by Jochen Eisenbrand and Mateo Kries, 170–201. Weil am Rein, Germany: Vitra Design Museum, 2016.

Butler, Don. *The History of Hudson*. Sarasota, FL: Crestline, 1982.

Caplan, Ralph. *The Design of Herman Miller*. New York: Whitney Library of Design, 1976.

Carlisle, Kathleen Smith. *The Rampant Refugee*. New York: E. P. Dutton, 1946.

Carter, Brian. "Kahn's Industry: An Architecture of Integrated Design." In *Michigan Modern: Design That Shaped America*, edited by Amy L. Arnold and Brian D. Conway, 59–65. Layton, UT: Gibbs Smith, 2014.

"Christmas Present." *Detroit Free Press*, August 6, 1950.

City of Detroit v. Lothrop Estate Company. 99 N.W. 9 (1904).

Clark, Robert Judson. "Cranbrook and the Search for Twentieth-Century Form." In *Design in America: The Cranbrook Vision, 1925–1950*, edited by Robert J. Clark and Andrea P. A. Belloli, 21–33. Detroit: Harry N. Abrams, 1984.

Clark, Robert Judson, and Andrea P. A Belloli, eds. *Design in America: The Cranbrook Vision, 1925–1950*. Detroit: Harry N. Abrams, 1984.

Conway, Brian D. "Acknowledgments." In *Michigan Modern: Design That Shaped America*, edited by Amy L. Arnold and Brian D. Conway, 14–15. Layton, UT: Gibbs Smith, 2014.

Cooperman, Emily. "A Challenge to the Future: Eliel and Eero Saarinen and the General Motors Technical Center." In *Michigan Modern: Design That Shaped America*, edited by Amy L. Arnold and Brian D. Conway, 247–53. Layton, UT:

Gibbs Smith, 2014.

Cranbrook House and Gardens. "Our History." Accessed January 22, 2017, www.housegardens.cranbrook.edu.

"Cream of Young Society." *Detroit Free Press*, June 23, 1957.

Crumb, Edith B. "Grosse Pointe Architect Designs Own Home." *Detroit News*, September 24, 1948.

——. "Young Artist Converts Coach House into Studio." *Detroit News*, September 18, 1949.

"Debs Light the Sky." *Detroit Free Press*, June 24, 1957.

Defenbacher, D. S. "An Editorial Note." *Everyday Art Quarterly* 13 (Winter 1949–50): 13–14.

"Defying Frost and Storm." *Sports Illustrated*, January 23, 1956.

De Long, David. "Eliel Saarinen and the Cranbrook Tradition in Architecture and Urban Design." In *Design in America: The Cranbrook Vision, 1925–1950*, edited by Robert J. Clark and Andrea P. A. Belloli, 47–90. Detroit: Harry N. Abrams, 1984.

"Department Store Plugs Modern Design." *Business Week*, October 15, 1949.

Derrick, Robert O. Membership Files, the American Institute of Architects Archives. *The AIA Historical Directory of American Architects*, s.v. "Derrick, Robert O." (ahd1005300). Accessed January 25, 2017, http://public.aia.org/sites/hdoaa/wiki.

"Design Process at Herman Miller, The." Special issue, *Design Quarterly* 98–99 (1975).

"Detroit Architect Builds One House Where Two Stood Before, A." *Architectural Forum*, February 1949.

Doelle, Katie. "Historical Architecture of Grosse Pointe–114 Lothrop, the Elegant Regency Home Designed by Hugh T. Keyes." Higbie Maxon Agney Realtors. Last modified 2015, www.higbiemaxon.com.

Dunbar, Willis Frederick. *Michigan through the Centuries*. Vol. 4. New York: Lewis Historical Publishing, 1955.

Edwards, Leslie. "Competition, Collaboration, and Connection: Cranbrook in the 1930s." In *Michigan Modern: Design That Shaped America*, edited by Amy L. Arnold and Brian D. Conway, 160–67. Layton, UT: Gibbs Smith, 2014.

"Eero Saarinen's Masterpiece: The G.M. Technical Center." *Architectural Forum*, November 1951.

Eidelberg, Martin. "Ceramics." In *Design in America: The Cranbrook Vision, 1925–1950*, edited by Robert J. Clark and Andrea P. A. Belloli, 213–33. Detroit: Harry N. Abrams, 1984.

Eisenbach, Ronit, and Caterina Frisone, eds. *Ruth Adler Schnee: A Passion for Color*. Milan: Skira, 2011.

Eisenbrand, Jochen. Introduction to *Alexander Girard: A Designer's Universe*, edited by Jochen Eisenbrand and Mateo Kries, 10–15. Weil am Rein, Germany: Vitra Design Museum, 2016.

——. "The Whole World a Village: Alexander Girard and Folk Art." In *Alexander Girard: A Designer's Universe*, edited by Jochen Eisenbrand and Mateo Kries, 140–69. Weil am Rein, Germany: Vitra Design Museum, 2016.

Eisenbrand, Jochen, and Mateo Kries, eds. *Alexander Girard: A Designer's Universe*. Weil am Rein, Germany: Vitra Design Museum, 2016.

"Exhibition for Modern Living, An." *Everyday Art Quarterly* 13 (Winter 1949–50): 12–14.

"Factory Cafeteria." *Architectural Forum*, October 1944.

Farmer, Silas. *Grosse Pointe on Lake Saint Clair*. Detroit: Silas Farmer, 1896. Reprint, Gale Research, 1974.

"Fashions in Living: Where the Alexander Girards Live and Work." *Vogue* 139 (May 1, 1962).

Ferry, W. Hawkins. *The Buildings of Detroit: A History*. Detroit: Wayne State University Press, 2012.

——. "A Suburb in Good Taste." *Monthly Bulletin, Michigan Society of Architects*, March 1956.

Fitch, James Marsdon. "Like the Girards: State Your Problem Clearly and You'll Solve It with Originality." *House Beautiful*, February 1953.

Fletcher, Rosamond. "The General Motors Technical Center: A Collaborative Enterprise." In *Eero Saarinen: Shaping the Future*, edited by Eeva-Liisa Pelkonen and Donald Albrecht, 230–35. New Haven, CT: Yale University Press, 2006.

"For Modern Living Show Highlights Trends in Home Articles." *New York Times*, September 25, 1949.

Freeman, Gary. "Bootlegging across the Border." *Heritage: A Journal of Grosse Pointe Life* 1 (1985): 122–28.

Gallagher, John. *Yamasaki in Detroit: A Search for Serenity*. Detroit: Wayne State University Press, 2015.

"George Rieveschl, 91, Allergy Reliever, Dies." *New York Times*, September 29, 2007.

Girard, Alexander. "'For Modern Living': Show Highlights Trends in Home Articles." *New York Times*, September 25, 1949.

——. Foreword to *An Exhibition for Modern Living, September Eleventh to November Twentieth, Nineteen Forty-Nine*, edited by Alexander H. Girard and William D. Laurie Jr., with William A. Bostick, 5. Detroit: Detroit Institute of Arts, 1949.

——. Foreword to *Multiple Visions, a Common Bond: The Girard Foundation Collection*, iii. Santa Fe, NM: International Folk Art Foundation, 1982.

——. *The Magic of a People: Folk Art and Toys from the Collection of the Girard Foundation*. New York: Viking, 1968.

——. "Mr. Girard Answers His Critics." *Retailing Home Furnishings*, May 4, 1936. Alexander Girard Estate collection.

Girard, Alexander H., and William D. Laurie, with William A. Bostick, eds. *An Exhibition for Modern Living, September Eleventh to November Twentieth, Nineteen Forty-Nine*. Introduction by E. P. Richardson. Detroit: Detroit Institute of Arts, 1949.

"Girard Editorial." *Monthly Bulletin, Michigan Society of Architects* 27 (January 1953): 21–36.

"Girard's Clever Corners." *Interiors*, September 1949.

"Girard Story Shows How Homemaking Can Be an Art, The." *House Beautiful*, February 1953.Glassie, Henry. *The Spirit of Folk Art: The Girard Collection at the Museum of International Folk Art*. New York: Abrams, 1989.

"GM's Industrial Versailles." *Architectural Forum*, May 1956.

"Good Design 53." *Arts and Architecture* 70 (March 1953).

"Grosse Pointe Asks, 'How High the Fence?'" *Detroit News*, June 5, 1952.

Hakanson, Joy. "Girard Talks about Modern Living Show." *Detroit News*, July 24, 1949.

——. "Museum Reveals Plans for Modern Galleries." *Detroit News*, January 15, 1950.

——. "Public Reacts to 'For Modern Living.'" *Detroit News*, October 2, 1949.

"H&G's Hallmark House No. 3: A New Concept of Beauty." *House and Garden*, February 1959.

Harada, Jiro. *The Lesson of Japanese Architecture*. 1936. Reprint, Hartsdale, NY: Masterson, 2011.

Harris, Neil. "North by Midwest." In *Design in America: The Cranbrook Vision, 1925–1950*, edited by Robert J. Clark and Andrea P. A. Belloli, 15–19. Detroit: Harry N. Abrams, 1984.

Hastings, Robert. "Case Study of Sandwich Panel Design and Experience: The General Motors Technical Center." In *Sandwich Panel Design Criteria: A Research Correlation Conference*, 99–103. Washington, DC: National Academy of Sciences, 1959.

"Here Is How Alexander Girard Goes about Designing a House." *House and Home*, November 1952.

Hess, Alan. Foreword to *Michigan Modern: Design That Shaped America*, edited by Amy L. Arnold and Brian D. Conway, 16–19. Layton, UT: Gibbs Smith, 2014.

Hill, Eric J., and John Gallagher. *AIA Detroit: The American Institute of Architects Guide to Detroit Architecture*. Detroit: Wayne State University Press, 2002.

Hodges, Michael. *Building the Modern World: Albert Kahn in Detroit*. Detroit: Wayne State University Press, forthcoming.

Holleman, Thomas J., and James P. Gallagher. *Smith, Hinchman & Grylls: 125 Years of Architecture and Engineering, 1853–1978*. Detroit: Wayne State University Press, 1978.

"House at Grosse Pointe." *Architectural Review* 107 (April 1950): 247–51.

"House Hidden in the Woods, A." *Architectural Forum*, December 1951.

Hubred-Golden, Joni. "Lumen Goodenough, a New Kind of Pioneer." *Farmington Patch*, November 5, 2011.

Hyde, Charles K. *The Dodge Brothers: The Men, the Motor Cars, and the Legacy*. Detroit: Wayne State University Press, 2015.

"Inspiration from a Grand Design." *House and Garden*, June 1956.

"Jinx McLucas to Be Bride." *Detroit Free Press*, September 4, 1958.

"Jinx's Birthday Party." *Grosse Pointe News*, December 24, 1953.

Kaufmann, Edgar, Jr. "Alexander Girard's Architecture." *Monthly Bulletin, Michigan Society of Architects* 27 (January 1953): 19–20.

——. "For Modern Living, an Exhibition, the Detroit Institute of Arts: Then and Now." *Arts and Architecture*, November 1949.

——. "Hand-Made and Machine-Made Art." *Everyday Art Quarterly* 1 (Summer 1946): 3.

——. Introduction to "The Exhibition Rooms." In *An Exhibition for Modern Living, September Eleventh to November Twentieth, Nineteen Forty-Nine*, edited by

Alexander H. Girard and William D. Laurie Jr., with William A. Bostick, 72. Detroit: Detroit Institute of Arts, 1949.

——. Introduction to "Selected Objects in the Exhibition." In *An Exhibition for Modern Living, September Eleventh to November Twentieth, Nineteen Forty-Nine*, edited by Alexander H. Girard and William D. Laurie Jr., with William A. Bostick, 40. Detroit: Detroit Institute of Arts, 1949.

——. "Modern Design in America Now." In *An Exhibition for Modern Living, September Eleventh to November Twentieth, Nineteen Forty-Nine*, edited by Alexander H. Girard and William D. Laurie Jr., with William A. Bostick, 27. Detroit: Detroit Institute of Arts, 1949.

Kelly, Daniel T., Jr. *The Buffalo Tail: A Memoir, 1921–2010*. Indianapolis, IN: Dog Ear, 2012.

Kelly, Hank, and Dot Kelly. *Dancing Diplomats*. Albuquerque: University of New Mexico Press, 1950.

Kirkham, Pat. *Charles and Ray Eames: Designers of the Twentieth Century*. Cambridge, MA: MIT Press, 1995.

Kouwenhoven, John. "The Background of Modern Design." In *An Exhibition for Modern Living, September Eleventh to November Twentieth, Nineteen Forty-Nine*, edited by Alexander H. Girard and William D. Laurie Jr., with William A. Bostick, 10–26. Detroit: Detroit Institute of Arts, 1949.

Lacey, Robert T. *Ford: The Men and the Machine*. Boston: Little, Brown, 1986.

Lancaster, Clay. *The Japanese Influence in America*. Whitefish, MT: Literary Licensing, 2013.

Lange, Alexandra. "Alexander Girard in Columbus." In *Alexander Girard: A Designer's Universe*, edited by Jochen Eisenbrand and Mateo Kries, 276–319. Weil am Rein, Germany: Vitra Design Museum, 2016.

Larsen, Jack Lenor. "Alexander Girard." In "Nelson/Eames/Girard/Propst: The Design Process at Herman Miller." Special issue, *Design Quarterly* 98–99 (1975): 31–39.

Leck, Greg. *Captives of Empire: The Japanese Internment of Allied Civilians in China (1941–1945)*. Bangor, PA: Shandy, 2007.

Lipstadt, Helene. "The Gateway Arch: Designing America's First Modern Monument." In *Eero Saarinen: Shaping the Future*, edited by Eeva-Liisa Pelkonen and Donald Albrecht, 222–29. New Haven, CT: Yale University Press, 2006.

"Little Shop Grows Up, The." *Detroit Free Press*, November 20, 1938.

Locher, Mira. *Traditional Japanese Architecture: An Exploration of Elements and Ideas*. Tokyo: Tuttle, 2010.

Lutz, Brian, and Reed Kroloff. *Knoll: A Modernist Universe*. New York: Rizzoli, 2010.

Maraniss, David. *Once in a Great City: A Detroit Story*. New York: Simon and Schuster, 2016.

McCoy, Ester. "Charles and Ray Eames." *Design Quarterly* 98–99 (1975): 21.

McLucas, Scott. *Lucky Life*. Ponte Vedra Beach, FL: Susan the Scribe, 2013.

"Men Behind It All, The." *Detroit News*, October 5, 1958.

Miller, R. Craig. "Interior Design and Furniture." In *Design in America: The Cranbrook Vision, 1925–1950*, edited by Robert J. Clark and Andrea P. A. Belloli, 91–144. Detroit: Harry N. Abrams, 1984.

Miller, Will. "Eero and Irwin: Praiseworthy Competition with One's Ancestors." In *Eero Saarinen: Shaping the Future*, edited by Eeva-Liisa Pelkonen and Donald Albrecht, 57–68. New Haven, CT: Yale University Press, 2006.

Mock, Elizabeth B. *If You Want to Build a House*. New York: Museum of Modern Art, 1946.

MOMA. "Press Release: Good Design 1953 to Open at Museum with 250 Home Furnishing Items in Special Installation." September 23, 1953.

Monkhouse, Christopher. "The Miller House: A Private Residence in a Public Realm." In *Eero Saarinen: Shaping the Future*, edited by Eeva-Liisa Pelkonen and Donald Albrecht, 236–41. New Haven, CT: Yale University Press, 2006.

"Mrs. McLucas Dies on Visit to Missouri." *Detroit Free Press*, July 15, 1946.

"Museum Tells Plans for Modern Home Show." *Detroit News*, June 12, 1949.

"NBD Bancorp, Inc.—Company Profile, Information, Business Description, History, Background Information on NBD Bancorp, Inc." Reference for Business. Accessed June 2012, www.referenceforbusiness.com.

Nelson, George. Introduction to "Nelson/Eames/Girard/Propst: The Design Process at Herman Miller." Special issue, *Design Quarterly* 98–99 (1975): 6–9.

Nestor, Sarah, ed. *Multiple Visions, a Common Bond: The Girard Foundation Collection*. Santa Fe, NM: Museum of International Folk Art, 1982.

Nicholson, Emrich. *Contemporary Shops in the United States*. New York: Architectural Book Publishing, 1945.

"Nostalgia and Curiosity Produce Identical Results." *Grosse Pointe News*, January 16, 1947.

Noyes, Eliot. *Organic Design in Home Furnishings*. New York: Museum of Modern Art, 1941.

Nute, Kevin. *Frank Lloyd Wright and Japan*. London: Routledge, 2000.

Obniski, Monica. "Accumulating Things: Folk Art and Modern Design in the Postwar American Projects of Alexander H. Girard." PhD diss., University of Illinois at Chicago, 2015.

——. "The Theatrical Art of Displaying 'Good Design.'" In *Alexander Girard: A Designer's Universe*, edited by Jochen Eisenbrand and Mateo Kries, 202–30. Weil am Rein, Germany: Vitra Design Museum, 2016.

"Offices and Showroom Are Created from an Old Detroit Hamburger Stand." *Architectural Forum*, May 1947.

Oldham, Tom, and Kiera Coffee. *Alexander Girard*. Los Angeles: AMMO Books, 2011.

"Pavilion, The." Fundació Mies van der Rohe. Accessed January 22, 2017, http://miesbcn.com/the-pavilion/.

Pelkonen, Eeva-Liisa, and Donald Albrecht, eds. *Eero Saarinen: Shaping the Future*. New Haven, CT: Yale University Press, 2006.

Piña, Leslie. *Alexander Girard: Designs for Herman Miller*. Atglen, PA: Schiffer, 2002.

"Post-Concert Supper Party Planned for Monday by Mr. and Mrs. McLucas." *Detroit Free Press*, November 9, 1950.

Quinn, Bradley. *Mid-century Modern: Interiors, Furniture, Design Details*. London: Octopus, 2006.

"Retail Trade: Store into Institution." *Time*, March 1953.

Richardson, E. P. Introduction to *An Exhibition for Modern Living, September Eleventh to November Twentieth, Nineteen Forty-Nine*, edited by Alexander H. Girard and William D. Laurie Jr., with William A. Bostick, 7–8. Detroit: Detroit Institute of Arts, 1949.

Riley, Marguerite. "Radcliffe Tour to Tap Housing Lore." *Detroit Free Press*, September 26, 1948.

Riley, Terence, and Edward Eigen. "Between the Museum and the Marketplace: Selling Good Design." In *The Museum of Modern Art at Mid-century: At Home and Abroad*, edited by John Szarkowski and John Elderfield, 150–79. New York: Museum of Modern Art, 1995.

"Rough Drinker." *Grosse Pointe News*, January 30, 1947.

Ryder, Sharon Lee. "A Life in the Process of Design." *Progressive Architecture* 57 (1976): 60–66.

Schlanger, Jeff, and Toshiko Takaezu. *Maija Grotell: Works Which Grow from Belief*. Northampton, MA: Studio Potter Books, 1996.

Shaw, Virginia. "Career of George Lothrop Covers One Whole Country." *Detroit Free Press*, April 14, 1925.

Skarsgard, Susan. "Where Today Meets Tomorrow: The General Motors Technical Center." In *Michigan Modern: Design That Shaped America*, edited by Amy L. Arnold and Brian D. Conway, 104–13. Layton, UT: Gibbs Smith, 2014.

Smith, Elizabeth A. T. *Case Study Houses, 1945–1966: The California Impetus*. Cologne: Taschen, 2006.

Smith, Elizabeth A. T., Peter Gossel, and Julius Schulman. *Case Study Houses: The Complete CSH Program, 1945–1966*. Cologne: Taschen, 2009.

Socia, Madeleine. "A House of Hidden History." *Pointer News*, April 1996.

Social Secretary of Detroit: 1941 Edition. Detroit: Edgar C. Cox, 1940.

Social Secretary of Detroit: 1947 Edition. Detroit: Edgar C. Cox, 1946.

Social Secretary of Detroit: 1949 Edition. Detroit: Edgar C. Cox, 1948.

Social Secretary of Detroit: 1961 Edition. Detroit: Bruce E. Cox, 1961.

Social Secretary of Detroit: 1962 Edition. Detroit: Bruce E. Cox, 1962.

Spicer, Nicholas Goodenough. *Luman W. Goodenough and David Gray: The Story behind the Community Center, Visitor Center and Heritage Park*. Birmingham, MI, 1992.

"Storage Wall." *Life*, January 22, 1945, 64–71.

Sugrue, Thomas J. "Motor City: The Story of Detroit." Gilder Lehrman Institute of American History, Spring 2007. www.gilderlehrman.org.

"Susan W. Needham Wed to Architect." *New York Times*, March 15, 1936.

Taragin, Davira S. "The History of the Cranbrook Community." In *Design in America: The Cranbrook Vision, 1925–1950*, edited by Robert J. Clark and Andrea P. A. Belloli, 35–45. Detroit: Harry N. Abrams, 1984.

Taut, Bruno. *Fundamentals of Japanese Architecture*. Tokyo: Kokusai Bunka Shinko-kai, 1936.

"These Men Take Bank Directorates and Executive Posts." *Detroit News*, January 11, 1950.

"Tiny Virginia McLucas Eyes Horse Show Honors." *Detroit Free Press*, June 14, 1949.

Tottis, James. *The Guardian Building: Cathedral of Finance*. Detroit: Wayne State University Press, 2008.

"Tour of Homes Scheduled Oct. 15 by Radcliffe Club." *Grosse Pointe News*, October 7, 1948.

Vogel, Elisabeth. "Small Area of Pine Woods Remain in Grosse Pointe Farms." *Grosse Pointe Patch*, December 18, 2011.

Walker, Stephen G., Richard A. Holderness, and Stephen D. Butler. *The State by State Guide to Architect, Engineer, and Contractor Licensing*. Vol. 1. New York: Aspen, 1999.

Watson, Ben. Foreword to *Alexander Girard: A Designer's Universe*, edited by Jochen Eisenbrand and Mateo Kries, 4–7. Weil am Rein, Germany: Vitra Design Museum, 2016.

"What Is Modern?" *Pathfinder News Magazine*, October 5, 1949.

"Where to Buy Well Designed Objects." *Everyday Art Quarterly* 7 (Spring 1949): 3.

Whitney, Mark, ed. *Ruth Adler Schnee*. Troy, MI: Kresge Foundation, 2015.

"Who, Where and Whatnot." *Grosse Pointe News*, September 11, 1952.

Wilson, Chris. *The Myth of Santa Fe: Creating a Modern Regional Tradition*. Albuquerque: University of New Mexico Press, 1997.

Wittkopp, Greg. "Cranbrook Academy of Art: Architecture's Cradle of Modernism." In *Michigan Modern: Design That Shaped America*, edited by Amy L. Arnold and Brian D. Conway, 77–85. Layton, UT: Gibbs Smith, 2014.

Wright, Henry, and George Nelson. *Tomorrow's House: A Complete Guide for the Home-Builder*. New York: Simon and Schuster, 1945.

Yamasaki, Minoru. *A Life in Architecture*. Trumbull, CT: Weatherhill, 1979.

"Year's Work (Residential), The: Alexander Girard, Grosse Pointe, Michigan." *Interiors*, August 1949.

Index

About the Author

Deborah Lubera Kawsky completed her undergraduate studies at Smith College and her PhD in art history at Princeton University. She is an adjunct associate professor at Madonna University, where she teaches art history courses and leads European study-abroad trips. Her current projects relate to Detroit history, art, and architecture.